The hardcover edition of this book came with a boun copies of the worksheets you'll find in *Acceptance and Commitment Therapy for the Treatment of Post-Traumatic Stress Disorder and Trauma-Related Problems*. All these files are available to you as a free download at: 23338.nhpubs.com

This outstanding book offers clinicians a clear understanding of the traps of language and the paradoxical implications of trying to control our internal experiences. The authors bring years of experience working with survivors of trauma and a comprehensive grasp of their topic to this lucid explanation of acceptance and commitment therapy. Each of the treatment components is presented clearly and succinctly, yet integrated into a comprehensive whole. Illustrative case examples and session transcripts offer a vivid picture of the ACT approach.

—Chad LeJeune, Ph.D., author of *The Worry Trap: How to Free Yourself from Worry and Anxiety Using Acceptance and Commitment Therapy*

The ABCs *of* Human Behavior

Behavioral Principles *for the* Practicing Clinician

JONAS RAMNERÖ, PhD

NIKLAS TÖRNEKE, MD

Context Press
New Harbinger Publications, Inc.

Publisher's Note

Care has been taken to confirm the accuracy of the information presented and to describe generally accepted practices. However, the author, editors, and publisher are not responsible for errors or omissions or for any consequences from application of the information in this book and make no warranty, express or implied, with respect to the contents of the publication.

Distributed in Canada by Raincoast Books

Copyright © 2008 by Jonas Ramnerö and Niklas Törneke

New Harbinger Publications, Inc.
5674 Shattuck Avenue
Oakland, CA 94609
www.newharbinger.com

Acquired by Catharine Sutker; Cover design by Amy Shoup;
Edited by Jean Blomquist; Text design by Tracy Carlson

Library of Congress Cataloging-in-Publication Data

Ramnerö, Jonas.
  The ABCs of human behavior : an introduction to behavioral psychology / Jonas Ramnerö and Niklas Törneke.
    p. ; cm.
  Includes bibliographical references and index.
  ISBN-13: 978-1-57224-538-9 (hardback : alk. paper)
  ISBN-10: 1-57224-538-7 (hardback : alk. paper)
  1. Clinical psychology. 2. Medicine and psychology. 3. Operant conditioning. I. Törneke, Niklas. II. Title.
  [DNLM: 1. Psychology, Clinical--methods. 2. Behavior Therapy--methods. 3. Conditioning, Operant. 4. Learning. WM 105 R174a 2008]
  RC467.R35 2008
  616.89--dc22

                    2007047459

17 16 15

15 14 13 12 11 10 9 8 7

Contents

PART 1
Describing Behavior

PART 2
Explaining Behavior

PART 3
Changing Behavior

Foreword

Behaviorism has a bad name in many circles. When people are asked why, they cite a number of dogmas that have achieved "truth" status even though they don't look quite so "true" when one looks carefully at original scholarly sources. Two of the most popular misconceptions are, first, that behaviorism denies thinking and feeling. The second is the notion that behaviorism seeks to break behavior into its most fundamental atoms and in doing so threatens to turn humans into machine-like automatons. If these caricatures are true anywhere in behaviorism, they are not true in the behaviorism of B. F. Skinner, and certainly not in the contemporary contextual behavioral account described in this book.

All of us have a fraction of the world to which only we have direct access. Others may see what we do with our hands and feet quite directly. They do not have such direct access to what we think, feel, imagine, and desire. Any psychology that does not address these matters is likely to be, and probably ought to be, rejected out of hand. In the middle of the last century, empirical psychology was running away from questions about this world inside the skin—in search of a so-called objective psychology. In striking contrast, B. F. Skinner quipped to the famous historian of experimental psychology E. G. Boring that "While Boring must confine himself to an account of my external behavior, I am still interested in what might be called Boring-from-within" (Skinner, 1945, p. 277). But, Skinner's was only one voice in behaviorism. And, many within the broader behavioral movement did call out for an analysis that was uninterested in our inner life.

During the nineteen sixties and early seventies, behavioral approaches dominated empirical clinical psychology. Inattention to cognition left an opening, and that opening was filled by the rapidly rising tide of cognitive psychology. The later seventies, eighties, and nineties saw the strong emergence of cognitive psychology in both basic and applied realms. In organizations such as the Association for the Advancement of Behavior Therapy (AABT), we saw the inclusion of cognitive interventions in behavioral treatments as well as the rise of wholly cognitive approaches. This transformation was sufficiently complete that AABT eventually changed its name to the Association for Behavioral and Cognitive Therapies.

There was another notable change during the same time period. Academic departments that trained psychologists began hiring an increasing number of cognitive psychologists—both basic and applied. Whereas during the sixties and early seventies the conversations in psychology departments were dominated by behavioral voices, this became less and less the case during the rise of cognitive psychology. This trend in the academy was so pervasive that some empirically-oriented clinical doctoral programs stopped teaching behavioral psychology except in the most cursory way.

Intellectual generations in the academy move very quickly. An individual gets their Ph.D. and a job as an assistant professor. Perhaps five years later, they produce the first of their own Ph.D.'s. In many academic settings, we are hiring people that are three or four generations away from professors who themselves had very strong training in basic behavior analysis. This is, of course, less true in some domains. Mental retardation and child behavior problems, for example, have often remained bastions of behavioral training. However, mainstream empirical clinical psychology has traveled a good long distance from its behavioral roots.

Some of this may have been a reaction to excesses: positions that were held too stridently or versions of behavioral psychology that truly did not take human cognition seriously. For whatever reason, the plain fact is that we now find ourselves at a point in time where many individuals providing mental health care were not well trained in behavior analysis. This might not be a terribly important issue, except that the emerging third wave behavior therapies, especially functional analytic psychotherapy, dialectical behavior therapy, behavioral activation, and acceptance and commitment therapy, all make case conceptualizations from a behavioral perspective. If therapists are interested in these emerging treatments, an understanding of behavior analysis is a critical asset.

There are a few approaches to behavioral training. Some are highly technical and provide extremely refined descriptions that are critical for basic laboratory work. Some distinctions that are important in tightly controlled experimental preparations may be less so outside the laboratory. It is unlikely that the concept of a changeover delay in a concurrent VI-2' /VI-2' schedule of reinforcement will be of much practical importance to a clinician. What clinicians do need is an understanding of the core of behavior analysis—an understanding of the functional relation between behavior and the contexts in which it occurs.

Ramnerö and Törneke have written a book that will serve several important groups. Individuals whose behavioral training happened a long time ago or was weak or not well integrated with clinical work, as well as those with no behavioral training at all, will find a gentle, nontechnical entry point into a functional contextual understanding of behavior. The book is filled with case examples that bring behavioral sensibilities to life in readily recognizable clinical contexts. For students interested in third wave behavior therapies, this book will make an excellent starting point in cultivating an understanding of behavior analysis. The book will also provide a theoretical basis for understanding the impact of many of our more traditional cognitive and behavioral practices. In my own capacity as a professor in a clinical doctoral program, I will make this book required reading for my students.

With kind regards,
Kelly G. Wilson, Ph.D.

Our Thanks

Writing this book comes at the end of a long succession of events. Over the years, many people have made contributions to what finally became this book. The scientific background is documented in the list of references. We want to take the opportunity here to thank a long line of teachers, colleagues, and students who for many years, or for shorter periods, have been in dialogue with us concerning the question of what psychotherapy is and how it is best conducted. Special thanks to Sandra Bates, Ata Ghaderi, and Gardar Viborg for their thoughtful comments on the early draft of the Swedish manuscript. Thanks to Steve Hayes for taking the book abroad; Liza Ask and Sandra Bates for contributing to the translation process; and Jean M. Blomquist for her editing of the text. To everyone at Context Press and New Harbinger Publications, thank you for all your work in bringing this book into being. Last but not least, we want to thank our clients, former and present, who together with us have struggled with the question of how to understand what we do and how to change the things we want to change.

Building on Behaviorism: Cognitive/Behavioral Therapies, Behavioral Psychotherapy, and Functional Contextualism

Even though this book is based specifically on learning theory and has behaviorism as its point of reference, we believe there is a need to start by relating its content to the wider world of both behavioral and cognitive therapies. Let's turn to that topic now.

COGNITIVE/BEHAVIORAL THERAPIES

Cognitive and behavioral therapies have undergone significant development over the past twenty years. Scientific support has grown along with interest from society at large. The therapies are practiced in different ways, but therapists typically use a mixture of techniques from both perspectives, most of the time under the heading of CBT (cognitive behavioral therapy). However, there is an inherent tension in this mixing. While traditional behavior therapy is a clinical application of learning theory, cognitive therapy is based on a model of information processing. Of the two, the cognitive model has dominated, at least since the 1980s, the theoretical aspect of CBT. One probable reason for this dominance is that several successful treatment models have developed from a cognitive perspective. Another might be the fact that classical learning theory has had problems dealing with some typically human phenomena, such as the power and function of thought. Even though behaviorism and well-researched principles of learning are implicit in the CBT tradition, the epistemologically more critical view of science in the tradition of behaviorism has often been pushed into the background.

In the last few years, interest in classical learning theory has increased. Several new treatment models, explicitly based on behavioral philosophy, have developed. The best known is probably DBT (dialectical behavior therapy). At the same time, there has been a growing debate about the scientific foundation of CBT. One argument suggests that the current models lack a solid foundation in basic experimental science. If so, this would contradict the idea that therapy should be an application of principles of learning that are known from, and tested in, empirical research. Without this link with research, theory easily becomes more an elaboration of folk psychology rather than being a part of a progressive scientific movement (O'Donohue, 1998).

Criticism of the psychology of information processing has often been raised from a behavioral perspective. For us, the essence of behaviorism is its tradition of fostering an epistemologically critical view of science. This line of thinking has grown out of functionalism, where the function of the organism's behavior in relation to its context is the central focus. This is so whether we focus on the survival of the species or study the learning of an individual organism. Behaviorism is also anchored in a pragmatic tradition in which the value of knowledge is ultimately determined by its usefulness. Behaviorism, then, is not primarily a psychology. Rather we see behaviorism as a philosophy and a tradition of epistemology that serves as a foundation for psychology. From this standpoint, the critical view of knowledge inherent in the tradition becomes evident. A behavioral perspective redefines what the object of study for psychology is. From this perspective, one questions whether psychology should be the study of hypothetical structures in the "mind." More importantly, one also questions whether descriptions of these hypothetical constructs can lead to meaningful knowledge about what governs human behavior and if they have any utility in helping change behavior.

The death of behaviorism has been proclaimed many times, and each time the proclamation has come, we think, a bit too early. The tradition of being critical of a commonsense view of knowledge is still very much a relevant issue, particularly in the area of psychotherapy. In the United States, the behavioral trend in psychotherapy, commonly referred to as clinical behavior analysis, is evident. It is characterized by both a return to tradition and by innovation. There is a strong emphasis on classical learning theory—respondent and operant conditioning—as the basis for psychological change. At the same time, there is a focus on addressing areas that have been underdeveloped in traditional behavior therapy, such as the therapeutic relationship. Recent basic research on language and cognition is also being used to develop new intervention techniques, resulting in new areas being targeted.

BEHAVIORAL PSYCHOTHERAPY AND BEHAVIORAL PSYCHOLOGY

Having said that, it ought to be clear that this book is based in the same tradition as classical behavior therapy. At the same time, it will hardly escape the reader that we as authors are influenced by the somewhat different models of behavior therapy that have developed in the last fifteen to twenty years. We have already mentioned DBT. Others are ACT (acceptance and commitment therapy), BA (behavioral activation), and FAP (functional analytical psychotherapy). Although there are separate models, we want to put our focus on the behavioral tradition and the functional understanding of human behavior more generally. Our aim, thus, is not to present a set of different models of psychotherapy. We want to present a particular perspective, applied to a specific situation—the situation usually called psychotherapy. This perspective, shared by the therapies mentioned, is a development of traditional behavior therapy leading to more behavior therapy and, sometimes, behavior therapy done in new ways.

Just to make sure we are not misunderstood at this point, let's be clear: we are not suggesting a new form of therapy by calling this "behavioral psychotherapy" (BPT?). Actually, one of the peculiarities of the behavioral tradition seems to be that every extension comes with a new name and acronym. However, to us, *behavioral psychotherapy* is simply a meaningful descriptive term that can be used synonymously with *behavior therapy*. The first term has a more clear theoretical meaning, but *behavior therapy* is precisely this: psychotherapy from a behavioral perspective. Behavior therapists have traditionally disliked the word "psyche." And it is indeed strange to talk about therapy for a "psyche" at the same time that this concept is regarded as an unfruitful basis for science. Historically, the term "behavior therapy" was created as a reaction to "psychotherapy." At the same time, there is a sound behavioral tradition of using acts that work, and this includes using words that work. We describe something that is done, a particular kind of behavior. This type of behavior is usually called psychotherapy. The word "psychotherapy" has become synonymous with psychological treatment. So why not use the more apt term: behavioral psychotherapy?!

In using this term, we do not wish to take an extreme position that would exclude many others. Rather, we see behaviorism as a vibrant and fruitful basis for the practice of psychotherapy. This practice readily includes techniques that do not have their origins in learning theory. This means that a reader who is used to another model of psychotherapy will probably be familiar with some of what we write about in this book.

OUR JOURNEY TO WRITING THIS BOOK, OR HOW DID WE END UP HERE?

We both started our journey, independent of each other, through the landscape of psychotherapy using a psychodynamic map. We read books by Kohut, Kernberg, and others, and tried to practice what we read. One of us was training to be a psychologist (Jonas), the other a psychiatrist (Niklas). This was back in the 1980s when the cognitive map was growing in general usage. We were both attracted to its promise of increasing the impact of empirical research on psychotherapeutic work. We did our separate training in psychotherapy, reading Beck, Clark, and others, and continued to work with clients. At this point, we were still independent of each other. Our continued interest in the empirical base of psychotherapy led us both to a deepening interest in the behavioral contribution, and suddenly we found ourselves on fruitful ground—a little sparsely populated maybe, but full of life, both old and new. There we met, and in our conversation about what we found, the idea of this book was born.

Our Intention

This book is an effort to answer some of the questions we have encountered while teaching in different contexts and in trying to clarify our own positions. One of the most common questions has been this: where can one read more about this? It has been difficult to give a good recommendation. The older literature is often complicated and is either focused on experimental research or has areas of application other than psychotherapy. More recent books are either on research only, or are focused on one specific model of behavioral therapy. So where can you read about the basic perspective of behavioral psychotherapy? Hopefully we can now say, "Here!"

As we began our writing, we wanted to fill several gaps. We wanted to write a fairly easily accessible introductory book on clinical behavior analysis/behavioral psychotherapy, a book that presented the challenges that this perspective contains. We wanted to write a basic book on how learning theory can work as a basis for clinical conceptualization/analysis. We wanted to stress the position of analysis: the theoretical understanding of human behavior and how practical clinical techniques can be derived from the theory.

Choices We Have Made

In our presentation of behavioral psychology, we've had to make several choices. One, and this has been a painful one, is to abstain from presenting the experimental basis for the theories and concepts used—and we do this while presenting a perspective in which this is explicitly stated to be the raison d'être for the position we've taken! The alternative, however, would have turned out to be a different book than the one we wanted to write—the one that is now in your hands.

Other choices are about how particular words should be used. This is so because behavioral psychology in a sense is not one psychology but many. Words are used in different ways, and usage sometimes even reflects opposing positions. The choices we've made mean that you might find the same terms used in other ways in other texts. This is inevitable in such a broad tradition as behaviorism. If you want a name for the specific position we take, the most common name is radical behaviorism, the same position that, later in this introduction, is described by the more modern and specific term "functional contextualism."

WHAT BEHAVIOR IS

Everything in this book is about behavior. Because that word can be used in different ways, it would be wise to explain our usage of it from the start. In accordance with radical behavioral tradition, *behavior* means everything an organism does. Behavior is not only what we easily can see another person doing, such as lifting an arm or talking to someone, but also the things we do on the inside, such as when we think, feel, or remember. This differs from how this word is used in everyday language. The reason we use the word in this way is because we want to keep these phenomena together, and because we believe they are best understood and influenced using the same principles. We won't take time at this point to argue in more detail for our definition. Hopefully our use of the word "behavior" will be clarified as you work through the book. We just want to make our use of the term "behavior" clear so you don't misunderstand what follows.

Behaviorism takes interest in something done—an action. Our book should also be read from this perspective. We want to share something we do: observing the behavior of clients and using a functional analysis of that behavior as an integrated part of clinical work. We also want to present behaviorism as a way of taking an epistemologically critical stand. This is not for its own sake, though. We believe this serves the purpose of producing a sound, scientific psychology. In therapy, this also works as an invitation to reflect on our own behavior as therapists as we ask ourselves these questions: What am I doing? What can I observe, and what can I influence?

These questions—or, more accurately, our answers to them—underscore the importance of functional contextualism in behavioral psychotherapy. Let's look more closely now at this perspective and its role in therapy.

A FUNCTIONAL PERSPECTIVE: OUR CLINICAL STARTING POINT

Six clinical cases are woven throughout the book. They illustrate both theoretical concepts as well as strategies of treatment. Different aspects of each case will be emphasized for educational purposes. The cases are not real, but they do reflect general situations that most psychotherapists probably recognize as authentic. The purpose is both to use everyday examples for illustration of the principles and to show how understanding and change are tightly connected in a psychotherapy based on learning theory.

Let's start our exploration of human behavior and functional contextualism with a few clinical vignettes based on these six cases:

- *It is Friday afternoon on Ward 11, an emergency care unit at the psychiatric clinic. The staff discovers that Jenny has disappeared from the ward despite the fact that she is not permitted to leave on her own. She cut her wrists three times last week, so the staff is extremely troubled that she is gone.*

- *Anna is starting to see her relationship with Peter as increasingly hopeless. They hardly speak to each other anymore. On weekends, when Peter has been drinking, they usually end up fighting. Anna doesn't want their four-year-old daughter to go through this anymore.*

- *Marie describes being uncomfortable when she is the focus of attention. She constantly struggles with thoughts that others will realize how nervous and insecure she really is. At times, she feels as if she is facing her own execution.*

- *Mirza says that he woke up again last night with the same nightmare. He really doesn't know how long he can stand the memories and the nightmares—the images from the night the militia came to their village, the last time he saw his brother.*

- *Alice didn't get much done at work today. Her heart was beating irregularly, and she's worried that there might be something seriously wrong. She feels this way despite the fact that her doctor told her that her health is okay. And now, because she didn't get much done today, she's also worrying about all the work she has to make up.*

- *Leonard didn't get off to work again today. He has been on sick leave, due to depression, for quite a long time. Even though he had agreed to work part-time, he just can't motivate himself to follow through.*

If we work in clinical settings, we all recognize examples like these. We could have chosen others. The critical thing for the moment is not the content of these examples. The critical thing, right now, is what we are doing: we are observing and describing people, people who are behaving. We ask ourselves, "Why are they doing this?" Or expressed differently, we observe behavior and try to explain it. This means that we are taking a perspective. All attempts to create knowledge about people imply taking a perspective, a priori. The perspective we take here could be called *a functional perspective*, that is, a perspective that focuses on the function of a particular behavior as it appears in a particular situation.

FUNCTIONAL CONTEXTUALISM

For a moment, let's leave the clinical setting and move out into everyday life. We observe a man, Mr. Smith. Every morning around 7:30, he leaves home and drives his car to work. When he walks from his front door to his garage, he passes by his neighbor's window, where Mr. Brown sits looking out while having his morning coffee. Mr. Brown, who has been retired for a couple of years, likes to take his time having breakfast and reading the newspaper. Mr. Smith waves his hand discreetly while simultaneously nodding his head and making a slight movement with his mouth without producing any sound. Mr. Brown replies by raising his cheek and forming his mouth into a smile. This is a behavioral sequence that is repeated with a high degree of predictability, day after day. Now, why is Mr. Smith doing this? What is the purpose of this behavior? We are trying to figure out the function of the behavior.

The greeting behavior emitted by Mr. Smith is responded to by Mr. Brown. The behavior is followed by a consequence. Here we have identified an elementary behavioral sequence in its context. It is a behavioral sequence that has a function in maintaining an everyday relationship between two neighbors. We could easily assume that if Mr. Smith disliked the consequence, he would stop greeting; this assumes, of course, that there are no other consequences which maintain the behavior that we would need to consider. It is indeed the fact that Mr. Smith finds it quite awkward if he looks away or otherwise ignores his neighbor as he passes by his window. When this has happened in the past, it has evoked an uncomfortable feeling. He is afraid that he might hurt Mr. Brown's feelings in some way. By greeting him every morning, Mr. Smith effectively avoids this mildly aversive event. We could probably find a number of other functions for this behavior. For the moment, though, we'll simply say that a single behavioral act may have *multiple functions*.

Mr. Smith could substitute his waving with a discreet bow, the raising of his arm to lift his hat, or by uttering the words "Hi there" without threatening the mutual relationship between the two neighbors. So here we find other behaviors that easily could acquire the same functions. We say these behaviors are *functionally equivalent*, or that they belong to the same functional class. This is an important distinction. Behaviors that look different may be functionally alike—that is, they may have the same or a similar purpose.

On the other hand, behaviors that look alike may have different functions in different situations. Consider the situation where Mr. and Mrs. Smith go shopping. Since

Mr. Smith finds the women's department rather uninspiring, he usually waits outside the store. To pass the time, he watches younger women and waves his hand while simultaneously nodding his head and making a slight movement with his mouth without producing any sound. When Mrs. Smith sees this from inside the shop, she will probably not accept the excuse that this is the same behavior Mr. Smith emits outside his neighbor's house every morning. In one sense, Mr. Smith would be correct in asserting that it is the same behavior. His behavior outside the shop looks identical to his behavior with Mr. Brown. It has the same form. We would say that topographically it is the same behavior. However, it is reasonable to assume that Mrs. Smith will argue that, in this situation, the same behavior has a different meaning. We agree with her. Said another way, a behavior can only be understood when considering the specific environmental circumstances within which it occurs. Topographically identical behaviors can be different behaviors from a functional perspective.

We have chosen the word "context" to depict these environmental circumstances. It is in the context that we search for causes of behavior, or, more specifically, in the context where the behavior occurs now and the context where this or similar behaviors have occurred in the past. Therefore, two things are central to the task of describing, understanding, and influencing behavior: the function of a particular behavior and the context within which it occurs. Understanding the function is to understand the purpose of a behavior—that is, its consequences. And consequences occur in the context. This is a perspective that is called *functional contextualism* (Hayes, 1993).

When Mr. Smith returns from work, he often sees Mr. Brown in his garden. Mr. Brown is usually busy trimming the hedges, raking his gravel walk, or otherwise tending his neat little garden. Mr. Brown stops what he is doing and utters phrases like "Good evening" or "How are you doing?" Since Mr. Smith, like many other living organisms, is equipped with the ability to discriminate between different situations that call for different behaviors, he will not emit the behavior he performs in the morning. He senses it would not be a sufficiently rewarding experience for Mr. Brown, and Mr. Smith would probably feel impolite. Instead, from a broad repertoire of potential behaviors, he chooses to reply with verbal statements such as "I'm fine, thanks" or "Just great!" Sometimes these behaviors are supplemented with a few words about the weather or encouraging remarks about Mr. Brown's pansies. It is the same suburbia, the same people, the same distance from the front door and garage, yet a different context.

DIFFERENT PERSPECTIVES, DIFFERENT QUESTIONS, DIFFERENT ANSWERS

We have chosen a certain perspective in order to study behavior. We could choose other perspectives to study the same phenomena. The ambitious young neurophysiologist might choose to equip Mr. Smith with a newly designed mobile PET-scan that would allow him to measure the blood flow in different parts of Mr. Smith's brain during his waking hours. Let's suppose he finds an increase in activity in certain parts of Mr. Smith's brain when he passes by Mr. Brown's window. The researcher may draw the conclusion that there are specific sites in the brain involved in coordinating discrete muscle movements in social situations that have a low level of novelty. The behavior emitted is thus caused by the identified activity in the brain. This is also an explanation of Mr. Smith's behavior, but it is a different explanation from the one suggested by the functional perspective. From our perspective, the fact that Mr. Smith uses a part of his brain when he greets his neighbor is no stranger than the fact that he uses his arm. From a functional perspective, the neurophysiologist has described how the organism known as Mr. Smith behaves rather than why.

Let's suppose that Mr. Smith is also the object of study by a personality researcher who makes him complete a vast number of questionnaires. The researcher finds that Mr. Smith tends to score high on dimensions such as "sociability," "interpersonal attentiveness," and "social desirability." The researcher concludes that Mr. Smith has a socially oriented personality. His persistent greeting behavior is thus explained by this personality. Again we see an explanation, but this time it's not from a neurophysiological point of view. Here the explanation focuses on something that Mr. Smith possesses: a personality. The personality researcher is interested in the more stable and constant aspects of Mr. Smith's behavior. Reasonably speaking, a specific personality is something you have all the time. Our interest in understanding Mr. Smith's behavior from a functional perspective, however, focuses on its variation across circumstances and situational specificity.

Different perspectives pose different questions, and they do so with different purposes. If a doctor meets a patient who complains that his throat aches when he talks, the doctor probably won't ask questions like these: "When do you talk? Who is present when you're talking? What do you say? How do you say it? What reactions do you get from others?" Instead the doctor will probably say, "And how long have you had this aching when you talk?" Then he will probably look at the patient's throat. This will give the doctor relevant information for his task. However, if the patient's complaint is "People don't seem to understand me!" the previously posed questions—"When do you talk?" etc.—seem suddenly relevant.

We formulate our questions in a way that can be considered adequate for gathering information in regard to a given task. Our neurophysiologist might have formulated his questions with a broader goal in mind. Suppose he is interested in tracking down the neurobiology of social-motor performance. He wishes to understand the patterns of impulse transmission in the brain and wants to be able to gather useful information for developing pharmacological agents that could effectively target these processes in disorders where disturbances in motor-communicative performance are important. That he specifically is studying Mr. Smith greeting Mr. Brown is not of crucial importance. Likewise, the personality researcher formulates his questions to be able to separate Mr. Smith from the rest of the population and categorize him according to personality traits—maybe for the purpose of finding social personality characteristics that could be useful in the interest of vocational recruitment.

A host of researchers from all kinds of perspectives could be gathered in Mr. Smith's neighborhood. The sociologist finds the greeting sequence as an example of the fragmentation of politeness in postmodern human interaction, the psychoanalyst sees in Mr. Smith's behavior the infant's wish for approval from a distant father figure, and many more that we don't have the time to describe here. They all ask their questions—and get their answers. And they are all involved in an intense debate over who is right and who is in possession of a true causal explanation, a debate often conducted with sentences that begin with "In essence, this is …" or "Basically, this is …" They all tend to speak of the cause as if it were something independent from the person who is observing and inferring.

But of all these perspectives, which one comes closest to "the true cause" of the actual behavioral event? Well, to answer that question we need to clarify what we mean by "cause." If we search in the philosophy of science, we will find different and competing assertions of what constitutes a causal explanation. This in itself should invoke a humble attitude toward asserting the existence of "true causes" as distinct from other kinds of causes.

Choosing a perspective is a starting point that eventually directs the questions we pose and therefore the answers we get. Even scientists can be understood as intentional organisms. So "truth" is then not a quality of something in the world that we can claim to have discovered. Rather, truth could be considered as an answer or answers that lead us further in pursuing our questions and intentions. This is the basis of a *pragmatic truth criterion*, a foundation of functional contextualism. According to this criterion, a statement is considered true to the extent it fulfills a practical purpose. In the present case, that overarching purpose is to predict and influence human behavior. A perspective is chosen a priori. Like other decisions, these choices precede the scientific and clinical process, and these decisions cannot be justified. In essence, they are choices.

In a way, this process looks like the one you go through when buying tickets to a soccer game. What seats should you choose? Maybe you should choose seats on the east side of the stadium. From there, you can see the entire field and you'll also get to sit in the sun. On the other hand, it can be quite irritating to have the sun in your eyes. What about the west side? It's also a good place for viewing the entire game, but it may be a little chilly in the shaded sections. In both cases, the seats are rather far from the goals, where most of the action takes place. Maybe you should sit on the south side, behind the goal of the opposing team. That will give you a great place for watching your team taking shots at the goal. But you could also choose the north side of the stadium to catch a good view of the home team's defense. An alternative would be to take into account the price of the tickets. Or another alternative is to sit where your buddies usually sit. Ultimately this is about what you want from the game. It would be very difficult to assert that any one perspective gives a better view in an absolute sense. It is ultimately about the purpose you have when booking the ticket. If there is a definite purpose (like watching your home team's defense), you could argue for the superiority of certain seats. But that would be a choice, and different spectators may choose differently.

So the core question of "best perspective" is a question of a philosophical nature, a question of utility, or a question of preferences. It is not a question that is amenable to a direct empirical test. But given a certain perspective, there are essential questions such as "Will treatment with drug X, which affects certain parts of the brain, be efficacious?" or "Are people with a Y-personality especially suitable for certain kinds of jobs?" This is where the empirical test is critical for the claim of effectiveness once the questions have been formulated. Our purpose is to understand and influence behavior. What will lead us there? Again we have a question that can be meaningfully and empirically tested in a vast variety of instances.

INFLUENCING BEHAVIOR

Mr. Smith is really quite dissatisfied with the formality of his conversations with his neighbor. He has very few friends and, based on their limited interactions, he thinks that Mr. Brown seems like a good guy. He would like to get to know him a little better. But Mr. Smith is worried that he might assume responsibility for his elderly neighbor who lives all by himself. Will he be able to live up to this responsibility? And beyond that, he thinks that it might seem a little awkward if he suddenly appears more interested in getting to know Mr. Brown. After all, they have been neighbors for many years now.

Mr. Brown, on the other hand, has lived much of his life as the one others depended on. He's used to being important to other people. He really misses that these days. His life is quite empty now that his kids are grown and his wife passed away. He's often had the thought that he could fix up Mr. Smith's garden. It would be nice to do something that mattered for someone else. But, throughout his life, Mr. Brown has gotten used to people asking him to do things. It's always been that way.

Now, if we would like to make a change in the relation between these two neighbors, I guess we could all come up with suggestions. Mr. Smith could put aside his concerns and ask Mr. Brown to come over for a cup of coffee. Mr. Brown could be more active in offering his services rather than waiting to be asked. Or he could buy some extra pansies and ask if the Smiths would be interested in his planting them in their garden. Or Mr. Smith could …

We could easily come up with a long list. The common denominator in these suggestions would probably be that ultimately they describe a change in behavior in order to contact new consequences in the environmental circumstances where these two persons exist. These suggestions will not be formulated in terms of changing a process that is hidden in a deep, mysterious part of these people.

Now, to be honest, the suggestions we have come up with can hardly be said to require formal training in a thorough analysis of human behavior. But thus far, our ambition has only been to establish the basis of the perspective we chose to take: a functional perspective, a perspective that has great relevance for working with human beings.

THE PURPOSE OF OUR PERSPECTIVE

The purpose of our perspective, as we will demonstrate in the following chapters, is to understand and influence human behavior. The basis for this lies in analyzing the behavior within the circumstances, or in the context, where it occurs. Of special interest is the understanding of the consequences of certain behaviors, that is, the function of those behaviors. This does not, of course, exclude the possibility of other perspectives. As human beings, we act purposely, that is, to achieve certain consequences. Ultimately, our chosen purpose is to best serve the people who seek our help. Our clients ask for help because they want change in their lives. Whatever best serves this purpose is considered to be truth in this process. This is a pragmatic truth criterion.

So, equipped with this perspective, we return to the ordinary life of clinical practice: to Jenny who is cutting her wrists; to the relationship between Anna and Peter; to Marie's social fear; to Mirza and his flashbacks; to Alice and her worry; and to Leonard, who didn't make it to work. It seems rather unlikely that mere advice would make a substantial difference in their lives. The fact that simple advice would not work could be considered part of the definition of a clinical condition (Öhman, 1994). But it is under these circumstances that we ask the question "Why are they behaving as they are?" That is what we will explore in the chapters that follow.

WHAT LIES AHEAD IN THIS BOOK

Three main sections follow. The first, Describing Behavior, deals with what can be observed when humans act, and how we as therapists should sort out what we see and what people tell us (chapters 1 and 2). The basic model of functional analysis is then presented (chapter 3). In the second part of the book, Explaining Behavior, we present the basic principles of learning. This is partly a review of well-established and often-used principles—respondent conditioning (chapter 4), operant conditioning (chapters 5 and 6)—and partly a presentation of more recent findings on human language and cognition (chapter 7). Part 2 ends with our presentation of an enhanced functional analysis including these more recent findings (chapter 8). The third part, Changing Behavior, focuses on clinical practice. Three chapters contain general strategies of psychotherapy (chapters 9, 10, and 11) and the last two present more specific strategies and techniques (chapters 12 and 13). We do not intend this book to be a treatment manual, but we still want to give you some practical guidelines that grow out of the functional perspective. In the end, this is what our professional lives are all about: what we can bring to our work with our clients.

PART 1

Describing Behavior

CHAPTER 1

Topographical Aspects of Behavior

The task of clinical behavior analysis is to formulate the problem in a way that increases the possibility for change. The individuals who seek our help usually show up with their own idea or conceptualization of the problem, for example:

- Marie wants help to overcome her "lack of self-confidence."

- The staff finds Jenny troublesome because she is so "self-destructive and manipulative."

- Peter and Anna want counseling for their "hopeless marriage."

- Leonard is referred to a therapist for treatment of his "persistent depression."

FORMULATING THE PROBLEM

All of the statements above contain a problem-formulation—the kinds of formulations we use in everyday language. Professional language is often quite similar to this, even if different words are used. Let's start by looking at Marie. What is she describing when she uses the expression "lack of self-confidence"?

I guess I've never been one of those who love speaking in front of a group. But it has gotten so much worse in the last few years. Now I can hardly sit down and have a cup of coffee with a colleague. It's even hard to go out if I know that I'm about to see someone. The worst part about it is that I never know what they're thinking. They must think that I'm kind of strange or something like that.

Marie describes a number of behaviors:

- She avoids situations where she has to speak in public.

- She avoids having a cup of coffee with colleagues.

- She thinks twice about going out if she is going to meet people.

- She worries over what other people might think about her.

- She thinks that others might find her strange.

To Marie's description, we could also add observations made by the therapist: while talking, Marie rarely makes eye contact and she tends to sit slightly turned away from the therapist. We now have started to formulate her problems in terms of observable behavior. It should be noted that most of these observations are not made by the therapist. They are made by Marie herself. The therapist has never seen her avoid speaking in public or having a cup of coffee. Neither has she seen Marie hesitating to go out. But we could assume that if the therapist were present in these everyday situations, these behaviors would be observable by the therapist. Marie, on the other hand, has made direct observations. It is her behavior. To call something *observable behavior* means that someone can actually observe the behavior in question. In a therapeutic context, this someone will most often be the client. This underlines the notion of therapy as a collaborative task, where the therapist largely depends on clients' observations of their own behavior.

However, it is not the case that Marie comes to therapy with a list of observable behaviors that she considers the problem. Her definition of the problem is that she lacks self-confidence. When asked about her withdrawn and avoidant lifestyle, she explains, "It surely must be that I lack self-confidence somewhere deep inside." To her, the lack of self-confidence becomes a cause of her behavior.

Let's consider how we might detect this problem with self-confidence. How could we observe it? We can observe Marie's avoidance, her hesitance, her behavior in social situations. The more we observe, the more behaviors we will detect. But we will never actually see any "self-confidence."

We easily end up in circular reasoning when lack of self-confidence is treated as a cause of her behavior. How can we conclude that she lacks self-confidence? The only thing we can do is to return to what we can observe: her behavior!

But what about Marie herself? Can she observe her lack of self-confidence? The answer is the same—she can only observe her behavior. She probably will be able to observe some of the events accessible to an outside observer: that she lowers her gaze, that she avoids meeting other people, and so on. But she will also be able to observe events that are inaccessible to an outside observer: that she is thinking about things, that she is remembering things, that she is feeling something in a certain situation. But in those cases still, it is what she is doing that is being observed.

The "self-confidence" that we so often refer to in everyday language is not there to be observed as a thing in itself, let alone a thing that one could have too little or have too much of. Instead we are referring to a label that may conveniently summarize a number of behavioral events. It is like a name. This name works in about the same way as when we use the word "bouquet" to denote a bunch of flowers that are put together in an arrangement. If we remove the flowers, the bouquet no longer exists. The bouquet was nothing in itself, but merely a convenient term to summarize what we could observe. It is important to note, however, that arguing that the bouquet does not exist as a thing is not the same as saying the word "bouquet" is meaningless. On the contrary, labels or words like "bouquet" allow us to conveniently talk about these flowers without referring to every single one of them as separate objects. Thus, this way of talking makes communication easier. However, just as a bouquet itself does not gather together a number of flowers, a lack of self-confidence does not set in motion a series of observable behaviors. This kind of reasoning, where we apply illusory explanations by simply naming phenomena, occurs frequently in everyday language. It should be noted, however, that it is also commonplace in psychological and psychiatric conceptual systems. Now let's take a look at Leonard's situation:

> Leonard hasn't been outside his apartment for the last two days. He spends most of the time on his couch in front of the TV, flipping between the afternoon shows. He goes to the store only after running out of food or cigarettes. But he hasn't been eating well for the last few weeks. He spends most of the time ruminating over his divorce, thinking about what went so wrong between him and Tina. He told his brother that life feels so meaningless. If it wasn't for his kids, he'd probably just kill himself.

Again we have a description of a number of behavioral events. In this case, these behaviors are characteristic of Leonard's life at the moment:

- He rarely leaves the apartment.

- He spends time on the couch in front of the TV.

- He eats irregularly.

- He ruminates.

- He experiences lack of meaning in his life.

- He thinks about suicide and at the same time about his children.

So, we ask ourselves, why is he behaving like this? Because he's depressed. But how do we know he's depressed? Because he's … And again we come back to descriptions of behavior. Basically this follows the same logic as Marie's lack of self-confidence. We attach a label to a number of behavioral events and then come to see the label as the cause of those events.

NAMING IS NOT EXPLAINING

Does this mean that a functional perspective is incompatible with using diagnoses in clinical case conceptualizations? Absolutely not. As previously stated, these labels are convenient terms and can be useful as such. It simplifies communication if we label Marie's difficulties as "social phobia" and Leonard's as "depression" instead of using a detailed list of observable behaviors when describing them. This, of course, assumes that we share a mutual understanding of these concepts with the listener. In the same way, it is easier for Marie to explain to a friend that she lacks self-confidence rather than stating all the behavioral events this term refers to. The problem that lurks among these abstractions is when they acquire a character as if they were something that Marie *is* or *has*, as if there were a property or thing inside her that could be treated as an entity separate from her behavior. It becomes even more problematic when this hypothetical entity is treated as an agent that is capable of governing the individual's behavior. Labels like these conveniently summarize, but they are not explanations.

Labels or concepts like these are useful because they can influence our behavior in a general way. If we are told that the person we will meet "suffers from depression" or "lacks self-confidence," this will probably influence how we act toward that person when we meet him or her. Although these general concepts speed up communication, they do so at the expense of individuality and detailed description. The word "bouquet" can correctly be applied to an armful of luscious red roses or a meager bunch of half-faded dandelions. If you want a bouquet to express your appreciation to someone dear, you'd be ill-advised to choose the latter even though you could, by indisputable logic, argue that they qualify as the same general concept as the roses: a bouquet. The problem with labels is that they may contribute to less effective action.

In psychotherapeutic settings, generally speaking, it is far from self-evident that these labels lead us to effective interventions. We do not know where the self-confidence is situated, and even less how to fix it when there is a "lack" of it. This puts us very much in the same position as Marie. Her self-confidence becomes a mysterious inner entity that needs to be repaired. But if we instead look to the list of observable behaviors, it becomes easier to identify strategies for change.

COVERT OR OVERT: IS IT JUST BEHAVIOR?

It is common to think that focusing on behavior means that private events, such as thoughts and feelings, are rendered unimportant. This is definitely not the case, and we would like to expand a bit further on this. In the observations we have gathered from Marie and Leonard, we mention behaviors like worrying, thinking, and feeling. These are phenomena that are located inside the skin of these individuals. From a functional perspective, these phenomena are not special, that is, they are not uniquely different from other kinds of behavior. They are, just like the other observations, something that these individuals do. They are examples of *covert behavior*.

The difference is that these private events do not lend themselves to direct observation by an independent observer. They are only accessible to direct observation by the person who is doing the behaving. To the rest of us, the private events can only become indirectly accessible when the person tells us about them or in some other way expresses what is going on beneath the skin. This does not render these observations less important. The difference lies in how easily they can be verified. Most of the time, it is easy to agree on whether a person cries or not, or if a person screams. But how can we agree on whether that person is mourning or feeling pain? We are still referring to something the person is doing, but this "doing" is not accessible to verification by an outside observer in the same way as the person's *overt behavior*. If we, as outside observers, are to gain meaningful access to these inner observations, we must share the same verbal "code" as the direct observer. For example, when I feel anxiety, do I refer to the same inner sensation as you do when you say you feel anxiety? And how do I know that I am hungry in the same way as you are?

Now sticking to observable behaviors alone can feel incomplete. It is as if you miss something genuinely human that is inherent in the expression "self-confidence" or the graveness in "depression." And, indeed, the phenomena we are referring to are not easily expressed in a few words depicting the person's behavior. We can be sure that the more we pay attention, listen to, and talk with our client, the more we will be able to observe; a richer and more complex picture evolves. However, it is not a picture of some other kind of material. It is just behavior, but it is more behavior!

THE MEDICAL MODEL

Let's consider the physician who has met a patient who complains about his throat aching when he talks. By our definition, the observation "experiencing pain while talking" would qualify as a behavioral event. In this scenario, the physician will probably look down the patient's throat to see what it looks like. In clinical psychology, we have grown used to a similar practice in a metaphorical sense. Human problems are to be understood by looking into the individual in the search for an underlying pathological element. But when we do this in psychology, we tend merely to formulate hypothetical constructs—constructs that do not contain any further observations of what the person is doing or under what circumstances. The medical model (see fig. 1.1) rests on a rather straightforward logic, and this relatively simple model is considered integral to the success of Western medicine (Sturmey, 1996).

Figure 1.1 The Medical Model

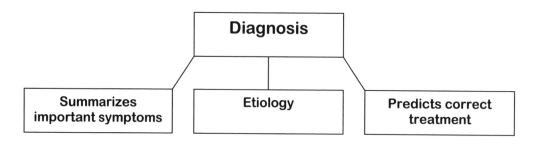

The physician does his observations by noting symptoms (which may well be behavioral data). The patient tells him about his sore throat, and this could be supplemented by confirming redness and a whitish fur on the palate (symptoms). He assumes that this could be a case of tonsillitis, since all the symptoms seem to point in that direction. It would then be reasonable to conclude that the cause of this is the presence of streptococci (etiology). This could easily be verified by taking a throat culture. This additional information is, however, not behavioral data. What has been identified is instead something that could be regarded as circumstances under which the problem is likely to occur. The conclusion is that, to cure the infection, treatment with antibiotics would be a proper intervention. The medical model works in an impeccable fashion in this case. But what if Marie tells us about her feelings of insecurity in the presence of others, how she finds it difficult to express herself when she gets nervous, and how she dare not approach her colleagues during lunch breaks (symptoms). If we were to obtain further information about her fears and avoidance, we would be able to conclude that she suffers from social phobia (diagnosis). But what can we say about etiology? Our present knowledge might point in the direction of inheritance or learning factors, that is, her personal history or special circumstances in that history. But there is no objective indicator or special test to confirm that it was her lack of self-confidence or that she had a disordered self-image somewhere inside. When searching for this, we are, at best, just observing more behavior. At worst, we are just inventing new words.

From the general diagnosis, there are a multitude of possible therapeutic strategies. Even if we can give an authoritative recommendation on treatment of choice for social phobia, the diagnosis does not tell us a great deal of what the treatment will be specifically directed at in Marie's case. As you may notice, the medical model does not work as well in this instance. This has also been found to be the case with lifestyle disorders such as hypertension, obesity, cardiovascular disease, and so on (Sturmey, 1996). In spite of this, the medical model has had a huge impact on the field of psychological treatments across a range of theoretical orientations. This is true even among approaches that share few other common assumptions. In a functional model, we do not gather behavioral observations primarily for the purpose of classification. We do it for the purpose of understanding the nature of the relationship between the individual and the environment and through this understanding to better equip ourselves to contribute to a process of change. The topographical description of behavior will serve as a starting point for this.

AND THY NAME SHALL BE …

We tend to see the process of naming, or attaching the proper label to, human misery as a matter of great importance. This can easily acquire an almost magical property of being able to capture the essence or truth that lies hidden inside. We see evidence of this in Jenny's case.

> *At Jenny's ward, there has been a divisive argument over whether her "lack of impulse control" is a sign of a "borderline personality disorder" or if she is acting out in a "histrionically manipulative" fashion. Others insist that her problems are really a "prolonged adaptation disorder with narcissistic features." It seems almost as if it is impossible to agree because of professional differences.*

Whether Jenny cuts her wrists, yells at the staff, or collects the pills that are in her cupboard is not debated. These events are not only observable, they can also be agreed upon by independent observers. What is not hidden from the eyes is more easily agreed upon. Whether Jenny actually is sad when she says so is a question that can evoke many answers. The staff cannot, of course, see her "sadness." Jenny is the sole observer of her sense of sadness. The essential descriptive task in a clinical situation like this is not to decide what she is or has but rather to describe what she does.

OBSERVING AND CATEGORIZING BEHAVIORAL EXCESSES AND DEFICITS

To continue with our task, we need a way to organize the observations we make when we work on a viable problem-formulation. We make a basic distinction between behaviors that occur too frequently (excesses) and those that don't occur frequently enough (deficits) (Kanfer & Saslow, 1969). This distinction provides, at least at first glance, a relatively easy way of categorizing behavior.

Behavioral excess may be defined as a behavior or class of behaviors that can be considered problematic due to excess in frequency, intensity, duration, or to their occurrence in inappropriate situations. Here are some examples:

- Hand washing twenty-five times a day (frequency)

- Hand washing with steel wool and detergents (intensity)

- Hand washing thirty minutes at a stretch (duration)

- Interrupting a conversation to go to wash one's hands because the topic could be considered "dirty" (occurrence in inappropriate situation)

A *behavioral deficit* is a behavior or class of behaviors that can be considered problematic due to deficits in frequency, intensity, duration, or their lack of occurrence in situations where they would be beneficial for the individual. Here are some examples:

- Washing hands once a week (frequency)

- Washing dirty hands without using soap or any cleansing product (intensity)

- Washing dirty hands for just a few seconds so they will not be clean (duration)

- Without washing visible dirt from hands, being seated at a formal dinner (lack of occurrence when it would be beneficial)

Thus, it is not the behavior of "washing hands" in itself that is the basis for categorization: it is the inappropriateness of the behavior in a given situation. In the previous examples, it is obvious that it is "too much" when we use the term "excess" and "too little" when we use the term "deficit." But does this mean that we have identified a norm for adaptive hand washing? How often do people wash their hands? Twice a day or five times a day? How long do they wash their hands? And what should be a normal cleansing product? Actually, we do not know of any data that could, in an objective way, tell us what the behavioral norm for all people should be. It is probably safe to assume that there would be substantial variation in what would be considered "normal." The examples above depart in an obvious way from what most of us would consider normal behavior, and that makes them easy to categorize as excesses or deficits, especially since these behaviors would have adverse consequences for one's skin, way of life, and social functioning.

An Excess—of What?

But where is the cutoff for an excess behavior, and where does a deficit begin? Can excesses and deficits occur together? Let's consider some examples. Jenny is cutting her wrists, which can cause a serious threat to her health. This is a behavioral event that is excessive as soon as it occurs. Once is enough to be considered too much. We would not consider wrist cutting in terms of relative variations in the population. It is not an act that, in principle, every person is expected to perform under certain circumstances and thus a problem only when it exceeds a certain frequency. Also, in clinical settings we are bound to consider it as behavioral excess due to its potential harmfulness in the same way that we are bound to consider drug abuse or physically abusive behavior as excesses. The laws and ethical guidelines we follow as clinicians lead us to define such behaviors as excesses regardless of circumstances.

Let's return to the problems of Anna and Peter and try working on a useful formulation of the problem. Their own formulation is that they have a "hopeless marriage." Here we immediately run the risk of perceiving their marriage as if it was a thing that had acquired a quality of hopelessness. You probably will not be very surprised when we advocate that a more viable avenue is considering what behaviors are getting in the way of them living happily together. The primary task will be to observe what they are doing. The available observations come from two perspectives: Anna's and Peter's. A third perspective can be added: observations made by the therapist.

When this couple is encouraged to define their relationship problems in terms of observable behaviors, Peter puts forth their frequent arguing (excess) that is followed by long periods of silence (here defined as excess, but it could equally well be understood in terms of deficit). He is sad that Anna does not want to have sex with him (deficit), and he does not think she shows him the respect he is entitled to (deficit). Instead, she continuously makes unreasonable demands of him (excess).

Anna, too, says that the worst part is the frequent arguing (excess) and the silence that follows. She says that she does not get any appreciation from Peter for what she does (deficit) and that he does not spend time with their daughter (deficit). Anna describes how she has to put up with him constantly working long hours (excess), and lately she has become really worried about his drinking habits (excess).

We have now taken a substantial step forward toward reaching a more viable formulation of the problem than their initial description of "hopeless marriage." But it is also an improvement over the label "relationship problem" that might be the label we would prefer as clinicians.

Another observation is made by the therapist. Both Anna and Peter's descriptions of problems include behaviors that the other person does, or they both do together. Neither identifies behaviors they do alone that could be causing problems. That is a deficit in both of their repertoires, noted by the therapist.

When the couple is invited to comment on the other's description, they note that they agree on two things: the excessive arguing and the silence that follows. However, Anna says, "I just don't get why you have to bring that sex issue up when our relationship is the way it is. Sure, I respect that your work is important, but it is always given priority over us." And Peter comments, "Okay, I've been drinking too much lately, but the pressure has just been too much for me these past few months. But how can I spend more time with our daughter? As soon as I have a day off, you take Lisa and go over to your sister's place!"

Clearly they will also have comments on these comments and so on. We will, however, stop at this point and, like the therapist, note a behavioral excess for both of them: finding arguments in how the other's behavior causes problems in their relationship.

The issue of Peter's consumption of alcohol has also been raised, and it would be difficult to ignore this. So for a moment we put our analysis of the other problematic behaviors aside and focus on this. Anna says, "I think he's turning into an alcoholic." This is a profound concern for her, especially when taking Lisa into consideration. Now we are not primarily interested in what to call Peter but rather in what he does. In this case, what he does is drink alcohol. How do we assess what is "too much" in this case? Peter's drinking habits could be related to existing knowledge about average consumption levels in the population and to the existing knowledge of the risk for long-term adverse health consequences due to excessive alcohol consumption. From a functional perspective, yet another aspect becomes important. Both Peter and Anna define their quarrels as an excess that is definitely unwanted. These quarrels tend to occur more often in association with discussions connected to Peter's drinking: both discussions about his drinking and discussions that take place when Peter is under the influence of alcohol. Peter himself says he likes "to have a drink and relax," but when the actual consequences are examined, you will see that this is rarely the case. Drinks tend to be followed by fighting more often than relaxation. It could thus be argued that his behavior does not really work very well in regard to its desired effects. Neither does it work well in regard to other important objectives in his life. At this point, our topographical analysis has led us to functional aspects, and these aspects provide a further basis for categorizing Peter's drinking as a behavioral excess.

CATEGORIZING BEHAVIORAL EXCESS

We have now identified a number of grounds for categorizing behavior as an excess:

- It departs substantially from a generally agreed upon norm.

- It is associated with suffering and impairment of daily functioning.

- It is associated with known health-related risks.

- It is a behavior that is attached to certain legal and ethical issues.

- It is a behavior that is incompatible with important values for the person.

This might give the impression that working with this kind of categorization results in well-founded and logically impeccable judgments, but this is hardly the case. If we meet a person who spends two hours a day showering, this is an obvious excess (given that the person does not have a very convincing explanation for this). If we, on the other hand, meet a person who showers for fifteen minutes every other week, we would probably agree that it is a deficit. But what's the normal rate? Well, we guess that most people would say once a day. Do we need to do this for our survival and to abstain from becoming socially repulsive? We doubt it! Is this a rate that is vital to our physical health? Hardly! But still, we tend to perceive this as a normal rate. This is worth considering since sooner or later we will run into this question: Who decides what is an excess and what is a deficit? Most often the answer will be that you do, together with your social group. Consider what is normal regarding the following:

- The frequency of intercourse with people other than one's spouse

- The amount of time a toddler's parent spends at work

- The duration of mourning after a broken relationship

- The extent to which deeply personal topics should be discussed in public

But if this kind of categorization is to a large degree subjective, should we even do it? The answer has to be yes, basically because it is not possible to avoid categorization. As humans, we assess, make judgments, and categorize. It is as though this is a fundamental part of being human. For clinical practice, it is important to do this in a way that it is open for discussion and criticism, and in a way that helps clients clarify what they are doing and what they want and need to change.

A Deficit—of What?

We can observe an individual's behavior and sense that something is missing. Take, for example, the depressed person's lack of activity, the shy person's short and quiet answers that make it hard to hear what he says, or the person who does not show up for scheduled appointments. Similar to the categorizations described above, we could take the same stance in regard to deficits. The individual does not perform or too infrequently performs behaviors that would be beneficial for health or social adaptation or that would be functional in the service of personal values. But would we be able to observe a behavioral deficit? It could be difficult, given it would require that we possess a thorough knowledge of exactly what behaviors should exist in an ordinary repertoire. What we can do, in collaboration with the client, is to state behaviors that would be functional in regard to desirable life changes. What are identified as behavioral deficits could actually be seen as ideas for behavior change.

Excess or Deficit—What Is It?

The distinction between excesses and deficits may seem straightforward and obvious. As we will see, however, making the distinction involves several decisions. The first decision is choosing one's perspective. Let's look at this in Alice's case.

Alice is in one of her "periods" when she avoids almost everything. "Nothing's working anymore," she says. For several months, she's had no problems going to work. But then all of a sudden she just feels unable to manage these trips, and when her fiancé doesn't give her a ride, she stays home. She says she has turned "antisocial" again. By this, she refers to the fact that she avoids being around people, even if these are coworkers or friends. She says that she doesn't want to have to explain to others "why I am like this."

Let's go back to the task of observing. What does Alice do? Let's focus on two observations:

- She avoids traveling to work by herself.

- She avoids situations where there are plenty of people.

When confronted with the task of categorizing these and similar behaviors, the question arises: Are these excesses or deficits? She avoids too much, but that implies that she does not do certain things enough. This question is interesting because it turns our attention to the function of the descriptive analysis.

If, in Alice's behavioral repertoire, we identify a class of behavior that reasonably could be labeled "avoidance" and if these behaviors occur with a frequency that somehow is associated with impairment, they will fall in the category "excess." Our analysis will then focus on these and put them in a theoretical context where we can explain the function of these behaviors.

From a pragmatic point of view, however, in therapy it could be reasonable to talk of the same phenomena as "deficits." Alice rarely travels alone and rarely allows herself to be in social situations. By defining these as deficits, they are indirectly understood as behaviors where an increase in frequency could be assumed to be beneficial. So, in order to facilitate life changes, it seems more straightforward to do more of these deficit behaviors than to do less of the more abstract "avoiding." The categorization of deficit is also intuitively closer to Alice's own definition: "Nothing works anymore." Theoretically, though, we will be interested in understanding the class of "avoidance." Seeing this as an excess also guides the clinician toward the observation that "avoid" and "can't do" do not necessarily imply an absence of behavior. "Doing nothing" is often an extensive activity.

The Relation Between Excess and Deficit

Jenny's behavior is seen as very worrisome at the ward. Apart from cutting her wrists with whatever sharp objects she can find, she yells abusively at the staff and causes disruption by repeatedly requesting to leave the ward on her own. However, when these behaviors are not occurring, the staff describes her as "fairly invisible." She spends most of her time by herself but does very few activities. She seems to find it difficult to ask for things, whether it is ordinary things such as unlocking the kitchen or talking to a staff member when she doesn't feel good.

The behavioral excesses are obvious because they constitute a serious threat to her well-being and they are aversive to the people around her. In these cases, interventions are often directed at the excesses—interventions aimed at making her stop. But parallel to this, several deficits can be observed (see fig. 1.2).

Figure 1.2 Excesses and Deficits: Jenny

Excesses	Deficits
■ *Cutting herself* ■ *Yelling obscenities* ■ *Nagging*	■ *Spending time with others* ■ *Taking initiative to do things on her own* ■ *Asking for things*

Drastic excesses are always a reason for considering deficits in the behavioral repertoire. The connection between them also provides a ground for raising hypotheses about the function of these excesses. In the same vein, watching Alice, we can see the interdependence between excesses and deficits (see fig. 1.3). When one class of behaviors increases in frequency, it corresponds to decreases in another. This furthers the analysis by providing a basis for establishing their functional relationship to each other.

Figure 1.3 Excesses and Deficits: Alice

Excesses	Deficits
■ *Worrying about her health* ■ *Worrying about how other people might evaluate her*	■ *Managing to get to her job on her own* ■ *Being in social situations when there are plenty of people around*

OBSERVING EMOTIONS: HOW DOES IT FEEL?

It might be worth taking a moment to consider what to do with the observation of emotions. We have gotten to know Marie who has defined her problem in terms of "lack of self-confidence." She also tells us that she "feels a lot of anxiety." This obviously sounds like an excess, though a covert one. But what is Marie observing? She senses something on the inside that her *verbal surroundings* (that is, the cultural context that uses a certain language) have taught her to label "anxiety." When does this become an "excess"? Well, we are now entering an area with a complete lack of normative data and explicit guidelines. How is life supposed to feel? Can we be sure that it really is anxiety she is feeling? The key here is that Marie describes her suffering, and this suffering poses an obstacle to the life she wishes to live. These are the kinds of things that bring people to seek therapy: the feeling is too much, too little, or maybe not there at all. We are constantly facing the questions of what is too little, too much, or if clients' emotions correspond with what they say they feel.

It could hardly be considered meaningful to try to settle these questions in an absolute sense. The client's report could in principle be regarded as valid. We would have a difficult time finding arguments to invalidate it. On the other hand, we should keep in mind the fact that what we label anxiety is simply one aspect of the problem-formulation, and it should by no means be regarded as the most central part. And it is important to note that when the intensity of feeling states is considered the problem, an intuitively tempting solution seems to follow, as we see in these examples:

■ "If I only could get rid of this anxiety, I would be free from my problems."

■ "If I only could feel motivated, I would get on with my life."

In reality, however, these intuitive solutions may be a part of the problem.

HOW MUCH DETAIL DO WE NEED?

How detailed should an adequate description of behavior be? We said that Marie is isolating herself and suggested that this involves several behavioral events:

■ She is most frightened of the informal meetings and lunch breaks at work.

■ She always brings her own food to have an excuse to eat alone.

■ She plans activities to keep herself busy so she has excuses for not going out after work.

- She stays away from situations where she thinks that her colleagues may bring up ideas about social activities.

We now have a more detailed picture than the description of "isolating herself." The isolating is not an event that is observable in itself but rather is a description that refers to a consequence (becoming isolated) of the behaviors above. Of course, it would be possible to go into more detail about how she prepares and eats the lunch she has brought with her and how she plans her activities. If we wanted to go into extreme detail, everything could be expressed as muscular movements. But there would be nothing gained at that level of detail. We need to be detailed enough only to get our analysis working, which means understanding what happens in a way that allows us to influence it.

However, we should be alert to the kind of abstractions that we get so used to that we tend to perceive them as if they were observable events: "acting out," "fulfilling needs," "forming attachment." Do we know what the person is doing when we use these phrases? We cannot teach clients to "fulfill" their "needs." We can, however, teach them a number of skills that would increase the likelihood of getting what they consider, or what is considered, to be needed. These skills need to be specified to the extent that we can perceive them as functional units at a level where they can be learned. Thus, the level of detail is governed by pragmatic considerations.

HYPOTHETICAL CONSTRUCTS, OR WHAT ABOUT THE SELF-CONFIDENCE?

Nowhere in our descriptive analysis have we found that the client shows a deficit in "self-confidence" or an excess in, using rather circular logic, a "lack" of self-confidence. It is important to be alert to hypothetical constructs that do not add further observations. It is so easily said that the passive person has a deficit in "motivation," the anxiously withdrawn person has a deficit in "courage," and the person behaving angrily has an excess of "aggressiveness." But this restating is just another version of "naming," and, as we said earlier, naming is not explaining. A good rule of thumb is to search for verbs instead of nouns. Ask clients what they are *doing* rather than what they *are* or *have*.

FUNCTIONAL FOR LIFE

In the process of clinical problem-formulation, we are moving from a diffuse and commonsense description of problems to a description expressed in terms of observable behavioral events in order to get a clearer picture of what the person is doing. But in order to decide whether these behavioral events are problematic or not, we need to consider what is beneficial for the person. Problem behaviors are behaviors that are dysfunctional in relation to living consistently with one's own values and goals. Ultimately we want to promote behaviors that are functional in that sense. Functionality is not inherent in a behavioral event; it exists only in relation to something. We could assume that all behaviors are functional in relation to something, or else they would not be there. We are searching, however, for behaviors that could be functional for clients, in getting to the life they seek.

- *Marie would like help to overcome her lack of self-confidence. She thinks this would enable her to seek a new job. And she is so tired of feeling lonely and isolated on weekends.*

- *The staff is really worried that Jenny might seriously hurt herself. They've seen too many young girls develop cutting habits and wish that they could help her. Jenny herself wants to be discharged from the ward.*

- *Alice wants to be the way she was before she became so "anxious."*

- *Peter and Anna are not really sure what they want, basically because they thought the therapist's question "What do you really want?" was a prompt to come up with a solution to their problems. They agree, though, that if they didn't have the problems they have, they would like to be a family.*

At this point, we do not have exact and well-defined goals to govern the process of change. The formulation and mutual agreement on the goals for the therapeutic work is a later part of the clinical process. What we do have are rather vague formulations of a direction in which to go as we pursue our analysis. We need to clarify these formulations, and we learn more about how to do that in chapter 10. Let's now move on to the topic of how the temporal and situational variations can be used in the process of gaining knowledge of behavior.

CHAPTER 2

Observing Behavior: When, Where, and How Much?

Every act performed exists in space and time. When a person describes behavior, there is always a "where" and a "when." In order to gain an understanding of the function of behaviors, we need to know how the behaviors "move." When do they increase in frequency? When do they decrease? The variation in any given behavioral event supplies us with important clues when searching for the factors that govern the event.

But there is an additional purpose in observing and measuring behavior. It will supply a point of reference for considering the extent of a problem. We will also have a basis for making comparisons between individuals. A person who isolates himself in his apartment seven days a week, in a sense, has a bigger problem than one who does it three days a week. And we might not consider the person who does it once a week as having an "isolation problem" at all. But our primary interest in topography is not the comparison between individuals. What is more essential is the variation for a given individual. This will provide relevant information for the task of exploring what governs behavior and its functions, and if interventions applied are appropriate. If the person who isolates himself in his apartment seven days a week reduces this to five days, this would be a reduction by almost 30 percent. He would still be isolating himself, but this variation provides us with important information of a change process.

So let's return to some of the expressions our clients have used to describe their suffering:

- "Constant quarreling"

- "Everything seems hopeless"

- "Worry all the time"

- "Totally unconfident whether I'm able to …"

When we describe problems, we tend to use generalizations like these. But this creates difficulties. Someone might object that, in an objective sense, the generalizations are not true. We prefer to stress that these kinds of generalizations have a limited ability to guide us in a process of change. The cues they offer for the individual to understand how his behavior works are sparse. They are more like statements saying that the behavior does not work.

If we, for instance, look at Peter and Anna, we see that their quarreling is not constant. Since they both work, they do not see each other for most of their waking hours (which, at most, allows some minor arguments over the phone). Is it then the case that they quarrel as soon as they meet? If the answer is yes, this would still be a more specified description than the one we started off with. But is this the case? Probably not.

In order to get a clearer picture of their problem, we have to ask two very relevant questions: "How often?" and "How much?" We would like to see the variation, in time and space, of their behavior. This is not a process that, in some clever way, aims at proving that they are wrong about the frequency of quarreling when they say "constant." The issue here is to open them up to the possibility of understanding and change. "Constant" provides little opportunity for this. Still, this statement has a function. We often use such generalizations to communicate emotional messages. Perhaps when Peter and Anna say this, it reflects their despair over all the time spent in seemingly endless quarrels over the trivialities of everyday life. And even though their statement may be considered valid in that sense, we will try to explore the situation further in order to catch the nuances of variation in the actual behavior to which it refers. It will be crucial to find ways to observe the variation in Peter's and Anna's arguing in order to understand it functionally and to gain an understanding that opens the way to a constructive process of change. But these observations are also needed in order to measure the result of such a process.

MONITORING BEHAVIOR

First, we want to learn more about the frequency and intensity of the problematic behaviors in our clients' lives. This is called measuring a *baseline*.

In order to do this, the therapist gives Peter and Anna the task of monitoring their quarrels: when and how they occur. According to the couple, this ranges from irritated comments to situations where they both yell at each other. There has never been any physical violence, but they do say things, such as sarcastic comments, in order to hurt each other. The therapist gives them a "quarrel diary." They each get one, not only to avoid arguments about the monitoring itself but also because the therapist thinks it will be interesting to compare their respective registrations (see fig. 2.1).

The couple has also defined the extended periods when they remain silent as a problem. Would it also be possible to monitor this in a diary? A problem is that this might be trying to observe a "nonbehavior," even though we stated earlier that "doing nothing" should be regarded as an activity. Taken the other way around: when or how

Figure 2.1 Monitoring of Problematic Behavior: Quarrel Diary

Date	Place	What happened?
6/4	The kitchen, after dinner	The usual nagging over work time vs. family time and who's responsible for what
6/7	Over the telephone	Arguing about who's going to pick Lisa up

would we be able to conclude that there are fewer or shorter periods of silence? The answer, of course, is this: when they are talking to each other more frequently. So it would be a potentially valuable thing if they could monitor infrequent but desirable communicative behaviors. This is a class of behaviors connected with their difficulties in settling everyday concerns such as who is going to pick up their daughter, what time Peter will get home from work, and whether Anna will take their daughter to visit Anna's sister on the weekend. Peter and Anna have agreed that they have a definite deficit in the constructive handling of these kinds of topics. So they are asked to register their conversations about something that has happened or those dealing with specific family concerns.

Figure 2.2 Graphic Representation of Problematic Behavior

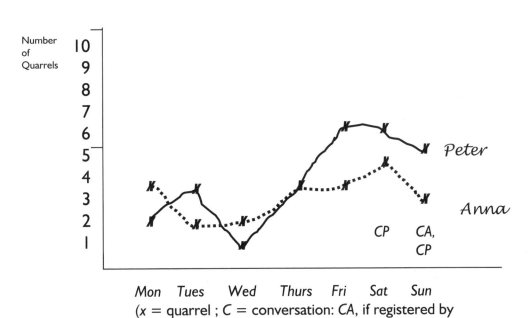

(x = quarrel ; C = conversation: CA, if registered by Anna; CP, if registered by Peter)

After the first week of monitoring, the couple and the therapist sit down and look at their observations so far. From the registrations, the therapist, together with Anna and Peter, can follow the fluctuations in frequency and the character of the quarreling. The therapist notes that Peter has a higher estimation of the number of quarrels than Anna has (see fig. 2.2). The frequency escalates Friday afternoon and evening, and continues at an elevated level during the weekend. Thus far, the weekend seems to be the period of the most frequent arguments, which is perhaps due to the simple fact that they are together more. When considering the frequency of conversation, they find they seldom talk. Anna notes two conversations. Peter notes one, and one of the conversations Anna notes, Peter has labeled as a quarrel. However, they both agree about one conversation Sunday night that concerned whether Peter could pick Anna up before the therapy session. Now we can say that we have a one-week baseline for two classes of behavior, the quarrels and the constructive conversations, that are considered central in their relational problems. A closer inspection of how these behaviors "move" in time and space will give important information for understanding their functional relationships.

How Monitoring Affects Behavior

Someone might wonder if there isn't a risk that the intensity and frequency of the quarreling will decline if you are expected both to write every occasion down and to discuss the quarrels with your therapist. These are socially undesirable behaviors, so you might think twice before emitting them. Likewise, if you write down every occasion of everyday conversation, will not the likelihood of these events increase by the very fact that you've been instructed to record them? In other words, could there be a problem with reactivity of measurement? The risk is obvious! It is even very likely (Heidt & Marx, 2003). If the purpose were to achieve an estimate in an uninfluenced objective manner, that would be a problem. By studying behavioral events, these events are often likely to be influenced by the very fact that we are studying them. Disregard the question of whether it would be possible to study behavior in a totally detached way, free of influence, because the overarching purpose here is to understand and to influence. Above all, the monitoring process should be designed to be useful in that way. The monitoring process will contain an inherent tension between the interest of studying behavioral events as they appear in our clients' lives in order to understand them, and the fact that what we observe possibly will change by the mere fact that we are observing.

So, what do we do when we give Anna and Peter this monitoring task? Observing one's own behavior can constitute a powerful intervention. Beyond that, a new social context—that of Anna and Peter bringing their quarrel diaries to and discussing them with their therapist—is created in this process of observation. This is likely to make the quarrel diaries and discussion of them an even more powerful intervention.

"Isn't this manipulation?" someone might ask. We are inclined to agree that it is. In experimental science, the word "manipulation" does not carry the negative connotations that it has in everyday life and language. In experimental science, it simply means "influence," that is, you intently make a change in ("manipulate") one variable that somehow is under your control in order to observe how it influences other variables. If we accept this definition of "manipulation," the self-monitoring process can be seen as something that manipulates the situation. The behavioral event (quarreling) could be influenced by the fact that one is requested to monitor it. But above all, the monitoring process provides information about the problem at hand (in this case, the quarreling) and how it might be affected. For most of us, the word "manipulation" leaves a bad taste in our mouths. It is much more appetizing or acceptable if we instead say "influence" and pose our questions this way: what is it that we are influencing and in what way are we influencing it? And even if we persist in using the word "manipulation," we are not referring to a process of making people do things that oppose their own goals and values. On the contrary! When it comes down to the core processes, all human interaction is manipulation. We cannot interact without influencing one another.

Observation of Covert Behavior

In Peter and Anna's case, there are tangible excesses and deficits to track in the monitoring process. But what about Leonard's case? He has a passive lifestyle, and passivity also characterizes his relationship to the therapist. The central task is to find the variability in behavior behind expressions like "my life is so hopeless." In session, Leonard tends to answer questions about variability in a negative way, as we see in the following exchange:

Therapist: How have things been since last week?

Leonard: Not so good, I guess.

Therapist: Has there been any day that's been a little better?

Leonard: No, it's mostly the same.

Therapist: You haven't done anything that's made you feel better, or worse for that matter?

Leonard: Not really, it's been pretty much the same all the time. But I had a hard time coming here today. Things just felt hopeless.

We could take this as a descriptive statement about Leonard's life. Depressed people often describe their lives as if they did not contain any variation at all. And still, from an independent observer's point of view, this is hardly the case. Does this invalidate the content of the statement? When the therapist asks Leonard to describe the past week, he describes the picture he recollects, which is a general and rather diffuse picture that lacks detail and specific information. Providing this kind of generic memory has been found to be a phenomenon that is associated with depression (Williams, 1992).

We need a different kind of information than what Leonard reports in this diffuse way. If Leonard was attentive to his life, there are plenty of things that would be important for his therapist to know. For example: What activities occur during an ordinary week and what emotion accompanies them? During the week, is there anything that is associated with experiencing satisfaction? What events are followed by lowered mood, and how does Leonard cope with these events? As a part of his treatment, there could be a long list of valuable observations that Leonard could monitor (see fig. 2.3). And, as before, there are three basic questions we always come back to: What does Leonard do? Under what circumstances does he do it? What consequences follow upon his doing it?

Figure 2.3 Leonard's Activity Monitoring Sheet

	Morning	Noon	Evening	Night
Monday	Sat at home and watched TV (moody)	Took a nap, called brother (felt down, miserable!)	Made a stew (felt quite proud of myself)	Lay in bed a long time before I fell asleep (anxiety)
Tuesday	Slept till 10:00	Visited work (really tough, but satisfied afterward)	Watched TV, fell asleep on the sofa	Tried to read, had a hard time falling asleep. Thought of the kids.
Wednesday	Woke up early (anxiety)			

As you can see, one of Leonard's frequent activities is his ruminating over different aspects of his problems—especially ruminating on the pain he might have inflicted on those close to him. Here's what Leonard says about that:

> Over and over again I go over the issue of what I've given my kids. How will they manage their lives? Other kids' dads don't sit at home, feeling miserable like I do. I just can't understand why I should feel this way. Of course, things have been pretty rough on me since the divorce, but feeling this bad … I just don't get it. You know, I think a lot: What if I never come out of it? What if I never get well?

In everyday language, we would say that Leonard suffers from guilt, and it is so easy to start treating this "guilt" as if it were a thing somewhere inside of him. If we approach this from a behavioral point of view, we want to know what Leonard does. What is he doing when he goes over (and over and over) the issues of "guilt," "whose fault," "why," and "how things will turn out"? Two aspects—content and activity—are of particular interest. Concerning content, Leonard's therapist needs to ask this question: What is he ruminating over? That aspect is perhaps the one that is most easily accessed because that is usually what the client will tell us. But equally important is considering ruminating as an "activity," that is, what is Leonard doing when he ruminates? When is he ruminating? Does he do other things while ruminating? What follows after ruminating? What does he do then and how does that feel? These aspects usually are less accessible, basically because clients do not attend to them a great deal. This, in turn, might partially be due to the fact that attention is focused on the content and the suffering associated with it.

Behavioral Approach Test

Up till now, we have presumed that the analysis can be built upon continuously occurring behavioral events that are relevant for self-monitoring—events that would allow us to assess not only the extent of a problem but also to what extent the problem has been influenced by treatment. However, for many problems we encounter, observations made on a daily basis are less viable and not as relevant to our central concern.

Let's consider, for example, Alice's difficulties in getting to work, which are due to the anxiety associated with traveling by herself. What should we observe? We could monitor the number of days she actually gets to work, but how informative would that be for our purposes? As a therapist, you would probably like to have a more detailed picture of what goes on when she is confronted with the demand to travel by herself. When her fiancé is not away, he usually gives her a lift. If Alice feels worried and if he is in town, she sometimes calls him and asks for a ride. She also sometimes walks the two miles to work, if she can arrange with a friend of hers who lives halfway along her route to meet her so they can walk the last part of the way together. Taking the bus is out of the question in the morning because it is so crowded, and she doesn't have a driver's license, so she can't drive herself. Alice also has a problem with predicting whether her chosen mode of transportation will work or not. Sometimes, Alice says, walking or taking her bike is no problem, but other times it seems just impossible for her to leave home. She says, "I get nervous just at the thought of going all by myself." People around her are puzzled about what Alice can do and what she cannot do because of her anxiety disorder. This is especially true since everyone agrees that when she is at work she performs very well. So what should we observe? A central aspect of her problem seems to be her ability (or inability) to deal with situations that evoke anxiety, and it would be helpful if we could gain information about and insight into this more quickly than by observation of her spontaneously emitted behavior. One way is to use a behavioral approach test (BAT) in which the subject—in this case, Alice—approaches situations she fears; the situations are presented in a graded or hierarchical manner (those that evoke the least fear are presented first, and so on). In Alice's case, her therapist takes a map and marks the route from Alice's home to her workplace. Alice is then instructed to walk as far as she can. She puts a mark on the map at the place where she stops. In addition, she takes notes on the emotions that she experiences and the thoughts that she has on her walk as well as her motives for turning back. After this information is noted, she is free to return home.

You can use this kind of approach test—a thorough BAT would include several situations that invoke increasing levels of fear—for any number of situations that a client avoids due to fear. The client, with assistance from the therapist, ranks the situations from the easiest to the most difficult. For Alice, apart from walking alone to her job, she also fears going by car unless she knows the driver well. Her fear increases if she has to sit in the backseat. But by far the worst for Alice is going long distances by bus, especially if the bus is crowded. These situations constitute a sample of fear-relevant situations for Alice that could be arranged in a hierarchy to serve as a base for a BAT. She is then instructed to approach as many of these situations as she is prepared to. This should be done in a graded fashion while simultaneously noting her reactions. This will provide you with important information. In particular, the level up to which she is prepared to approach the situations will give you a personally relevant estimate of her freedom of movement. You can return to this estimate to evaluate the treatment and determine its efficacy by repeating the procedure. We'll return to creating a hierarchy of feared situations in chapter 13 when we discuss this as a useful tool for organizing exposure treatment.

Observation by Others

Now let's turn to Jenny and see what we might be able to learn about her situation. Jenny's self-destructive behavior is a behavioral excess that is potentially accessible as data for therapy. Questions on how often, under what circumstances, and on the seriousness of her actions could be formulated in a way that allows monitoring. Ultimately Jenny would be the one to handle this monitoring, but in a situation like hers, it is often people around her who report on the problem. In an institutional setting like Jenny's, an important task of the staff is to monitor in order to grasp or understand a behavior labeled "self-destructive." The staff should ask these questions: What is it Jenny does? When does she do it (that is, what is the precipitating situation or what happened prior to her action)? What happens after she does it? See figure 2.4 for an example of a chart that might be developed to monitor self-destructive behavior.

Self-destructive behaviors are often so drastic that other people in the same social setting simply can't ignore them. But at the same time, it should be remembered that it is equally important to gather wider observations, especially of behaviors, which are not

Figure 2.4 Monitoring Chart for Self-Destructive Behavior

Time	What happened before?	What did the person do?	What happened afterward?

quite so dramatic, that would be helpful to increase. In Jenny's case, we would be most interested in communicative behaviors that pose no threat to her well-being.

Taking a wider perspective in our observation rather than focusing exclusively or primarily on the most conspicuous behavioral excesses is vital when we deal with people who come to us for treatment because of infrequent but socially undesirable acts like exhibitionism or violent crimes. These are two classical examples of behaviors for which it is difficult to estimate a baseline. An infrequent behavior could require an unduly long period of observation to gather information concerning when and where the behavior occurs, and to make an estimate of reliable change over time. In this case, it may be much more informative to observe deficits. What does the exhibitionist's normal approach behavior to the opposite sex look like, and when does it occur? Concerning violence, we might search for behaviors—such as involvement in drug-related activities or spending time in high-risk situations—that set the stage for violent acts. We monitor behavior in order to understand the individual who acts. His or her actions will gain comprehensibility if we consider the variation they show. By monitoring behavior and observing the circumstances that lead to variations in the behavior, we will more easily access the function of that behavior. This in turn will not only help us to influence the behavior but also help us to assess the extent to which this attempt to influence has been successful.

RATING SCALES FOR BEHAVIOR EVALUATION

In clinical work, one of the most common ways to gather information suitable for evaluation is to use rating scales. These may consist of forms where a person other than the client rates the client's difficulties in a given format. However, more common is the use of different self-ratings. We will only touch on this topic briefly here, as a more thorough presentation lies outside the scope of this book.

Let's consider a scenario where you conduct treatment. Before the treatment process is initiated, you ask the client, "How are you feeling?" You proceed with your intervention, and afterward you ask, "And how are you feeling now?" Now you could compare the answer from the first occasion with the one from the second. But there is a problem: the questions are not identical. It could be the case that adding "and" and "now" affects the answer in a predictable manner.

A rating scale supplies a way of avoiding this potential problem by asking the same questions in the same way and in the same format. Notice that the logic here is similar to the logic of the behavioral approach test we described earlier. You study behavior in relation to uniform stimuli before and after treatment. A difference, though, is that the behavioral event—in this case, answering questions in rating scales—is unlikely to pose any central part of the problems that brought the person to therapy. Here it is interesting to see if the person's answers to the rating-scale questions correspond with other classes of behavior under other circumstances. If, for example, Alice's ratings on the phobic avoidance scale "P" correspond to her avoidant behavior in everyday situations such as when she tries to go to work, we capture something relevant; otherwise, we do not.

An advantage with using rating scales is that they allow us to make comparisons with other people or even an entire population. We are able to collect normative data that will increase the interpretability of individual scores. We can compare Leonard's score on the depression index "D" with what people in general answer, or with the scores of people who have been diagnosed as depressed, because we possess these data. Using rating scales enables us to relate responses to a norm and to make comparisons with other kinds of treatments. Rating scales can be useful in an individual treatment also because they do essentially what clinicians do: they ask questions. This has the potential of providing us with an extra pair of spectacles that can help us in drawing attention to information that we have not attended to as well as to point out directions that we ought to investigate further.

At the same time, we would like to draw your attention to the fact that psychometrics, the measurement of behavior and psychological abilities, often takes a different vantage point compared to the functional perspective we are describing here. The logic behind psychometrics often rests on the assumption that observable behavior is considered an indicator of an underlying construct or inner entity. For example, the scores from a number of subtests that a person completes in order to assess "intelligence" will not primarily be considered interesting due to the observable behavior in the situation where the test is taken. It is the hypothetical underlying construct of "intelligence" or intellectual ability that is sought. In the same vein, the scores on the depression index "D" may be assumed to represent an underlying depression and the phobic avoidance scale "P" may be treated as an index of the underlying phobic disorder. In a functional perspective, underlying hypothetical entities are not used for explanatory purposes. But still, rating scales are a useful and practical way to use one behavior (that is, answering questions in a rating format) to make a statement about probable behavior in other situations.

EVALUATION OF CLINICAL PROBLEMS

In the task of analyzing clinical problems, we now have taken two steps. First, we defined the problem in terms of observable behavior. Second, through monitoring, we estimated a baseline of the appearance of that behavior or behaviors. But beyond having gathered information that is a necessary prerequisite for understanding the problems presented, we also have set the stage for developing a design that can assist in evaluating our treatment.

If we now equate A with the baseline and if B indicates our introduction of the intervention we've chosen in order to influence a particular behavior, then we have two conditions to compare: a control condition (baseline) and an intervention condition (see fig. 2.5).

Figure 2.5 A-B Design: Baseline and Intervention Conditions

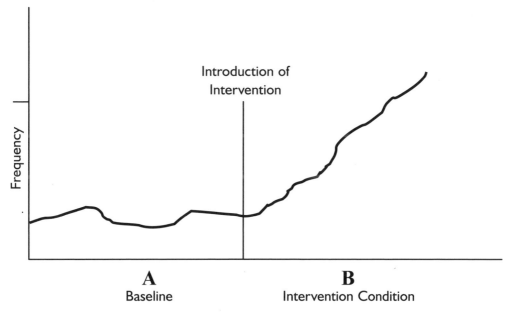

Here we see a hypothetical curve that invites us to make an obvious interpretation. The behavior at hand occurs at a stable level during baseline, and when the intervention is introduced, the frequency escalates to a higher level. The temporal contingency supports the assertion of causality between intervention and change. Now a curve like this, which offers such ease of interpretation, may not be the most common pattern in a therapeutic setting. We have, for example, already discussed the possibility of monitoring having an influence on behavior, which is illustrated in figure 2.6 below. Let's return to that situation now (see fig. 2.6).

Figure 2.6 A-B Design: Baseline Influenced by Observation

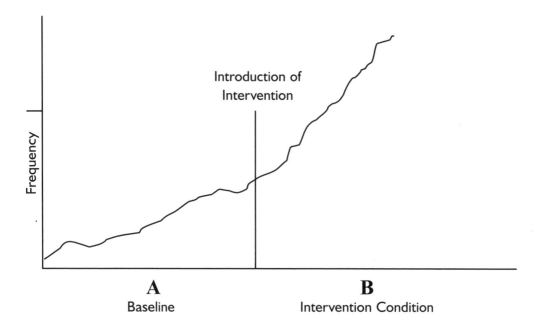

Introduction of
Intervention

Frequency

A
Baseline

B
Intervention Condition

Figure 2.7 A-B Design: Intervention Results Inconclusive

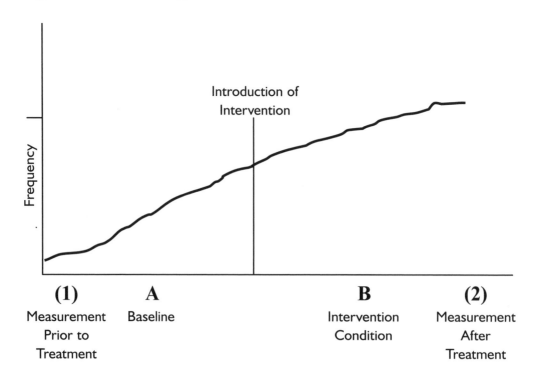

Introduction of
Intervention

Frequency

(1)
Measurement
Prior to
Treatment

A
Baseline

B
Intervention
Condition

(2)
Measurement
After
Treatment

In this case, it is not as obvious what happens when the intervention is introduced, but when looking at the slope of the curve, it becomes reasonable to conclude that the intervention has had an effect over and above that introduced by mere observation. But how about the next one? See figure 2.7.

In this case, we would clearly run into difficulties in asserting that it is the intervention B that influences the behavior under study. However, it should be noted that if we only had done singular measurements prior to (1) and after (2) treatment, we would see a significant difference that we might be inclined to attribute to our treatment method. However, a more careful analysis would provide no basis for concluding that the intervention was responsible for the effect. There's a substantial risk that we would uncritically accept the more favorable interpretation. This is a rather typical situation in a great deal of treatment evaluations. We observe a positive effect that occurs during treatment and then ascribe this effect to our specific method without any firm evidence for this.

If we now add another period of observation, after the intervention, we will have further possible conclusions to draw about the effects. See figure 2.8.

Figure 2.8 A-B-A Design: Intervention Reversed—Behavior Decreases

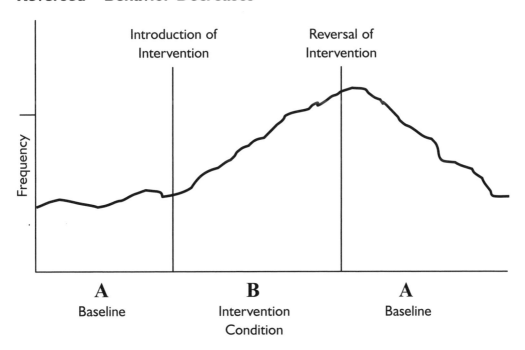

Here we see a curve that may convey important information about the intervention. When the intervention is introduced, we observe an increase in the behavior at hand, but when it is reversed the behavior returns to the baseline. This boosts our conviction that we've identified a factor of influence. In the example below (fig. 2.9), we can see

Figure 2.9 A-B-A Design: Intervention Reversed—Behavior Stable

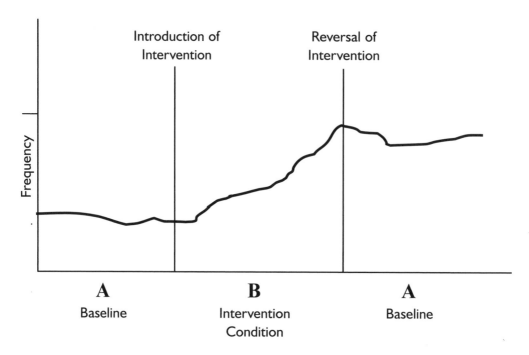

how the behavior at hand stays at the same level even after reversal of the intervention. This indicates the kind of learning process we strive for in psychotherapy—a process of learning that remains steady after we have withdrawn our active part in it.

We now have an option of reintroducing the intervention, which results in an A-B-A-B design. See figure 2.10.

This design increases the probability that it really is the intervention that has had the effect on the behavior, if the effect is repeated. It would indicate that we are able to control an important governing factor. In a study of senile patients in a residential setting (anecdotally conveyed to one of the authors), a change in the way the residence was furnished seemed to benefit the social interactions of the patients. However, the treatment design demanded that the intervention—the new way of furnishing—be reversed. This change upset relatives of the elderly residents because they, too, had noticed the beneficial effects of the new way of furnishing and the subsequent negative effects when the intervention was reversed. But when the new way of furnishing (the intervention) was reintroduced, the relatives were satisfied. The researchers were also satisfied because they now had a design that allowed them to draw clear inferences concerning the effects of environmental control of important social behaviors in the senile.

The evaluation strategies described above have mainly been used in settings with a high degree of control over environmental circumstances. But their usefulness should

Figure 2.10 A-B-A-B Design: Reversal and Reintroduction of Intervention

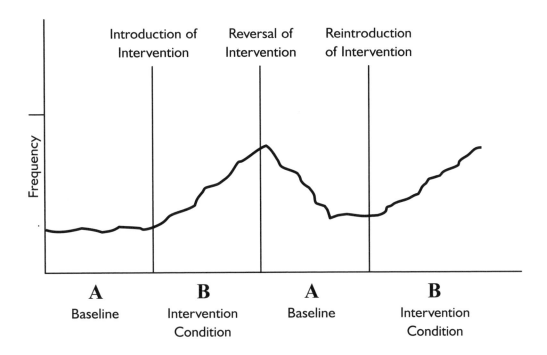

be acknowledged over a wide range of treatment settings that offer opportunities for an experimental approach to evaluation. Therapies often by nature contain breaks, interruptions, or changes in interventions that invite studying how the clients' behavioral repertoires evolve under different circumstances (Hayes, 1981).

What we have described here is the basis of an experimental design that could be used with single subjects (Hersen & Barlow, 1976). This experimental approach has been an integral part in the formulation of the psychology of learning. But it is also a methodology that has great potential for researching vital questions in psychotherapy, far beyond the areas of behavior therapy and applied behavior analysis that have classically been its domains (Hayes, 1981). It provides a methodology that, in combination with well-validated scales of measurement, allows the description of treatment in scientific terms even though we treat singular clients. This will make room for scientific evaluation of the everyday work of various therapies, and this evaluation will no longer be limited to large-scale group studies that few of us will conduct (Kazdin, 1981).

By going through some of the principles and practical tools of observing and registering behavior, we have cleared some ground for what is the core of the functional perspective: understanding behavior in the context where it occurs. So that is where we turn next.

CHAPTER 3

Knowing Your ABCs

Any behavioral event occurs in a context, and it is there we will observe it. We cannot understand human behaviors like talking, walking, or singing an aria if we consider them strictly out of context. They would be incomprehensible events. This is, of course, also the case with clinical behaviors. We cannot understand "avoids," "argues," or "self-mutilates" if we do not consider the context in which these behaviors occur.

It is important to keep in mind that topographical analysis is limited to describing different behavioral events, but it has no explanatory purpose. It does not have the capacity for explanation. Therein lies the danger in perceiving topographical summations (like diagnoses) as the explanation of the very descriptions they summarize. The criticism you sometimes hear about behaviorism, that it is "superficial," would be correct if our story were to end here, and we only were interested in the topographical description of behavior. In that case, we would end our analysis with lists of behavioral events that would bear no connection to the world in which they exist. This kind of analysis would list a lot of acts, but those acts would be incomprehensible. It is in the context where they occur that we will be able to form an understanding of particular behaviors. But we also need to know this context to be able to take on the scientific goals of prediction and control. It is the context that adds depth to the behavioral observations we make.

Because of this, we will need further information in order to describe the context. This leads us to what is called contingency or sequential analysis. For the remainder of this book, we will refer to this as "ABC analysis."

ABC ANALYSIS: ANTECEDENT, BEHAVIOR, CONSEQUENCE

We all have learned the importance of knowing our ABCs, and we think this rule is worth establishing in our clinical work as well. The focus up till now has been on what is found under "B" in that sequence: the observable behavior. "A" denotes an antecedent, that is, an event that occurs prior to the behavior at hand, and "C" denotes a consequence that follows the behavior.

Thus, the ABC analysis has three parts, and the function of those parts is to assist the therapist in exploring the circumstances that govern the behavior at hand. They are aids to answering the therapist's questions concerning the world of human behavior.

BEHAVIOR: WHAT IS THE PERSON DOING?

Since it is the act, the behavior, we want to explain, our first question is "What is the person doing?" In order to move on to the question "Why is he or she doing it?" we will need some further observations before we can come up with a reasonable answer to that question.

ANTECEDENT: WHEN DOES THE PERSON DO IT?

So, after the first question, which gave us B (the behavior, or what the person is doing), the next question is "When does the person do it?" or "In what situation does the person do it?" We are asking for A, the antecedent.

Now, the phrasing of these questions might give an impression that we would settle for a certain point of time or place in order to gain proper understanding of antecedent events. But what we really are looking for under the category "antecedent" is a broad spectrum of external and internal stimuli. The question might be better phrased like this: "In the presence of what does the person do it?"

CONSEQUENCES: WHAT HAPPENS AFTER THE PERSON DOES IT?

The third question is "What happens after the person does it?" or, more properly, "What events follow upon doing it?" We are looking for C, the consequences of the behavior.

From a functional perspective, the question of consequences is vital. If we are to explain behavior, we must detect its function. What purpose does the behavior serve? That question is identical to asking what the consequences of a behavior are. This is crucial because behavior is governed by consequences of earlier, similar behavior. We will take a closer look at these functional relationships in chapter 5, but even prior to that we need to search for possible consequential events that might stand in relation to the actual behavior.

We are searching for consequences (C) because therein lies the answer to the question "Why is the person doing this?" It is important to understand that all consequences do not have the same controlling or influencing function on a given behavior. It is far from self-evident which consequences are controlling and which are not. This implies that in an analysis we start by searching for possible consequences with a broad question: "What events follow the behavior?" This means starting with an open investigation of several possibilities. But in the end, the consequences we are interested in are those that have actual controlling functions. This is the essence of a functional perspective.

The basic rule is simple: Where do we find B? In its context, between A and C!

Figure 3.1 ABC Analysis

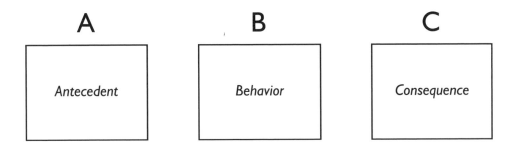

Observation of Antecedents (A) and Consequences (C)

In the presence of A, B leads to C. If we were to make any more conclusive statement on the validity of the application of this formula, we would need to conduct controlled experiments that allow us to actively manipulate the antecedent and consequential events. In a clinical situation, we rarely have the opportunity to make a thorough investigation from a scientific standard to establish the validity of the presumed contingency. But what we are doing when we formulate an understanding of a client's behavior and lay out possible ways of change is following a model that stems from the experimental idea.

We have three basic areas to explore—A, B, and C—in the process of analysis. Let's turn for a moment to Alice's situation to see how we might begin our analysis:

> *When Alice feels unsure whether she will be able to get to work by herself, she calls her fiancé and asks for a lift. Usually she gets one.*

Out of a range of potentially fear-related behaviors, we have focused on the particular act of calling her fiancé and asking for a ride which occurs in the presence of her feeling uncertain before going to work on her own. The event that follows as the consequence of this act is simply that she gets a ride.

Figure 3.2 ABC Analysis: Alice

Antecedent

Feels uncertain about whether she will make it to work by herself

Behavior

Calls her fiancé and asks for a ride

Consequence

Gets a ride

When Marie is confronted with the situation where she will have to attend a meeting, she gets very nervous. She usually arranges to get busy with something else that prevents her from going to that meeting. This momentarily reduces her feelings of nervousness.

Figure 3.3 ABC Analysis: Marie

Antecedent

A meeting that evokes nervousness

Behavior

Gets busy so she won't be able to attend the meeting

Consequence

Decreases the nervousness

Notice in this particular example how A has two sides to it. It is an external event, which is constituted by the meeting and all of its components, and at the same time it contains an internal event: Marie's feelings of nervousness. So the complete antecedent (A) event harbors public events like the observable situation (the meeting) as well as private events that are observable solely by Marie (her feelings).

Let's look at yet another example and especially consider the consequences:

When Alice gets too far away from home, she gets very nervous (A). Then she turns back (B), which momentarily makes her less nervous (C).

As we can see here, the consequence is something that is diminished, namely Alice's nervousness. But that is not the only consequence: Alice also becomes disappointed with herself that she did not make it to work. She eventually gets more worried over the possible reaction from her colleagues at work and increasingly troubled over how she will manage to go to work in the future. All of these are consequences that she does not want to have. But, for the moment, these consequences are not the critical ones when it comes to the behavior at hand: turning back. In this case, it is Alice's first reaction that is critical: a sense of relief when the nervousness diminishes. Any behavioral event may have several consequences. However, every possible consequence that may be identified does not have a controlling function for the behavior at hand. In this case, we can see that the immediate consequence (diminished nervousness) "wins" in the competition with the consequences that occur later (for example, becoming disappointed with herself).

In any human behavior, A, B, and C respectively are far from self-evident. We cannot identify them in a predetermined fashion. Instead, human behavior is like a weaving where the threads of different actions continuously and continually intertwine with each other. What we usually do is to extract sequences in a way that permits analysis. An example of this is our attempt to understand what happens when Peter and Anna discuss how to spend their weekend and end up in a quarrel (see fig. 3.4).

Figure 3.4 ABC Analysis: Anna and Peter

Note that the consequential event that occurs following one behavior (starting a discussion) is another behavioral event (quarreling). This leads further to another sequence.

Figure 3.5 ABC Analysis: Anna and Peter

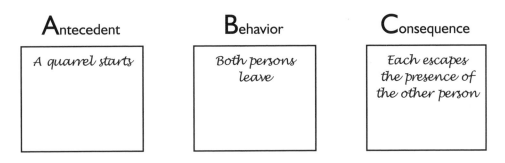

Getting away from another person can be understood both in terms of ending the quarrel as well as diminishing the anger that is experienced in the presence of that person. But now Peter and Anna have put themselves in a new situation. They start the weekend with avoiding each other, which in itself is an antecedent for yet other behaviors. We can be fairly certain, for example, that this antecedent is not likely to lead to an increase in constructive planning behaviors. This in turn is an antecedent event for … And life goes on!

Peter and Anna's behavior also provides an illustration of different kinds of consequences, that is, short-term versus long-term. In the short run (when the couple gets away from each other after starting the quarrel), the behavior is followed by something they strive for: a decrease in the unpleasant experience of quarreling. Years of experimental research have shown that consequences that occur closely to behavior easily acquire strong controlling functions. But at the same time, the long-term consequences of this behavior lead Anna and Peter further away from what they really want. Avoiding each other might lessen some immediate strain, but it is hardly a behavior that in itself is functional if they strive for a better and closer relationship. This is why they are seeking help. They will readily acknowledge behaviors that pull them apart, but mere acknowledgment does not equal behavioral change.

This is the essence of ABC analysis: We start with something that is done, an action (B). We search for the events in the presence of which the action takes place (A) and the consequences (C) that follow. Since the purpose of analyzing behavior goes beyond mere description (topography) and ultimately is an analysis of function, we are especially keen on identifying the consequences that have a controlling, or influencing, function. How do we identify these consequences in a credible way? In order to do that, we need to have a better understanding of how these functional relationships work. We will return to this issue in chapter 5 on operant learning or conditioning.

Consequences: A Way to Influence

The central point we're emphasizing here is that in trying to understand behavior, we must always consider the context in which it is emitted. In a treatment setting, we will never be able to place ourselves outside of this context. In the examples above, we have described ABC analyses of what the clients told us about what was going on in their lives. But we are also, together with the client (or clients), involved in a sequence of events that can be analyzed in the same way. We, as well as the client, behave (B) when we meet. We say what we say and do what we do in the presence of certain circumstances or antecedents (A). And what are the consequences of our behavior in the treatment setting (C)?

Sometimes the ethical value of a practice that attempts to influence human behavior by a deliberate adding or subtracting of consequences is questioned. However, since our mere presence in a therapy room or on a ward affects (and effects) consequences, this is hardly a reasonable question. Instead, these questions should be posed: What consequences result from our interaction? How do those consequences affect specific behaviors and under what circumstances? We are not able to step outside of this context! If we try to do so, we merely provide other antecedents and consequences. In itself, life means that we are in constant contact with the consequences of our own behavior. Simply stated: "The one who lives will get to C."

Long-Term Consequences

As we saw in the examples above, any behavioral event is followed by several consequences. The immediate ones more easily acquire controlling properties than the long-term ones. When Alice returns home, for example, this lessens her anxiety. This consequence has acquired a controlling property in establishing an avoidance behavior, even though in the long run this avoidance increases her anxiety concerning how to manage her job and her life. When Peter and Anna get away from each other in the midst of a quarrel, this lessens the negative affect momentarily, in spite of the long-term consequences of increasing difficulties in a number of areas and an increasing sense of hopelessness in their relationship.

As we've already said, a characteristic of long-term consequences is that they tend to have weak controlling properties. The immediate consequences, on the other hand, tend to dominate. But Alice, Peter, and Anna all notice negative long-term consequences and compare them to more desirable ones. Alice would like to worry less and manage her job more effectively on a regular basis. Anna and Peter would like to be able to constructively solve their marital problems and have a close and meaningful relationship. The importance of these desired consequences in therapeutic work is obvious. It is in their quest to reach desired outcomes that people come for treatment.

From a theoretical point of view, however, using desired consequences as an explanation of behavior is tricky. Consequences that have controlling properties are consequences that have followed upon earlier behavior. And a desired consequence may be an event that you have not yet experienced. Can such an event acquire controlling properties of behavior, or is this by definition impossible? To answer these questions, we must turn to the field of human language and cognition, and to how these processes work. It is through the acquisition of verbal abilities that behavior can be ruled by circumstances that have never been experienced. We will return to this topic in chapter 7 when we consider "thinking for better or for worse."

ESTABLISHING OPERATIONS: AN ADDITIONAL FACTOR IN BEHAVIOR ANALYSIS

One of the authors attended a presentation on different applications of psychological procedures in geriatric care. One speaker (whose name, unfortunately, is forgotten so we can't give the credit deserved) presented a study where features of the behavior of the nurses affected the inclination of the elderly to unnecessarily press the alarm button. They compared two different conditions. The first was this:

Figure 3.6 ABC Analysis: Geriatric Care— High Emotional Responsiveness

They then switched over to another condition:

Figure 3.7 ABC Analysis: Geriatric Care— Low Emotional Responsiveness

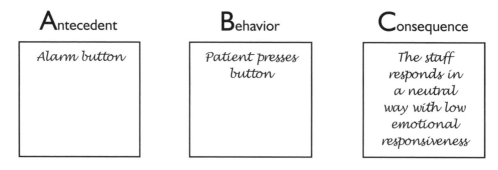

As you've probably already figured out, the first condition was associated with substantially greater inclination to press the alarm button. The conclusion was that the excessive button pressing was under social control. Another presenter was quite upset with this study and claimed that it really just demonstrated the superficiality of behavior analysis since it ruled out such a fundamental variable of human condition as loneliness. Without taking this variable into consideration, you could not understand the behavior. Who was right?

We would say that both were right from a behavior analytic point of view. The button pressing was under control of social consequences, as shown by the first presenter. However, we do not know if this contingency would be valid in a group of socially stimulated and not-so-lonely elders. The second presenter had shown that affecting this variable was a way of decreasing behavioral excess as well.

Figure 3.8 ABC Analysis and Function of Establishing Operations (EO)

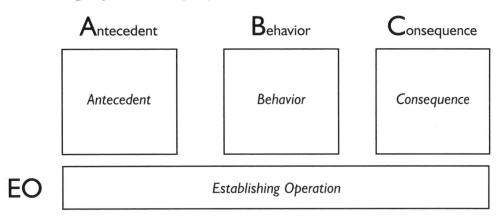

Here we are dealing with an additional factor in behavior analysis known as an *establishing operation* (EO) (Michael, 1993). See figure 3.8. An establishing operation is a factor that affects what is normally called motivation. It is something in the context of a specific behavior that affects the controlling function of a certain consequence in that very context. In the example above, the experience of loneliness, or the context of deprivation of contact with other humans, changes the rewarding experience of someone turning up as you press the alarm button. This works as a ground for the behavioral event. It is a part of the antecedent circumstances, but for practical reasons it can be regarded separately from A, B, and C. Still, it is an important factor that influences the contingency. As other factors in the context of a particular behavior, an establishing operation is a factor that potentially can be manipulated in order to change a behavioral sequence. Let's consider the following example to understand what function an establishing operation fulfills (see fig. 3.9):

Figure 3.9 ABC Analysis: Eating a Hamburger

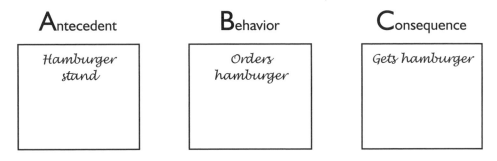

This situation would be completely different if I came from a big dinner or if I was starving. If we consider hunger as an establishing operation, this will affect all three areas in the contingency: It will make the hamburger stand more salient in the field of attention (A). The aromas emerging from it will have stronger appetitive functions. It will affect my ordering-from-the-menu behavior and possibly also the intensity in the verbal behavior used to convey my order at the counter (B). Last but not least, it will affect my subjective experience (C) when taking a bite from the juicy hamburger. Consider how the same sequence might be altered if I'd come directly to the hamburger stand from a big dinner. It should be noted that EO could be regarded as a motivational prerequisite, but it does not preclude A nor C when we are trying to explain a behavioral event. The event still occurs in a given situation and is followed by given consequences.

We can often consider basic physiological processes—such as satiety, hunger, and fatigue—as establishing operations. But we can't limit this important but perhaps somewhat circumscribed aspect of behavior analysis to physiological processes alone. What if the person who passes the hamburger stand is a vegan? This will also affect all three areas: the salience of the hamburger stand in the stimulus field (A), the behavior (B), and the experience of biting into the juicy hamburger (C). Values can have important implications for the contingencies in which human behavior is to be understood. A starving vegan could very well abstain from ordering a big, juicy burger because he or she dislikes the principles of the modern meat industry. Realizing that values, and what are generally called assumptions, can be powerful in affecting contingencies leads us once again to the area of language and cognition, something that will be dealt with in chapter 7.

When running lab trials in experimental psychology where the behavior of different animals is studied under the reinforcement of food agents, you would see to it that the animals are not satiated at the trial. If they were, they wouldn't be interested in tasks that would make food available. In the same way, socially stimulated geriatric patients might be less interested in pushing an alarm button that makes a nurse available to ask what they want. (Concerning the geriatric patients' button pushing, we don't think anyone would seriously recommend addressing the problem by training the nursing staff to be less nice to patients.) We will return to how these establishing operations can be central when planning treatment for clients, for example, in chapter 8.

TALKING ABOUT BEHAVIOR IN ITS CONTEXT

Doing these kinds of ABC analyses is not an activity solely located in the world of private events inside of therapists. It is something that is a highly viable tool in the therapeutic dialogue. The purpose, then, is to make ABC analysis useful for clients' understanding of their own behavior. Here's how that might happen in a session with Marie:

Therapist:	So you left the office yesterday?
Marie:	Yeah, I just couldn't take the situation anymore.
Therapist:	What happened?
Marie:	I got this e-mail that said everyone should brief the group about the status of their projects later that afternoon. I just felt that it would be impossible to talk in front of all those people.
Therapist:	So what happened when you read that e-mail?
Marie:	I froze instantly. I just don't want them to see how nervous I get.
Therapist:	So you get the message, you freeze, and then start worrying about them noticing that you get nervous in this kind of situation.
Marie:	Yeah.
Therapist:	What did you do then?
Marie:	I thought for a while that I might say I wasn't ready yet or that I might leave early and say that I must have missed that e-mail.
Therapist:	But you didn't do that?
Marie:	No, I said I didn't feel well, and that I had to go home and go to bed.
Therapist:	What happened then?
Marie:	What do you mean? I went!
Therapist:	What happened inside you?
Marie:	First, when I got out of the office, it felt as though a huge weight had fallen from my shoulders. But, you know, I didn't even get to the parking lot before I started worrying.
Therapist:	Worrying?
Marie:	Yeah, this has to be presented to the group. What do I do next time? I can't say that I'm ill every time there's a briefing. That'll soon be pretty suspicious. And besides that, I get so darn disappointed with myself when I just don't do things like this, when I just don't do what's expected of me.

Here the therapist can provide an analysis of the behavioral sequence at hand:

Figure 3.10 ABC Analysis: Marie

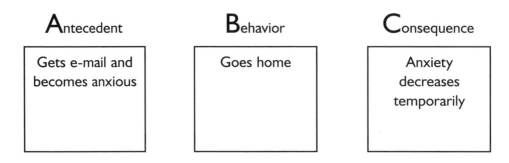

Antecedent	Behavior	Consequence
Gets e-mail and becomes anxious	Goes home	Anxiety decreases temporarily

Therapist: So if I've got this right, this seems to be about you getting this e-mail that makes you really anxious. And when you leave the situation, this lessens your anxiety, at least temporarily. It could be seen as a kind of escape. Is this something that you recognize from other situations in your life?

Marie: Well, you could say that's what my life's about: escape. I quit my last job just because I didn't dare take on the task of leading the group meetings. And now I'm moving in that same direction in this new job.

The consequence of diminishing anxiety would not be so problematic if it were the only consequence. Here you can see the importance of tracking down the difference between short-term and long-term consequences. And again, as we see in this conversation between Marie and her therapist, we find the immediate consequences to be in control:

Therapist: So this first experience of "a huge weight" falling "off your shoulders" doesn't seem to be the only consequence.

Marie: No, in the end, I just make a mess out of it and that causes so much worry. But I just can't force myself to do it. You see, this makes me pretty desperate!

Therapist: We can conclude that what you gain in getting rid of anxiety is gained at the expense of quite a lot in life.

Marie: Yeah, that's an understatement.

An ABC analysis becomes an intrinsic part of clinical work and an important source of insight. However, since the process is aimed at understanding the person's actions in the context where they occur, it might be more reasonable to call it "outsight" than "insight." Stated in theoretical terms, we refer to this process as *discrimination*, that is, discrimination of actions as well as the circumstances that control them. (We will discuss the term "discrimination" more thoroughly in chapters 4 and 6.)

We study humans who are feeling, acting, willing, and seeking meaning. That is what our psychology is about. Theories provide principles for exploring and assessing this in everyday clinical work. This leads us into the study of theories of learning, which, as we already stated, is needed in order to do ABC analysis in a meaningful way. So that is the topic to which we now turn in order to access these theories as tools for us and our clients.

PART 2

Explaining Behavior

CHAPTER 4

Learning by Association: Respondent Conditioning

Does the name Pavlov ring a bell? Ivan Pavlov was a Russian physiologist who worked at the end of the nineteenth century. He was the first to describe and analyze the kind of learning that is called *respondent conditioning,* learning based on association (Rachlin, 1991). The same principle of learning is sometimes called classical or Pavlovian conditioning. To this very day, Pavlov's experiments with dogs are probably the best-known psychological experiments, at least to the general public. Initially he wanted to examine the change of secretion in the mouths and stomachs of dogs as they were fed. During the experiments, Pavlov noticed a complication: the dogs in his laboratory, without any food being presented, secreted saliva and gastric juice when he entered the room. This caught his interest, and he started the experiments that ended up making him one of the most famous people in psychology.

Dogs have a natural reaction when food is presented to them. They salivate. They don't need to learn this; it is among the reactions that are biologically given. The famous experiments of Pavlov consisted of his attempts to systematically examine the reactions that he initially had noticed by chance. Just before the bowl of food was presented to the dogs in his laboratory, he rang a bell or struck a tuning fork. When this was repeated several times, Pavlov noticed that the dogs started to salivate when they heard the bell, regardless of the fact that no food was presented. A stimulus that was neutral from the start (the sound of the bell), that is, a *neutral stimulus* (NS), had obtained a function that was very similar to the natural function of the food. The reaction of the dogs was conditioned so that the sound of the bell became a *conditioned stimulus* (CS). The learned reaction it elicited is called a *conditioned response* (CR). The natural contingency of a stimulus and a reaction that is elicited without learning, in this example the relationship between food and salivation, is the contingency of an *unconditioned stimulus* (UCS) and an *unconditioned response* (UCR). The word *stimulus* refers to an event that precedes the reaction we study (see fig. 4.1).

Figure 4.1 Respondent Conditioning

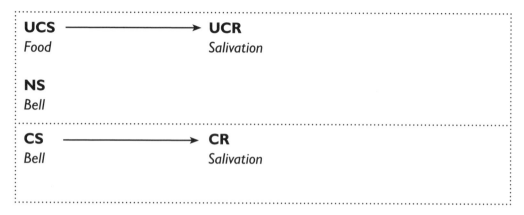

UCS ⟶ **UCR**
Food   Salivation

NS
Bell

CS ⟶ **CR**
Bell   Salivation

Another example that is often cited as a prototype for respondent conditioning is the naturally occuring eyeblink. If we direct a puff of air toward the eye of a human, the individual responds with an eyeblink. That this is an inborn response is hardly questioned. The puff of air is a simple stimulus that elicits the response. If the puff of air is reliably preceded by a tone, the tone will acquire some of the stimulus functions of the puff of air. Consequently the tone will elicit an eyeblink even when it is no longer followed by a puff of air. A stimulus, which at the start is neutral in this regard, acquires the functions of another stimulus, or at least part of those functions. Once again we have described a conditioned stimulus and a conditioned response. This is in contrast to the puff of air, which is an unconditioned stimulus, and the eyeblink that followed, which is an unconditioned response. If a puff of air is directed toward our eye, we blink. We don't have to learn that. The blink has a biological function—it protects the eye (see fig. 4.2).

Figure 4.2 Respondent Conditioning of the Eyeblink

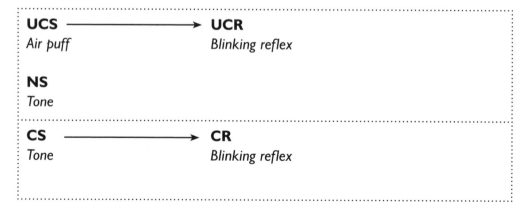

UCS ⟶ **UCR**
Air puff   Blinking reflex

NS
Tone

CS ⟶ **CR**
Tone   Blinking reflex

THE RELATIONSHIP BETWEEN CONDITIONED AND UNCONDITIONED RESPONSES

What then is the relationship between the conditioned and the unconditioned response? Are they the same? At first, it might appear as if they are, for example, in Pavlov's experiment. In both cases, the dog salivated. Pavlov interpreted it that way; the same response was elicited in both cases. It soon became apparent, however, that the conditioned response often is weaker than the unconditioned. Later research has also made it clear that these are not identical reactions (Rachlin, 1991; Rescorla, 1988). If we, for example, look closer at the chemical constituents of the saliva in the dog's conditioned and unconditioned responses, we will see that there are differences. It seems as if the dog has better discrimination than we might assume. The conditioned response is more like "the food will soon be here." The dog does not mistake the bell for the food; it reacts to the actual relationship between the bell and the food, which, up till now, has arrived just after the sound of the bell. Neither the unconditioned nor the conditioned response is restricted to simple salivation. Salivation is only an aspect of a complex reaction by which the dog's body is being prepared for receiving the food.

A way to summarize the function of the described process is to say that respondent conditioning gives something in the context or the environment of the organism a biological function it did not have up to that point. Something that, up to that point, had one function (or none at all) now acquires a new one. It is easy to recognize that this is an essential process for any species. Respondent conditioning creates an opportunity for changing the behavior of the organism and thereby contributes to adaptation and survival. A small child may run into the street without the experience of this being connected with danger. The child has a biological system that reacts to certain unconditioned stimuli (sudden cries, aggressive behavior from a parent) with fear (unconditioned response), but the child's system does not react to movement into the street as a stimulus for responding with fear. If a parent reacts with a scream or by showing aggressive behavior in this situation, the street (and/or other relevant stimuli) will become a conditioned stimulus which from then on can elicit fear (conditioned response). This will change the behavior of the child in relation to the street. Another example is that of a young man who is assaulted late one night at a restaurant downtown. A few weeks later when he returns to the same place, he experiences nausea, his heart beats faster, and he starts sweating. Through the process of respondent conditioning, an environment that used to be connected to pleasant feelings and memories now evokes completely different reactions.

THE RELATION OF BASIC AFFECTS TO CONDITIONED AND UNCONDITIONED RESPONSES

Our discussion above is part of elementary psychological knowledge. We have a range of hereditary responses, and the circumstances in which they are elicited depend on our particular learning history. Salivation and eyeblinking, however, are seldom a part of psychotherapeutic work. But what about other reactions—like emotions—that can literally occur in the blink of an eye. When an adult human is happy, angry, or scared, this reaction consists of several factors. As a whole, the reaction (or emotion) is not hereditary but to a great degree is shaped by the experience of this particular individual. At the same time, we know that parts of these affective reactions are common for all humans and can be shown to exist regardless of cultural and ethnic background. A great deal of research supports the idea that human beings are born with a small number of basic affects, or at least a set of emotional components, that are elicited automatically under certain circumstances (Ekman, 1992; LeDoux, 1996; Tomkins, 1982).

As early as the 1870s, Charles Darwin maintained that humans, like other animals, are equipped with a number of basic emotional reactions that serve survival (Darwin, 1872). Modern researchers don't agree on the exact number of these basic affects or which reactions belong to them, but there is a fair amount of consensus about the following five (Power & Dalgleish, 1997):

- Fear

- Sadness

- Joy

- Anger

- Disgust

The best-researched one is fear, which is of obvious significance for many of the problems people bring to psychotherapy.

What Constitutes Basic Affects?

Each basic affect has a particular visible expression (most easily seen in the face). The affects can also be separated by different physiological variables. They have the potential for particular types of actions or the predispositions for certain kinds of behavior. For example, when we are afraid, our heart beats faster, certain muscles are activated, and there are certain typical changes in blood flow (Ekman, 1992). This seems to be an integrated part of the experience of fear. When we notice we are afraid, our physiological responses have already been activated and we are prepared for certain behaviors, such as avoidance or escape (LeDoux, 1996). Our biology takes the lead here; basic affects don't need our conscious contemplation to be elicited by stimuli. Our basic affect of fear prepares us for immediate action. In the same way, the experience of disgust entails bodily preparation for distancing, and anger prepares for attack. When we notice our own anger, we are already ready to strike.

Emotional Reactions Based on Unconditioned Responses

This means that emotional reactions are based on unconditioned responses, formed by evolution. What do we know about the circumstances that elicit these responses, or, put in another way, what do we know about unconditioned stimuli? Our knowledge of this is limited. Most research is done on adults, that is, individuals with a long learning history. Concerning fear, there are data suggesting several eliciting factors that are not learned. Examples are objects approaching quickly, loud noises, and certain facial expressions of other people (Öhman, 2002). From an evolutionary point of view, it is not reasonable to assume that only one type of stimuli would elicit, for example, fear or disgust. If the reaction should serve survival, it would need to be activated in more than one context, even though the variation of the stimuli would not have to be extremely great to have an impact early in an individual's life.

We can use knowledge of respondent conditioning to understand how our emotional experience of the world is formed early in life. For example, regardless of what elicits an individual's anger initially, over time that person will make other associations that will acquire parts of the functions of the unconditioned stimuli, which will then in turn elicit anger. In this way, phenomena become associated with both external stimuli (actions of other individuals, smells, specific objects) and internal stimuli, such as other affects. Imagine a small child who, as she feels sad, is repeatedly confronted by a parent acting in a way that elicits fear in the child. Through respondent conditioning, the parent's action causes the child's affect of sadness to change into an eliciting stimulus for fear—or in plain language, the child learns to be afraid of her emotional reactions. As a possible example, this is something that was noticed by Marie's aunt:

> Marie's aunt has told her that she thinks Marie's parents were excessively worried when Marie was a child. The aunt remembers that when Marie was no more than a year old, she was a very active child, quickly crawling around the apartment where she lived. She seemed interested in everything, happily exploring her surroundings. The aunt remembers she thought it was sad to see how Marie's efforts to explore the world were interrupted by her parents in a way that seemed to scare Marie. When Marie heard this, she thought her childhood experiences might have affected how she reacts nowadays in situations that, for most other people, evoke interest and curiosity instead of the fear she experiences.

It is hard to tell if this experience really is the cause of Marie's problems. One thing is clear, though: respondent conditioning forms our reactions early in life and will affect our basic relationship to our environment throughout our lives.

External and Internal Stimuli

That states of affect can be elicited through respondent conditioning was recognized early in the development of behavioral science. John Watson, the man who proclaimed "behaviorism" in 1913, adopted early the conclusions of Pavlov's research and used them to explain the origin of fear in humans. To be frightened in the presence of one stimulus (for example, darkness) will make this stimulus capable of eliciting fear. We can see that these types of learned reactions are central for understanding, for example, how traumatized people react to certain stimuli (like the sound of a helicopter, the smell of smoke, or military uniforms). Traditionally in behavior therapy there has been a focus on external stimuli like these.

More recently, discussion about inner stimuli has increased. Inner stimuli can be affects, bodily sensations, or memories, for example. The term used for conditioning by such inner stimuli is *interoceptive conditioning*. Once again, Russian physiologists showed not only the possibility of this but also that this kind of learning was especially resistant to extinction, that is, it was hard to weaken or extinguish the association, once learned (Razran, 1961). This form of learning has become central in our efforts to understand certain anxiety disorders (Bouton, Mineka, & Barlow, 2001).

Biologically Prepared Learning

We are born with certain given responses to unconditioned stimuli, but our responses are more complicated than that. What we have called "neutral" stimuli are not always so neutral. Not all stimuli have the same capacity for conditioning and not all responses are as easily elicited by formerly neutral stimuli. In the example of the eyeblink above, to get the tone to elicit an eyeblink, the association of the tone (conditioned stimulus) and the puff of air (unconditioned stimulus) has to be made several times. However, to get a previously neutral smell to elicit disgust and nausea, you often need to experience only one occasion when the smell is associated with vomiting. Similar phenomena are described in affect research. It seems as if the organism is biologically prepared for certain kinds of learning (Öhman & Mineka, 2003). It is much easier to get a human to be afraid of snakes, heights, and darkness, for example, than for a range of other stimuli. But this is probably not only true for stimuli that we associate with specific phobias; the same also seems to be true about situations where we are examined by others, we are abandoned, or we experience unusual sensations in our own bodies. If someone has experienced a panic attack accompanied by chest pain while caught in a traffic jam, you can expect that person will feel fear once again if he or she experiences pain in the chest region or gets stuck in traffic. However, you would probably not expect the car's instrument panel or even the car itself to evoke fear or panic, even though these stimuli were very much present at the time of the panic attack.

Learning by association (respondent conditioning) is thus a combination of hereditary factors and the experience of each individual. What do we know about factors that govern the learning experience as such in respondent conditioning? Let's explore that question now.

FACILITATION OF RESPONDENT CONDITIONING

Conditioning involves learning to react to the relation between unconditioned stimuli and other stimuli that were previously neutral or irrelevant in a given context. Therefore, the character of the actual relationship is of decisive importance.

Facilitating Factors

As we look at the relationship between unconditioned stimuli and other, previously neutral stimuli, we must ask this question: which factors facilitate respondent conditioning? The following are crucial to the facilitation of respondent conditioning:

■ If the number of times that a conditioned stimulus (CS) occurs together with an unconditioned stimulus (UCS) is increased, the probability that the conditioned stimulus will elicit a conditioned response will increase. An example is the eyeblinking described earlier. The more the tone occurs together with the puff of air, the greater the probability that the tone will elicit blinking.

■ If the conditioned stimulus (CS) always occurs when the unconditioned stimulus (UCS) occurs, the tendency of the CS to elicit a conditioned response (CR) will be greater than if the UCS also occurs without the CS. For example, if the bell always rings when the dog is fed, the probability that the bell will elicit salivation will increase; this is unlike the situation where the bell only rings at certain times when food is presented. Or, if one person in a loving couple uses a particular perfume only in relation to sexual interaction, the probability will increase that the smell of this perfume will be sexually arousing for the couple.

■ The conditioned stimulus (CS) must precede the unconditioned stimulus (UCS), not the other way around. If you want to teach a dog to react to the word "cookie," you must say the word just before or as you give the dog a cookie. If you first give the dog a cookie and then say "cookie" after the dog has eaten the cookie, the dog will never learn the relation between the word "cookie" and the actual cookie, regardless of how many times you repeat the procedure. Respondent conditioning requires a certain fixed order in which the stimuli are presented. The CS must precede the UCS.

■   Another factor is the time interval between the conditioned stimulus (CS) and the unconditioned stimulus (UCS). If the interval is increased, the probability that the CS will elicit a conditioned response will decrease. If you say "cookie" a long time before the dog gets his cookie, the learning process will not work.

Notice that the actual relation is not the only governing factor. A strong biological predisposition can change this. Nausea is perhaps the clearest example. This is a reaction that is easily conditioned. Let's say you have had a delicious meal and later that night you get sick. The sensations of taste and smell that were a part of the meal can become a conditioned stimulus (CS) for a conditioned response (CR) of nausea despite the fact that several hours have passed between the smell/taste of the food and the relevant unconditioned stimulus (UCS) and unconditioned response (UCR). These sensations of smell and taste can now evoke disgust and nausea.

Further Conditioning: Second-Order Conditioning, Generalization, and Discrimination

A conditioned stimulus (CS) that results in a conditioned response (CR) can result in further conditioning. If a child was frightened in the dark and darkness has become a conditioned stimulus that elicits fear, another stimulus that exists in the context of darkness (certain sounds, for example) also can function as the CS and elicit fear, even though these sounds were not present in the original situation where the child was first scared in the dark. This is sometimes called *second-order conditioning*. The example of darkness, by the way, is yet another one in which biological predispositions play a part. Darkness is not "neutral" for humans but is another stimulus that we more easily learn to fear than some other stimuli.

Another very important factor that contributes to learning by respondent conditioning is *generalization*, the tendency for respondent conditioning to spread to similar stimuli. Let's return to Pavlov's dogs. Assume that a dog has been conditioned to react to the sound of a bell so that it salivates when the bell rings even though no food is present. Let's exchange the bell we have used up till now for a bell with a somewhat different sound. How different can it be for the dog still to salivate? The exact answer may vary depending on several factors, but the sound does not have to be exactly identical. It simply has to be "similar enough."

A small child who is knocked down by a dog and hurt will not only be afraid seeing that particular dog but also other dogs that are similar enough. If the child was knocked down by a German shepherd and the size of the dog is central as a conditioned stimulus (CS), we cannot be sure the child will be afraid of a dachshund. If the sound of the dog (barking) is central for the child, in this particular case a dachshund, the barking will serve as the CS and evoke fear, the conditioned response (CR).

Generalization means that the reaction will spread in such a way that other stimuli that share some formal characteristics with the original conditioned stimulus (CS) also can elicit the conditioned response (CR). A typical example is the person with a snake phobia who feels uneasy when seeing the garden hose lying on the lawn.

The opposite process to generalization is *discrimination*, the ability to react to differences between stimuli. We can also study this process in a classical Pavlovian experiment. If the dogs initially generalize so that they salivate when a range of bell sounds is presented, you can, by only presenting food with a particular sound but not with other (quite similar) sounds, get the dogs to increase their discrimination so that they only salivate when a more limited range of sounds is presented.

It's easy to see that generalization, discrimination, and the balance between the two are important for the organism in learning to adapt and survive. Sometimes it is very important to have a high degree of discrimination and only react to a very specific stimulus. An example would be a creature that needs to evaluate snow-covered ice where a difference in the shade of white indicates the relative safety or danger of walking on the ice. In another situation, generalization is of more importance, such as the case of an animal that lives with a high risk of becoming a predator's lunch. Then it might be wise to react to anything that moves.

Conditioned Forever, or Is Extinction Possible?

As has been made clear in our presentation of second-order conditioning, generalization, and discrimination, respondent conditioning is a dynamic process. From this, it follows that reactions that have been conditioned can also be weakened and disappear, what, as we mentioned earlier, is known as *extinction*—the response is "put out." In its most basic sense, extinction can be considered theoretically simple: end the relation between the conditioned and the unconditioned stimulus. Let's go back to Pavlov's dogs. If we continue to ring the bell repeatedly but no food is ever presented in relation to the sound, the sound of the bell will eventually not function as a conditioned stimulus (CS). This means that its ability to elicit the conditioned response (CR)—salivation, in this example—will end. If a small child who has been scared in the dark repeatedly spends time in darkness without anything frightening taking place, the probability increases that darkness no longer will elicit fear—that is, the function of darkness as the CS will end and it will not elicit the CR (fear). But the fact that extinction has taken place does not imply that the organism is back at square one. A reaction that is first conditioned and then extinguished is easy to recondition. Pavlov also showed this. He took two dogs—one that was first conditioned to salivate and in whom that reaction was then extinguished and another dog that had never learned the meaning of the bell. He exposed both dogs to a situation where the sound of the bell was once more tied to the acquisition of food. The first dog learned to react to the relation between sound and food much quicker than the second.

Here's another example. Let's say you're afraid of heights, but you still decide to spend a week putting a new roof on your house. If nothing scary happens to you during the roofing, your conditioned fear will probably subside during the week. Your experience of the distance from the rooftop to the ground loses some of its function as a conditioned stimulus (CS) and no longer evokes fear, your conditioned response (CR), or at least not as much as before. If, after finishing your roof repairs, you don't climb on your roof till the following summer, you'll probably feel more fear than you did toward the end of the week you spent working on the roof the previous year. However, it probably won't be as bad as when you started working on your roof the previous year—and it will probably take less time on the roof this year for your fear to subside again.

Respondent Conditioning and Psychopathology

It is easy to understand that the type of learning we've been discussing has relevance to many of the problems that cause people to seek professional help. We may, for example, have a client who comes to us because she is deeply fearful of going to the dentist. After many painful experiences at the dentist's office, certain smells, sounds (the drill, metal objects), and body positions (reclining in the dentist's chair) evoke unpleasant conditioned responses for her. Or we may have a client who comes to us because of posttraumatic stress. While living in a war zone, he experienced a range of events where painful reactions were elicited. Even though he no longer lives in the war zone, those earlier unconditioned stimuli and responses are now related to many phenomena that function as conditioned stimuli and then elicit reactions (CR) that are similar to the reactions evoked in the war situation (UCR). Let's look at this particular client's situation a little more closely:

> For a long time, Mirza and his family lived with increasing harassment from
> people around them in Bosnia. Eventually it turned into regular terror. The war
> came to the town where Mirza lived, and he saw people being assaulted and even
> killed. His older brother was taken away, and to this very day he has not been
> found. Mirza assumes he is dead. For several years, he lived with a daily threat
> of violence, maltreatment, and death. Both he and his parents were humiliated
> without being able to defend themselves in a reasonable way.

Now Mirza and his parents live in Sweden. Even though the present circumstances are good, he lives with the consequences of his past experiences. Ordinary events—different kinds of sounds, people in uniform, smoke, and fire— easily evoke pain and suffering. Some of these reactions seem easy to understand from a straightforward, commonsense point of view. That Mirza, for example, reacts to war scenes on the TV seems reasonable to most people. Other reactions follow a less obvious route. For example, the event of encountering Swedish police outside his house can evoke strong feelings. He knows that they pose no objective threat to him, but he still can't help reacting with intense fear. He even tries to reassure himself: "The police in Sweden have nothing to do with war, have they?" Mirza himself comes to regard his reactions as unnatural and hard to understand. "I know they are not here to harass me. Why do I react this way?"

To Mirza, there is a logical inconsistency in his responses. He reacts with fear, but from a logical perspective he can see nothing to fear. For Mirza's nervous system, however, there is no inconsistency. His reactions are based on respondent conditioning. They are not "logical," and "logical thinking" cannot do away with or govern his reactions. If we want to understand Mirza's reactions, we must consider his experiences of severe threat to both himself and his relatives. His reactions are formed by these experiences, even though the stimuli that evoke them today do not constitute an actual threat (see fig. 4.3). But the present conditioned stimuli have a formal similarity with stimuli in his historical experience, and in their presence his body mobilizes for action—either flight or fight.

Figure 4.3 Traumatic Conditioning

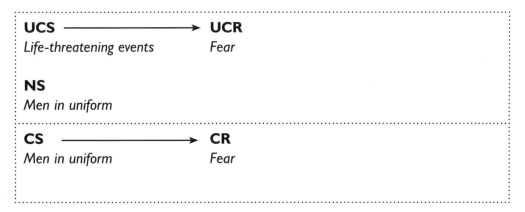

Problems with a less dramatic background, in an objective sense, can also be understood in the same way. It is not only with survivors of war and similar tragedies that we see the many problems and difficulties caused by respondent conditioning. Alice is an example of this:

Much has happened in Alice's life. For a long time, she has worked too much. The fact that she did not know, from one day to the other, in which department she was supposed to be did not make her work situation any easier. And then there was this thing with her fiancé, Bob, and the problems with her mother who has a drinking problem and calls almost every day. But that particular Wednesday, Alice was extra tired and upset. She noticed that her body was tense and felt "strange." In the evening, just after she had gone to bed, everything got worse. She felt extremely dizzy and her heart raced. She felt pressure on her chest, and she felt as if she could barely breathe.

Alice had what we call a "panic attack." In and of itself, panic is a normal reaction that can be evoked in anyone who is in a situation of immediate threat. We have this preparedness within the range of our basic affect system. In Alice's case, her panic attack was the result of a long period of stress. We can see this as a type of false alarm in a response system that was developed for life-threatening situations (Bouton, Mineka, & Barlow, 2001). The panic attack has, even though it is a passing experience, the ability to establish respondent conditioning, just as actual threats do. What becomes the conditioned stimulus (CS) then? Usually some of the most salient stimuli of the situation—like strong bodily sensations. This might also reflect what we wrote earlier about biological preparedness to react to changes in the experience of our own body. Let's take a further look at Alice's situation:

In the days following her panic attack, Alice continues to feel tense and tired. She still has just as much to do. Even though she doesn't experience another attack, she still feels a heaviness in her chest. But she finally calms down, and after a relaxed weekend, the exhaustion, tension, and heaviness in her chest are more or less gone. One night a few weeks later, Alice stays out late celebrating with a friend and, as a result, gets much less sleep than usual. As she gets ready to go to work early the next morning, she feels tired and senses some vague bodily discomfort. Suddenly as she walks down the hall, she feels dizzy, the sense of heaviness in her chest is back, her heart races, and panic hits once again.

How should we understand Alice's experience? At the time of this second panic attack, she was not exhausted the way she had been previously. She was tired, but the tiredness was due to lack of sleep. Alice thought she could manage one night with less sleep; she'd been short on sleep many times before and it was never a problem. But part of what Alice experiences "on the inside" as tiredness and somatic sensations connected with being tired can function as a conditioned stimulus (CS) and evoke a conditioned response (CR) in the form of, for example, accelerated heart rate and/or heaviness in the chest, regardless of the particular interpretations she makes of these phenomena. The interoceptive conditioning becomes a central part in the evolving vicious circle (see fig. 4.4):

Figure 4.4 Interoceptive Conditioning

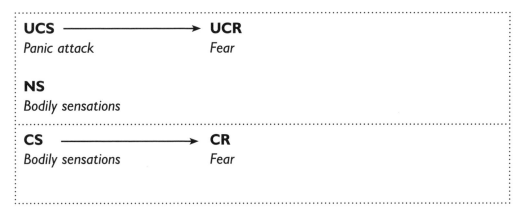

UCS ⟶ **UCR**
Panic attack   Fear

NS
Bodily sensations

CS ⟶ **CR**
Bodily sensations   Fear

Another example of how respondent conditioning can influence psychopathology is obsessive-compulsive phenomena. Here's another example from Alice's life:

> Alice has noticed recently that she is becoming more and more afraid of forgetting things. One example is with the stove. As she leaves the apartment, she often stops at the door and asks herself, "Did I turn off the stove?" She returns to the kitchen, makes sure the stove is turned off, and then heads for the door. Once she's at the door again, the thought comes back: "Let's see now, did I really turn it off?" Often she returns one or two more times to check.

Leaving aside the question of how Alice's obsessive-compulsive behavior started, it's easy to see how checking the stove over and over can result in respondent conditioning. The front door and/or the act of approaching it can easily become a conditioned stimulus (CS) that evokes anxiety. This, then, is an example of how respondent conditioning can become a part of psychopathology. It provides not only an explanation of how certain symptoms started but also how the same behavioral process can become a part of or increase existing problems regardless of how they started.

Avoidance and Escape

We have described how conditioned responses decrease or disappear when the relation between conditioned and unconditioned stimuli ends. When I climb onto the roof and expose myself to "the experience of height" without anything harmful taking place, I find that "the height experience's" capacity to evoke fear will decrease. Extinction takes place. This natural extinction process is prevented if I leave the roof when I start to feel afraid or if, remembering my earlier experience, I never climb it at all. To try to avert the unpleasant or aversive experience as it occurs is usually called *escape* and to not approach situations that are associated with such experiences is called *avoidance*. Often the term "avoidance" is used for both behaviors.

To avoid or to try to escape painful experiences is a very natural kind of behavior. It is natural to learn to avoid things that can be harmful. If we have eaten something poisonous or been attacked by a dangerous animal, it is helpful to avoid these things in the future.

Still, you can see how this process can become problematic with the behavior resulting in an effect that is opposite of the one desired. Not to climb the roof because climbing elicits fear has the short-term benefit of relieving me of something fearful now. If I might gain other possible advantages in the long run by climbing on the roof, I lose those possibilities when I abstain from doing so. Also, no extinction takes place, and if in the future I once again find myself on a roof (or another similar high place), in all probability I will once again meet my fear.

Many who seek professional help pay a much higher cost in their lives than simply not being able to climb on the roof. For example, if I have experienced the trauma of living in a war zone, I can't avoid everything that may possibly function as a conditioned stimulus for reactions to my hellish war experiences. Wherever I go, conditioned responses are evoked. If the anxiety is strong, it is easy to understand that a person tries to avoid that experience. Ironically, however, in the long run this very behavior maintains the anxiety responses as the natural extinction process does not take place. How, for instance, can Alice avoid her front door? Of course it's possible to do that, but it will have strange consequences. Those who've worked with clients with severe obsessive-compulsive problems know that people will indeed do many strange things when facing this kind of dilemma. Even though the experience of dirt, for example, can be very anxiety provoking if you have this problem, people who compulsively wash their hands can abstain totally from washing in an effort to escape getting stuck in rituals of hand washing. That some people with panic attacks become very passive (staying indoors, walking slowly) is consistent once you understand the vicious circle of conditioned stimuli, conditioned responses, avoidance, generalization, lack of extinction, and so on.

In these examples, other processes are also involved, processes that are better understood as a result of learning by consequences (operant conditioning). We shall return to this interplay of respondent and operant conditioning both in chapter 8 and in the last section of the book, Changing Behavior. At this point, we want to stress that the hopelessness in the avoidant behavior is due to the fact that the things the person avoids to a high degree are results of respondent conditioning. These responses are not under voluntary control and the path toward extinction is blocked by avoidance.

Respondent Conditioning and Thoughts

Thoughts we think, just like feelings, memories, and bodily sensations, are inner phenomena that can become a part of respondent conditioning. A thought can be a conditioned response (CR), thus being elicited by a conditioned stimulus (CS). If we say "September 11," surely you see certain mental images in your inner eye. This will not be as clear for most readers if we say, for instance, "October 7." But thoughts can also function as a CS and be the source of a CR. If you dwell on the images evoked, some of the feelings you had that day will come back to you.

This is of great relevance to clinical problems. Assume you have heard a judgment ("you are not normal") in connection to aversive experiences (unconditioned response, UCR). If you once again experience this judgment (or a situation that evokes such a thought of your own), the thought can elicit an affective response (conditioned response, CR) similar to the original one. One example of how thoughts can be a CR is a person with a long-standing problem of insomnia. Going to bed and lying awake with your head on your pillow has often been accompanied by thoughts of not being able to sleep. In time, the pillow (or the whole bed) can function as a conditioned stimulus (CS) for thoughts of not being able to sleep, and it will be impossible to go to bed without such thoughts (CR) turning up. The bed is now a CS for reactions that wake you up rather than putting you to sleep, which is the desired outcome in this situation.

The fact that inner phenomena such as thoughts, images, feelings, and bodily sensations are associated with each other and a range of external situations has great significance for human functioning. The reactions of a human being constantly undergo change due to the unceasing process of respondent conditioning that constantly alters the function the environment has for this particular individual. Something that up to a certain point was irrelevant gains an important function; something that had one function now obtains another.

We want to stress that respondent conditioning is still not enough to understand the phenomena we describe as "thinking." Respondent conditioning does take part in human language and cognition, but it is easy to show that this principle of learning does not capture the essence of it. The flexibility of human language and thinking is so much greater than this kind of conditioning can account for, as we see in this illustration from Marie's life:

> Marie has a vivid memory of the first time she clearly encountered the discomfort that now dominates her daily life. She attended church regularly and always sat in the back row. The first time she experienced the fear, it started rather unexpectedly as she sat there during a Sunday service. She noticed that she was sweating and that her face was flushed. Her heart started to race and she felt slightly dizzy. It was very unpleasant. After that, quite often as she sat there, the same discomfort came back. She valued attending the service and continued going, sitting in her usual place, with or without the discomfort—but mostly with it. She did not avoid the situation in which this was evoked, but she did stop going forward for Holy Communion. Since that time, her difficulties have spread to most parts of her life—but this is how it started.

How can we understand this? If we asked Marie, she would probably say something like "the Holy Communion, I could never manage that. What if the discomfort and my heart racing get worse and come when . . . ?" If we ask people in general, her argument and behavior would probably seem understandable. But if thoughts are primarily to be understood as respondent conditioning, Marie's behavior is very hard to explain. She had, at that time, no experience of the thing avoided. She had never felt this kind of discomfort or heart racing in connection to Holy Communion. The discomfort had never been worse than what she had experienced and the actual situation that evoked the discomfort was not avoided. It is as if her (and our) thoughts brought her to a place where she had never been before and got their functions from there. We will explore how this can be understood from a learning perspective in chapter 7. For now, it is enough to note that what is usually called thinking involves more than respondent conditioning.

CHAPTER 5

Learning by Consequences: Operant Conditioning

Imagine that you've installed a brand-new smoke alarm in your home. You feel safe just looking at the little white box on the ceiling as its red indicator light slowly blinks to tell you it's working properly. A few days later, the alarm goes off without warning—but there's no fire! You were just following the instructions in your new cookbook that explicitly states the spices must be dry-roasted in a preheated frying pan on the stove. But the alarm is not interested in the cookbook instructions; instead it reacts to the smoke and sends out its intense 110-decibel signal, carefully engineered to wake people from deep sleep wherever they are in the house. You jump up, your heart pounds, your entire organism is on alert—in other words, you're frightened.

While the alarm continues its loud and aversive screeching, you grab a ladder from the garage, climb up to the smoke alarm, and quickly push the button. Nothing happens. The alarm continues to screech as you pull it from its holder and remove the battery. At last, it gets quiet. How might you respond if someone asked you to explain your behavior in this sequence?

Other Person:	Why did you jump up?
You:	Because the alarm went off!
Other Person:	Why did you climb the ladder, pull the alarm from its holder, and remove the battery?
You:	Because the alarm went off!

The answer to each question is the same, but there are two different relationships between the activity of the organism (you) and the stimulus (the alarm signal). What's the difference? Your jumping up and your heart pounding occur automatically. In order to turn off the alarm, you probably put down the frying pan, perhaps under running water in the kitchen sink. You rush to the garage where you put that ladder the last time you used it. You could, in principle, go to the fridge and pour yourself a glass of milk before climbing the ladder—the process of turning the alarm off allows for a wide variety of actions. But your immediate reaction—you jump up and your heart starts pounding—would not vary a great deal from one time to another. Yet when it comes to actually shutting off the alarm, we could very well see a host of functional behaviors.

Let's say, for instance, removing the battery doesn't work. The alarm continues to screech. What will you do? Hit the box. Remove the entire back plate. Yank out the cord that's attached to its speaker unit. Rip out the wires from the power supply unit. But the alarm still screeches. When you finally slam it against the edge of your dining table, you succeed in silencing it. And there ends the behavioral sequence. A difference between the two kinds of responses, then, is that one (the respondent type) does not show a great variety while the other (the operant) does.

A similarity between the responses described is that both can be modified by experience. Let's say this evening you have a guest for dinner who lived through a war. He repeatedly experienced being awakened in the middle of the night by air-raid sirens, and he had to quickly gather his family and get them to a shelter. His reaction to the sudden screeching of an alarm would probably differ from yours. Chances are that his physiological reaction might be more intense and have the character of regular panic. Or let's say that you have found a clever way to turn the alarm off—perhaps by following the instructions in the owner's manual that tell you to push the button for ten seconds in order to turn off the alarm. If you knew that, you'd probably use this way to turn the alarm off.

Now let's return to our original scenario where you smash the alarm against the dining room table. When your family sees what has happened, they'll probably wonder if it was necessary to wreck the new alarm. Indeed, a reasonable and relevant question! But a question as to whether it was necessary to jump up and let your heart beat so rapidly does not really seem that relevant, especially not to our friend with wartime experiences. We are generally less inclined to assume personal responsibility for immediate reactions like these.

What we are trying to do here is map the relationship between stimulus and response. The different scenarios above describe two different relationships: respondent conditioning, that is, the learned immediate reaction to a stimulus, and operant conditioning, that is, the learned behavior of terminating the screeching alarm. Operant conditioning is the focus of our attention in this chapter.

WHAT IS OPERANT CONDITIONING?

Operant conditioning can be defined as the learning of instrumental behaviors, that is, behavior controlled by consequences. When people try to escape something (for example, a screeching smoke alarm), their efforts to escape imply that they are acting in order to change the circumstances, in this case to terminate an aversive stimulus in the form of a loud, screeching smoke alarm. In cases such as this, it is critical to understand that in similar situations that occurred earlier under certain circumstances, certain behaviors were followed by certain consequences. These consequences make it likely that a person will perform similar behaviors in similar situations under similar circumstances. In our historical experience, a certain relationship has been established between our acting and our experiencing certain consequences.

One way that we can understand the difference between respondent and operant learning is that it is similar to the distinction we make in ordinary language between "reacting" and "acting." Respondent behavior is classified by its relation to the eliciting stimuli that precede it, that is, it "responds" or "reacts" to the eliciting stimuli. Operant behavior, or "acting," implies a behavior that is purposeful or instrumental. Of course, operant behavior is also under the control of stimuli that precede it, which we previously described as being in the presence of certain circumstances. But operant behavior is, above all, understood as having a special relation to circumstances that occur *after* the behavior has been performed, that is, a special relation to the consequences that follow the behavior. For example, the fact that little Liza's salivation increases when her mother shows her the candy she just bought could be understood from a purely respondent point of view. The salivation response is reacting. But the fact that Liza shortly thereafter (when Mommy has left the kitchen) opens the cupboard where the candy usually is kept must be understood in another way—as operant learning. This response is one of acting, and it is a kind of acting that is influenced by the kind of consequences Liza experienced earlier when she has opened the cupboard (she acted) and found the candy (the consequence) that her mother thought she had hidden so cleverly. In short, she learned, when her mother buys candy, how she can look for it and maybe find it so she can eat it.

In operant learning lie possibilities to adapt to ever-changing circumstances in a way that inherited reaction patterns never would allow. If Liza's mother hides the candy in a new place, Liza can, for example, look for it until she finds it so she can once again eat it. She is learning by the consequences of her actions. This kind of learning opens up new possibilities of adaptation. We could not possibly have been biologically prepared for credit cards, electric wheelchairs, or cell phones, yet we are fully capable of learning to interact meaningfully with these things. Operant conditioning makes it possible for us to go beyond the slow process of the adaptation of the species made through changes in our basic biological endowment. It makes it possible for us to respond to ever-changing situations and inventions that were not even thought of when we were born.

HOW CONSEQUENCES AFFECT BEHAVIOR

Let's take a closer look at what it means to learn by consequences, that is, how consequences affect behavior. We'll start with a simple schema drawn from these basic possibilities: consequences can increase or decrease the likelihood of certain behavior, and consequences to certain behavior can be added or removed. This leaves us with four basic ways to affect behavior:

- **Positive reinforcement:** The addition (or increasing) of a certain consequence *increases* the likelihood of a certain behavior.

- **Negative reinforcement:** The removal (or lessening) of a certain consequence *increases* the likelihood of a certain behavior.

- **Positive punishment:** The addition (or increasing) of a certain consequence *decreases* the likelihood of a certain behavior.

- **Negative punishment:** The removal (or lessening) of a certain consequence *decreases* the likelihood of a certain behavior.

As given, these are purely functional definitions. They define the way in which a behavior is governed by its consequences. They do not, however, indicate what kinds of functions specific consequences might have. It's reasonable to ask what kind of consequences, when experienced, increase the likelihood of a certain behavior. For example, what kind of consequences would increase the likelihood that Liza would look for candy? However, we cannot determine solely by the objective features of an event, like the sweet-tasting properties of candy, what function a consequence will have on an individual's behavior.

You could, of course, assume from the start that certain consequences are aversive to people and therefore would have punishing functions, while other consequences are appetitive and would therefore probably have rewarding functions. But function cannot be reduced to a quality of the consequence itself. Function arises in the interaction between the person and the consequences. We'll discuss this a bit more somewhat later in this chapter.

It's important to remember that consequences, in and of themselves, are not the most important aspect of a functional analysis. The most important aspect is the effect of consequences on behavior. The expression "reinforcement" always refers to an increased likelihood of a certain behavior under certain circumstances, and "punishment" refers to a decreased likelihood of a certain behavior under certain circumstances. This is at the heart of the behavioral understanding. It also targets one of the most common misuses of these concepts as revealed in a comment like this: "We reinforce with all that we've got, but nothing happens with the behavior!" This statement gives us every reason to believe that it is not a contingency of reinforcement that is being described, at least not of the behaviors that they intend to reinforce. Verbal praise is a typical example where the quality of the event is often assumed a priori to have reinforcing qualities, hence it is easily overused with the intent of reinforcing but without monitoring actual effects on the behavior intended to be influenced.

A WORD ABOUT "POSITIVE" AND "NEGATIVE"

Positive and negative reinforcement cannot be equated with the adjectives "positive" and "negative" in an evaluative sense—that is, "positive" means good and "negative" means bad. This is probably the most common misunderstanding of positive and negative reinforcement. When using these terms, it is important to remember that "positive" means the addition (or increasing) of a certain consequence that has a reinforcing or punishing effect on behavior when it is added. "Negative" means that the removal (or decrease) of a certain consequence has a reinforcing or punishing effect on behavior.

Negative reinforcement is as basic and necessary as positive. When we put on a heavy knitted sweater in winter to avoid freezing outside, our behavior is under negative reinforcement since the behavior removes the aversive event of freezing. The same is true when we seek comfort in others when we're feeling sad, and these feelings are lessened by the presence of other people. Thus the comfort-seeking behavior is negatively reinforced. And if the reinforcer in taking drugs is the kick it brings, then the drug-taking behavior is under positive reinforcement. If the reinforcing properties that follow upon attacking and robbing people are the excitement and the extra monetary resources that come with assault and robbery, then the behavior is under positive reinforcement since the consequences of the behavior imply the addition or increase of these things for the person who attacks and robs people. But, as you can plainly see, there is nothing "positive" about these behaviors.

We hope this clarifies a bit the meaning of "positive" and "negative" as we use those terms in relation to operant conditioning. Let's look more closely now at a correct understanding of reinforcement and, in particular, positive reinforcement.

Positive Reinforcement: In the Presence of Antecedent (A), Behavior (B) Leads to Consequence (C)

As we said earlier, *positive reinforcement* is the addition (or increasing) of a certain consequence that increases the likelihood of a certain behavior. When you think about the term "positive reinforcement," you may readily associate it with situations such as teaching a dog to sit on its hind legs. When the dog sits on its hind legs, you reinforce this response by giving it a treat. For convenience and efficiency, though, you would be well-advised to first teach the dog to associate the treat with another stimulus: a pat or some verbal praise such as "Good dog!" Otherwise, if you give the dog too many treats, it may become satiated and lose interest in learning to sit on its hind legs (not to mention the risk of overfeeding the dog if this routine is repeated on a regular basis). In this example of training a dog to sit, we have a sequence that is a clear example of positive reinforcement (see fig. 5.1).

Figure 5.1 Positive Reinforcement: Teaching a Dog to Sit

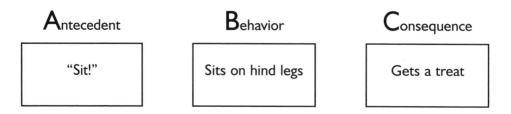

In this contingency, we can assume that the likelihood of the dog's behavior (sitting) increases in the presence of your giving the command "Sit!" since the behavior is reinforced by giving the dog a treat. The term "positive reinforcement" is sometimes equated with some kind of reward. But this understanding is incomplete and ignores an important, though perhaps subtle, aspect of positive reinforcement. Remember that we are studying behaviors that work in a given context. Let's say that you are a carpenter and you are asked to nail two boards together. Your behavior of "nailing" is reinforced by seeing the nails being driven into the wood and thereby attaching the two boards to each other. Positive reinforcement comes with the fact that you were able to do the task you were asked to do—nailing the boards together worked. This is equally true with the dog you were teaching to sit. From the dog's perspective, sitting on its hind legs "works"—that is, by sitting on its hind legs, it manages to get the human to give it a treat!

The learning principle of positive reinforcement, however, is not always seen as "positive" because of its association with control and manipulation. This association is not in itself erroneous, especially not if we use these words according to their scientific (and more neutral) definition. Then, control and manipulation simply mean that we can predict an event, and by changing one variable, we can achieve change in another. For example, we raise the amount of thermal energy in a container of water to bring it to a boil, and the water will thereby transform from liquid to gas. What has been manipulated is the amount of energy. In the same vein, we manipulate the context that surrounds our dog by imposing a contingency where a treat follows certain specified behaviors. In this way, the behavior of the dog is affected. But let's be clear on one thing: the dog affects you, the human, simultaneously. If the intended dog-training program we've just described were to be successful, this experience will also affect how you, the dog trainer, behave in the future (for instance, when training a puppy to sit on its hind legs).

Operant learning principles are not something we do to subjects. We do them together with the subjects. Being a part of a social environment involves influencing the behavior of others; that is a process that can be understood in operant terms. Let's say that you and I get together for coffee and I tell you about a problem that I ran into at work. I want to talk with you about it because you've handled similar situations. It feels good talking to somebody who understands these kind of things. While I talked, you listened. This led to you hearing my story, which put you in a position where you could respond to it. Then when you talked, I listened to the input you gave me about the situation, which in turn put me in a new situation to respond to, and on goes the conversation.

Figure 5.2 Mutual Contingencies: A Conversation

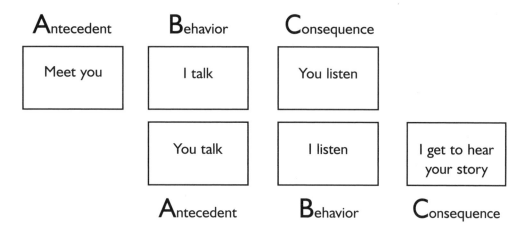

My behavior in this example is not elicited as a reflex to seeing you. It is more reasonable to understand the speaking as governed by the consequence of your listening to me. It is a functional sequence. For you, my talking constitutes a stimulus for the behavior "listening." It works: I talk, you listen. However, if you didn't listen to me, I soon would be inclined to stop talking. My behavior, therefore, is under the control of the consequences that follow it. But the consequences in this example do not come in the form of candy or dog treats. Instead, the consequences we're talking about here are the kind of reinforcers with which humans have extensive contact—interpersonal reinforcers.

In everyday language, we say that I speak with you because I "want" to. I would most likely not use that word if I were referring to a reflex response. Thus, operant learning is the study of voluntary behavior. But note that there is no "will" in the sense of an inner explanation of why the behavior is emitted. The "will" is rather a part of the act or the behavior at hand—that is, orienting the response toward certain consequences according to the relation between action and outcome that has been established in my history.

The image of B. F. Skinner controlling the behavior of rats and pigeons comes as the symbol of passive influence. But when we view it this way, we totally miss the influence these animals had on Skinner's life—that is, the influence was mutual. The behavior of Skinner was reinforced by the pigeons pecking in a pattern that he could discover, just as the behavior of the pigeons was reinforced by the fact that once in a while their pecking resulted in food dropping in front of them. Skinner's life would probably not have taken the course it did were it not for the influence these creatures had on his behavior. Hence, our earlier comment deserves to be repeated: Operant learning is not something we do to subjects. We do it together with them!

CONDITIONED REINFORCERS

In the example above, the dog learns to associate a stimulus (a treat) with a pat or the praise "Good dog!" Following this, the latter stimuli—the treat and the praise—can be used to reinforce behavior. Everyone who has visited a dolphin show has heard whistles sounding over and over. The dolphins are taught, through repeated trials, to associate the sound of the whistle with receiving fish. Gradually the trainer will be able to rely more and more on the whistle to influence the dolphin's behavior and increase the intervals between giving fish to the dolphins. For the dolphin, the sound of the whistle will come to mean something like "soon there will be fish" and this will function as a reinforcer. The whistle has the distinct advantage of not leading to satiety. But to continue to have its reinforcing properties, it must occasionally be paired with actual fish. We could, in a way, regard the whistle as a rudimentary symbol for fish. The dolphin reacts to an actual relationship between the sound of the whistle and fish that has occurred in the dolphin's personal history. As you will notice, this describes a relationship between two stimuli that is similar to that described in the chapter on respondent conditioning. The conditioned stimulus (the sound of the whistle) has been experienced in actual proximity to the unconditioned stimulus (fish) and thereby acquires a reinforcing function from the unconditioned stimulus. We refer to this type of reinforcer as a *conditioned reinforcer*.

GENERALIZED REINFORCERS

As human beings in a monetary economy, we learn to relate to money early in our lives. We learn to be satisfied when we receive money and disappointed when we lose it. Dolphins and dogs, on the other hand, tend to be notoriously hard to influence by monetary means—very much in the same way that raw herring and dog treats are rather impotent when it comes to influencing us humans. Money, in itself, fulfills no natural need. It is not edible, it doesn't protect us from cold, it isn't pleasant to feel against our skin, and it doesn't smell good. And yet we find it so very satisfying to have a pocket full of cash! By experience, we've learned to associate money with access to other stimuli. We can, for instance, buy fish with money. But money is not limited—that is, it doesn't have a restricted association—in the way that the sound of the whistle and the fish do for the dolphin in the dolphin show. Money gives us access to a variety of other stimuli. Throughout our lives, money has gained its conditioned qualities from a variety of sources: the joy of getting our weekly pocket money, the relief of finally receiving a student loan, the gratitude for being well paid, and so on. Money has great potential—that is, it is a means—for influencing us humans. Money, therefore, is a *generalized reinforcer* because it is a flexible means that denotes access to a host of primary reinforcers. Let's turn now to primary reinforcers and the role they play in operant conditioning.

PRIMARY REINFORCERS

A *primary reinforcer* is an unconditioned reinforcer. So what are the basic characteristics of a reinforcer that is not conditioned? These reinforcers fulfill basic human needs: food, water, shelter, intimacy, and sex. Stated differently, it is evolutionarily advantageous that the behaviors connected with these basic human needs be reinforced.

Someone might say, then, that what we need is a theory of human needs to understand why people behave the way they do. This is reasonable in the sense that if we analyze human behavior as ultimately in the service of survival, we could then regard learning theory as a theory about basic needs. But what we must keep in mind is that these "needs" are not observable events in themselves; often they tend to be a mere restatement of activity. For example, we draw the conclusion of a person's "intense need of proximity" from the fact that he intensely engages himself with behaviors that fulfill the purpose of gaining proximity, such as staying close to a trusted person and constantly checking out his or her location. What we observe is this activity, or behavior, and referring to a "need" adds no further observation: it is a restatement of the observed activity. Or, alternatively, we may draw that conclusion from human behavior in general. Sex seems to be a basic need, since humans are inclined to make substantial efforts to gain access to it. On the other hand, people do live perfectly sane and healthy lives without sex.

It is important to note that the basic needs of humans are not limited to those named above—that is, there are other needs or human events that have reinforcing properties that need not be conditioned. Studies of newborns are especially valuable for understanding primary reinforcers in humans, since we can assume that newborns have not yet established conditioned reinforcers to the same extent as grown-ups (Novak, 1996). What has been found is that imitative behavior has reinforcing properties in itself, such as when children produce sounds similar to those native speech sounds that are used by the people around them. This is also the case with motor behaviors such as crawling and walking. This implies that there is no need to add external reinforcers for them to develop, since the behaviors in themselves contain their own reinforcement. It has also been proposed that the early babbling in toddlers has a self-reinforcing quality. The sound of babble reinforces the behavior babbling. It is a rudimentary activity that eventually will enter a world of social control and be shaped into language. Some experiments also indicate that there is a reinforcing property for infants in exploring and discovering the association between their own behavior and consequences in the physical environment (Bower, 1977). This indeed sounds like a very attractive idea: we are born behaviorists (before we enter the world of social control)! Taken a little more seriously, these experiments hint that experiencing control might contain an element of these basic reinforcing qualities. It is easy, therefore, to see how these processes could serve useful evolutionary purposes.

REINFORCEMENT IN CLINICAL CONTEXTS

In clinical settings, it is often fruitful to look for consequences in the social context and in terms of emotional regulation. We can expect, for instance, to see behaviors that serve a function in avoiding painful experiences.

If we take self-injurious behavior as an example, these acts usually lead to massive attention from those in the same social context. Unfortunately such acts are sometimes trivialized by expressions like "she's just doing it to get attention." Treating self-injurious behavior in this way runs the risk of gravely devaluing one of the fundamental reinforcers for humans: being attended to by other humans. Even if attention in itself does not meet the criteria of being a necessity for survival, we learn as infants that if we are to be fed, it will be in the presence of the attention of another person. If we are to be warm, dry, and touched, this will occur accompanied by the attention of another person. Our experience of being loved usually takes place in a context of attention of another person. We all have the fundamental experience that attention comes with the fulfillment of our basic needs, and there is nothing trivial about that.

Let's return to Jenny's situation for a moment. What is the function of Jenny's self-injurious behavior? Our observations indicate that it occurs in the presence of the nursing staff. But what events follow upon the behavior? There are a multitude of possible consequential events, but let's begin with the most obvious one (see fig. 5.3):

Figure 5.3 Contingency: Positive Reinforcement and Jenny's Self-Destructive Behavior

Antecedent	Behavior	Consequence
In presence of staff	Engages in self-destructive behavior	Staff increases attention to Jenny

Here we assume that Jenny's behavior is under positive reinforcement and serves a function of maintaining attention from certain people. We could consider other positive reinforcers: her behavior provides an adrenaline kick in a stimulus-deprived environment and it provides a means of social control and influence. However, it is far from obvious that Jenny's behavior is solely under positive reinforcement (see fig. 5.4).

Figure 5.4 Contingency: Negative Reinforcement and Jenny's Self-Destructive Behavior

Antecedent	Behavior	Consequence
In presence of staff, as well as worry about being abandoned	Engages in self-destructive behavior	Increased attention, which simultaneously decreases worry

In contrast to the assumption of positive reinforcement above, here we assume that Jenny's behavior is under negative reinforcement. Jenny's actions provide access to other people, which might fulfill the function of lessening anxiety. Those of you that have toddlers (well, perhaps the rest of you also) know how persistent their behavior can be when you really do not have the time to attend to them. The aversive stimulus function that is contained in the event when an important person does not signal accessibility seems to have a powerful impact, and humans (toddlers and adults alike) act to terminate this event. We are approximating the concept of security, but formulated in functional terms. There are good reasons to assume that we are biologically predetermined for relating to and maintaining proximity to other people in that these consequences serve as primary reinforcers. If Jenny's actions provide access to the staff's attention, this in turn might function to decrease her anxiety.

So the question we face as therapists is whether any given behavior increases or decreases the presence of stimuli. This can often be difficult to separate in a clinical setting and you can assume that, as in the example of Jenny's self-injurious behavior, the behavior can both increase and decrease the presence of stimuli simultaneously.

Negative Reinforcement: In the Presence of Antecedent (A), Behavior (B) Will Lead to Not Having Consequence (C)

As we said earlier, *negative reinforcement* occurs with the removal (or lessening) of a certain aversive consequence and thus increases the likelihood of a certain behavior. Now let's look at this phenomenon in Jenny's situation.

Jenny's self-injurious behavior occurs in relation to an external, social context. In the same vein, we have described how influencing private events (like worry and anxiety) might provide a function to the behavior. Let's consider this track of inner experience a little further. Self-injurious behavior could also function as a means of subduing painful inner experiences.

Figure 5.5 Contingency: Negative Reinforcement and Jenny's Private Events

Antecedent	Behavior	Consequence
Wakes up in the middle of the night with painful images of being abandoned	*Engages in self-destructive behavior*	*Decreases momentarily the pain of the images*

The consequences that maintain Jenny's self-injurious behavior function through negative reinforcement. But how can we understand that inflicting pain might have reinforcing properties when pain is something humans usually want to get rid of? There are at least two alternatives: Jenny may experience the physical pain as more bearable than the pain of her memories, or she may "trade" an uncontrollable pain (for example, painful memories) for pain that is under her control (injuring herself). This could dampen the aversive experience of not being in control. Notice that even when we describe "dysfunctional" acts like self-injurious behavior, they are functional in a sense. It is possible to see some sense in them. At the same time, however, the drawbacks of this behavior are obvious: it is dangerous and could result in permanent physical damage. Beyond that, the consequences that govern Jenny's behavior—gaining the attention of people around her and dampening her painful inner experiences—only work in the short run. Self-injury may function to make other people attend to Jenny in an emergency situation, but in the long run that very same behavior runs the risk of scaring people off. And as a means of regulating affect, it is also only effective in the short run. It does not provide Jenny with a durable strategy for emotional regulation.

But Jenny's action tells us two things. First, she has a deficit of better adaptive strategies in her behavioral repertoire. Second, it tells us something about the situation where Jenny emits this behavior. Remember that operant learning is not anything we do to subjects—we do it together with them. Therefore, from a contextual point of view, the reasoning is erroneous when one explains a person's self-injurious behavior by saying "she is so manipulative." Instead, we need to search for the reinforcers that occur in this situation. Are we contributing to some of them?

As illustrated in the example above, a behavior may have multiple reinforcers. On the other hand, several behaviors may be functional in relation to the same reinforcer, as we will see below.

Functional Classes of Behavior

A *functional class of behavior* consists of several behaviors that serve the same function in contacting a certain reinforcer. In the case of Marie, we have observed that she experiences intense anxiety when confronted with various social situations. She often tries to escape or avoid altogether situations that demand social interaction. In this way, she diminishes her experience of anxiety (see fig. 5.6).

Figure 5.6 Contingency: Avoidance and Escape in Social Situations—Marie

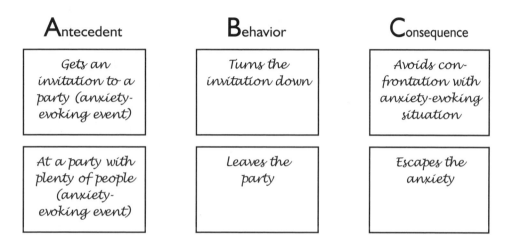

Antecedent	Behavior	Consequence
Gets an invitation to a party (anxiety-evoking event)	Turns the invitation down	Avoids confrontation with anxiety-evoking situation
At a party with plenty of people (anxiety-evoking event)	Leaves the party	Escapes the anxiety

Here we have two basic *functional relationships* (the relation between behavior and reinforcer): avoidance, when the function of a certain behavior is to avoid confronting an aversive stimulus, and escape, when the function of a certain behavior is to get away from or in some other way lessen the influence of a present aversive stimulus. Escape and avoidance behaviors function on negative reinforcement. By acting the way she does when invited to or when at a party, Marie diminishes, at least in the short term, experiences that she finds unpleasant.

There are many ways to accomplish this diminishment (see fig. 5.7). She could turn the invitation down, or, instead of turning it down, Marie could simply avoid showing up. Or she could schedule another engagement at the same time and thereby have an excuse not to attend. Or she could pretend that she misunderstood the time. The function of any of these behaviors is avoidance. And if Marie attends the party and becomes anxious, she has several options available. She could stay but keep herself at the periphery where the risk of being noticed is less; she could have several drinks so the intoxication lessens her anxiety; or she could sneak into the ladies room and take a tranquilizer. In all these instances, she remains in the social situation, but she acts in ways that serve the purpose of diminishing contact with an aversive stimulus. It should be noted that topographically diverse behaviors can have identical purposes for the individual, in which case we consider these behaviors *functionally equivalent*.

Figure 5.7 Contingency: Functional Classes of Behavior for Avoidance and Escape in Social Situations—Marie

Antecedent	Behavior	Consequence
Gets an invitation to a party (anxiety-evoking event)	1. Turns the invitation down 2. Doesn't go to party 3. Schedules another activity at the same time 4. Pretends to have misunderstood the time	Avoids the anxiety-evoking event

Antecedent	Behavior	Consequence
At a party with plenty of people (anxiety-evoking event)	1. Leaves the party 2. Keeps herself on the periphery 3. Gets drunk 4. Takes a tranquilizer	Escapes the anxious feelings

Collectively the behavior noted above is a functional class of behavior. Despite topographical dissimilarities, we consider these behaviors as a unit because of their functional properties, that is, escape is one functional unit and avoidance is another. This is an important characteristic of operant behavior: a multitude of behaviors can serve a singular purpose. Responses that are acquired by respondent conditioning do not show that kind of variability—for example, the physiological reaction that Marie experiences when she is anxious can be assumed to be fairly consistent from one time to another, in the same way as we discussed in the beginning of this chapter in relation to the fire alarm.

Operant Extinction: In the Presence of Antecedent (A), Behavior (B) No Longer Leads to Consequence (C)

Not every behavioral action is followed by consequences that function as reinforcers. In some cases, the behavior does not work and will then cease to be emitted, that is, it will be extinguished. This is analogous to the evolutionary principle of the survival of the species: those that successfully function in relation to the surrounding environment will survive; those that don't are likely candidates for extinction. Under *operant extinction*, the likelihood for a certain behavior decreases when it is not followed by certain consequences. Let's return to the dog we have been training and say "Sit!" The dog follows the command, but this time he does not get a treat (see fig. 5.8).

Figure 5.8 Operant Extinction: Dog Training

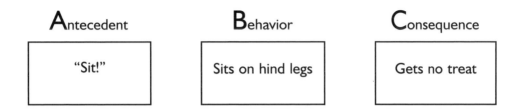

After a few times, the dog will cease to sit in response to the command. The behavior no longer serves the purpose of gaining access to the reinforcer that used to control behavior. The contingency has changed. Extinction can be formulated as follows: in the presence of A (antecedent), B (behavior) no longer leads to C (consequence).

Now let's return to our earlier example of my talking with someone about a problem I have at work. If the person I'm talking with no longer listens to me, the likelihood that I will go on speaking decreases (see fig. 5.9). This is an illustrative example because everyone recognizes how hard it can be to motivate oneself to continue speaking to a person who is obviously not listening. It illustrates that the essence of this analysis is to describe how what we speak of as "motivation" works. It works not as a mysterious inner force but as experiencing my acts in relation to the context.

Figure 5.9 Operant Extinction: A Conversation

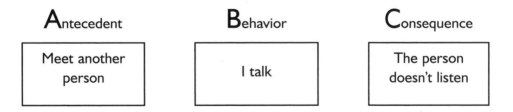

But here someone may object, "But if the other person doesn't listen, then you'll try harder and raise your voice!" Exactly! If I speak and the other person won't listen, my speaking behavior probably won't simply subside. Instead I will probably increase my efforts to make the other person listen, at least initially. Thereafter, if it doesn't work, I will probably give up. We vary and intensify our behavior when reinforcers that control the behavior do not appear in the way they have done previously.

When you do not listen to me and by doing so withdraw the reinforcer for my speaking, it may very well be that if I raise my voice enough, I could access the consequence that occurred earlier: you will listen to me! This phenomenon, called an *extinction burst*, has been shown in experimental studies of behavior.

The extinction burst is of vital clinical relevance. It is a process that can be observed in the escalation of different kinds of behavior. If a threatening behavior does not work, then I might try a little harder. If this new behavior works, we run the risk of having the reinforcement contingent on the new (and potentially more hazardous) behavior, as we see in Jenny's case:

> *On the ward, the staff has grown used to and tired of Jenny's acting out by superficially cutting the skin on her wrists. Since she is not considered to be severely suicidal, her behavior no longer evokes the same reactions from the staff. The next time Jenny cuts herself, she cuts deep enough to hit a blood vessel and has to be taken to the emergency room for stitches. Then the staff discusses the need for close surveillance of Jenny.*

Escalation of behavior is a potentially dangerous process. The removal of reinforcing consequences to achieve extinction is in reality a difficult balance. In the case of self-destructive behaviors, three things must be balanced: rules of legal responsibility, the tolerance of their own anxiety by the people around the client, and the goal of changing the contingencies so the establishment and maintenance of these behaviors are made less likely.

PUNISHMENT: THE ATTENUATION OF BEHAVIOR

The concept of punishment often leads to confusion since it exists in everyday language and is associated with aggressive correction and revenge. When it comes to learning theory, however, it is important to remember that we are talking about a relationship that has an effect on behavior. We are not using the word in some juridical or moral sense. Furthermore, it is easy to find instances of this effect on behavior in our own lives: We become less inclined to perform a certain behavior when it leads to pain, anxiety, or anything else that we might find unpleasant. In the same way, we become less inclined to behave in ways that lead to substantial losses of things that we value. From a learning theory point of view, a fine, for instance, is only considered a punisher if it has the effect of decreasing the unwanted behavior that was the reason for giving it. This is an important distinction to make: Learning theory refers to punishment as an actual effect on behavior. Everyday language refers to punishment as an event that is intended to correct behavior (or to be used for its own sake). So, in the context of this book, *punishment* is a consequence that decreases the likelihood of reoccurrence of the behavior that occurred prior to that consequence.

Positive Punishment: In the Presence of Antecedent (A), Behavior (B) Leads to Aversive Consequence (C)

Positive punishment is defined as the process where the likelihood of a behavior is decreased by the addition or increasing of a certain consequence. The prototypical example of positive punishment is the smack on the fingers that a child gets when reaching for the handle of a hot pot on the stove. But remember that functionally the term "punishment" applies equally well to the parents' harsh admonition or their yelling in fear. Both of these consequences may weaken the likelihood that the child will try to reach for the pot handle another time. Once again, we emphasize that "positive" in this context only means that something is added—an aversive consequence that decreases a behavior. The other possibility is that behavior is attenuated by the removal of certain consequences. This could be the case when it is an appetitive consequence—such as money, attention, or security—that is removed or decreased. Consequently, it would be labeled "negative punishment." Let's take a brief look at negative punishment now.

Negative Punishment: In the Presence of Antecedent (A), Behavior (B) Leads to Removal or Decrease of Appetitive Consequence (C)

Negative punishment is defined as the process where the likelihood of a behavior is decreased by the removal or lessening of a certain consequence. In this case, the prototypical example is a fine, such as a library fine for an overdue book. Since the undesired behavior (keeping a book past its due date) is followed by the confiscation of some of our financial assets, it should decrease our inclination to emit that particular behavior. Whether fining does serve that purpose is, however, another question, and it is a question of an empirical nature. Skinner himself pointed out the inefficacy of using punishment as a means of changing behavior (Skinner, 1953).

One problem with using punishment-based learning is that, by introducing the punisher, a stimulus that makes avoidance functional is introduced. This is apparent in many naturally occurring contingencies of punishment. If I feel a shooting pain in my back when I move, this decreases the likelihood of my moving (positive punishment). At the same time, however, it increases the likelihood of my resting or being still in order to avoid pain (negative reinforcement). If I become overwhelmed by anxiety when I approach other people, my inclination to do so will decrease (positive punishment). Inherent in this process is the fact that the inclination to avoid people in order to avoid anxiety increases (negative reinforcement). This close connection between introducing a punisher and reinforcing avoidance has the possible implication that when punishment is used for behavioral change, it might not have the effects intended. A parent who punishes a child who has told the parent about something bad he has done (such as breaking a lamp) runs the obvious risk that the child will learn to avoid telling certain things to his parents. Contingencies of punishment often have little control over the behaviors that are reinforced in their wake.

In spite of the problematic side effects, punishment as a solution seems to have an intuitive attraction to us humans (Sheldon, 1995). Even if our acceptance of corporal punishment as a means of control over undesired behaviors has decreased over recent decades, our belief in the harsh admonition, verbal threats, and aggressive confrontation seems to be solid. Unfortunately this is the case even in many clinical settings.

Human history is a history of punishment and aversive control. Our faith in these means to correct undesired behavior seems to be very resistant to the acknowledgment of its lack of effectiveness. If our children, for example, don't obey when we yell at them, we yell louder. And if this still does not work, we will try something that threatens them more. Ironically, as humans, we do not seem to have the same intuitive faith in positive reinforcement.

PUNISHMENT IN CLINICAL CONTEXTS

Consequences that have punishing functions have vast effects in people's lives. A clinical condition where this is pertinent is depression. A whole range of the phenomena that can be observed when a person is depressed could be understood as the effects of a life situation that has punishing functions (Martell, Addis, & Jacobson, 2001). Leonard is an example of this:

> Every time Leonard approaches his kids, he feels intense guilt over not having been the father he wanted to be. Because he feels this way, he tends to make fewer claims for the children to stay at his place. Instead, they get to stay at their mom's place, even at times that were agreed to be "his weekends."

We have just identified a sequence where Leonard's approaching his kids is under punishment. The punishing consequence is the experience of guilt that increases when he approaches his kids, hence it is positive punishment.

Figure 5.10 Positive Punishment: Leonard and His Children

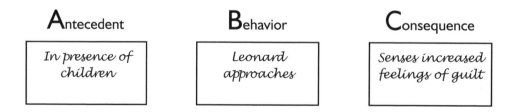

Antecedent — In presence of children

Behavior — Leonard approaches

Consequence — Senses increased feelings of guilt

And in this example, as mentioned previously, we see the interplay with negative reinforcement, where experiencing guilt functions as an antecedent for avoidance.

Figure 5.11 Negative Reinforcement: Leonard and His Children

Antecedent

Behavior

Consequence

| Feelings of guilt for his children | Lets the kids stay with their mom | Feelings of guilt decrease temporarily |

When avoiding the situation that evokes the feelings of guilt, the aversive experience decreases temporarily. But avoidance (not seeing his children) does not remove the circumstances (not having the regular contact with his children that he wishes to have) in which this experience of guilt occurs. On the contrary, the avoidance is likely to serve as a ground for an increased experience of guilt since having less time with his children is not what Leonard considers to be the behavior of a good father.

But Leonard's avoidance behavior will also have the consequence of him losing contact with important reinforcers. When the everyday interaction with his children decreases, he risks extinguishing parts of his behavioral repertoire that actually work in the contact with his children. (How, for instance, do you maintain the behavioral repertoire of talking with adolescents without regular practice?) This will be even more the case as they get older. The overarching consequence might be losing contact with that which he values the most: his children. So in Leonard's life, we see the formation of a context that contains a great number of aversive experiences that have potentially punishing effects. This will eventually attenuate a range of behaviors in his repertoire, even in situations that are not directly connected to his children, such as hanging out with friends (who all have families), socializing at work (where familial matters are a regular topic of discussion), or even going to work itself (which might acquire part of its reinforcing functions from providing for your family).

When people are depressed, their behavior is characterized by a marked decrease in adaptive actions. They are put in a situation that, from the perspective of learning theory, will be influenced by punishment and extinction on a broad front. Inactivity, frustration, low mood, and anxiety will be the natural accompaniment of this context (Martell, Addis, & Jacobson, 2001). This is reflected by the way depressed people often describe their lives: "Nothing's working anymore and everything feels so hard."

To analyze the functional aspects of behaviors in a clinical context is like following threads in a weaving. We gain an important understanding from this analytical detective work, because it enables us to better identify viable interventions. In Leonard's case, it is important that behaviors other than those that are primarily aimed at reducing the aversive experience of guilt are reinforced, especially those behaviors that are potentially functional in establishing a more durable and mutually rewarding relationship with his children. One of the main tasks for a therapist is to help Leonard in a process where he can endure the short-term punishing consequences (such as the feelings of guilt that are evoked when approaching his children) in order to contact those that are desirable from a long-term perspective (a stable, ongoing relationship with his children).

In this chapter we've focused on how consequences come to govern the behavior of the individual, but as we said in the beginning of the chapter, operant learning is also a process where behavior comes under the control of stimuli that precede it. We will elaborate further on that in the next chapter.

CHAPTER 6

Operant Conditioning: Stimulus Control

Operant conditioning is learning by attending to consequences. To understand the effects of these kinds of processes and how they affect our lives, we cannot solely consider the consequences (C). To learn from consequences is to put behavior under the control of antecedents (A).

The fact that a given behavior has been reinforced in a person's history does not mean that he or she will increase the frequency of that behavior in a random manner, at any time and any place. The experience of successfully using a hammer and nails, for example, does not imply that a person will start hammering nails in any and every situation. However, the likelihood of repeating this behavior increases in situations that are similar to ones where success has been experienced, such as doing carpentry work or hanging paintings on the walls.

The fact that behavior is reinforced implies that it comes under control of certain stimuli. Every time a behavioral event has occurred, it has occurred under certain circumstances. The individual acquires an experience in which different stimuli have preceded behaviors that have been reinforced. The behavior that has been reinforced under certain circumstances will be more likely to be emitted when these or similar circumstances occur again.

To illustrate this, we would like to tell a story of a complicated prank that occurred in Boston, Massachusetts, which has risen to the level of myth. The Boston area is home to two particularly prestigious higher education institutions: Harvard University and the Massachusetts Institute of Technology (MIT). These schools have a long-standing student rivalry (both in sports and off the field), and it is commonplace to witness the between-school student rivalry in the form of complicated and carefully constructed pranks.

The story goes that one year a group of MIT students sneaked into the Harvard football stadium to feed birds at several occasions over the summer. They blew a whistle and started spreading birdseed. Day after day, this was repeated: sneaking in to the arena, blowing a whistle, spreading seed. Birds came and feasted in ever-increasing numbers. Then the football season started, and everything was set for the first game. The spectators were seated, the players walked onto the field, the linesmen took their places, and the referee stepped onto the field to give the signal—that's right, by blowing a whistle—that the game could begin. We guess that you've already figured out what happened next. The football field was suddenly carpeted with birds coming to feast on the seed, just as they'd done all summer. What about the game? There were so many birds flocking to the field that the game could not begin. We're not sure whether this story is actually true; however, it does represent a creative application of learning theory that illustrates *stimulus control*, that is, how preceding events come to influence the probability of certain behavior.

The MIT students succeeded in establishing an antecedent (the whistle tone), which when present, increased the probability that the behavior emitted by the birds (flying down to the ground and pecking the grass to find seed) allowed contact with a reinforcer (food). The whistle tone had become what in operant psychology is labeled a *discriminative stimulus*—a stimulus, that when present, indicates that a given behavior is likely to be followed by reinforcement.[1] In everyday language, we would say that the birds perform this behavior in order to get food. We then overlook the fact that this expression contains a problematic way of reasoning from a scientific point of view. The presumed cause of the behavior (food) is temporally located after the behavior it should explain. Birds, like humans, are historical beings. It is hard to argue that a present behavior is under control of future events. Anyone who has watched the *Terminator* movies can see how difficult it is to do so.

It is not the fact that the birds will get seed that controls their behavior in the present situation. In fact, they do not get seed on the day of the game. It is the fact that they have gotten seed in similar situations that controls their behavior. They have a historical experience of reinforcement in the presence of a certain stimulus. You could search for similar examples in your own experience. We would guess that those examples are not about whistles, seed, and especially not about flying down to the ground. But they are probably about a subjective experience of being in contact with future events. That experience has been expressed in the following poetic way: "The past as the future in the present" (Hayes, 1992).

But don't the birds believe that they will get food? Is it their expectation that controls their behavior, or is it their intention? Are birds capable of believing, expecting, or holding intentions? We are hardly in a position to conclude that, since birds will probably never be able to tell us about their private events in a way that would even faintly verify these processes. We can, however, say that their behavior is intentional. But that is only a description of the fact that the behavior has a certain direction rather than a statement that supplies any explanation of it. The description of behavior in relation

---

1 Discriminative stimulus is usually written S^D. A stimulus that is associated with nonreinforcement is written S^Δ "S-delta." A stimulus associated with the likelihood of a behavior to be followed by punishment is written S^{D-}. All these stimulus functions are included under the label "antecedent."

to the context where it occurs has the advantage that it allows an understanding of variables that are potentially available for influencing the behavior. Both antecedents and consequences are variables that, in principle, can be manipulated. The purpose of a functional analysis is to better situate us for influencing the behavior of the people who seek our professional assistance to help them make a change in their lives.

CLINICALLY RELEVANT STIMULUS CONTROL

Anna knows that there is no use in telling Peter what she thinks about his drinking when he has been drinking.

The same sentence stated as an ABC contingency could be phrased: in the presence of A (Peter has been drinking), B (stating her opinion of it) does not lead to C (Peter listening to her). Anna's experience tells her that a behavior that often is useful (stating one's opinion) under these circumstances is unlikely to be followed by reinforcement.

But stimulus control in this case cannot be executed by Anna knowing what will happen. That would imply that she possesses supernatural powers. Anna does know what has happened every time she has done so in the past, however. In this case, stimulus control implies less likelihood that Anna will emit the behavior in that situation. Stating her opinion has been extinguished in the presence of the antecedent mentioned.

Stimulus control could also indicate a situation in which a certain behavior has previously been followed by a punisher. We can see this in the following situation:

Lately when Peter has tried to give Anna a hug, she has, somewhat sourly, said, "What do you want from me when you do that?" This has hurt Peter so much that he avoids seeking physical contact.

We can express the contingency for Peter's behavior as follows: in the presence of A (Anna), B (trying to physically approach her) leads to C (sour comments that are experienced as hurtful). The likelihood of him doing so will decrease because A has been associated with a punisher following his approaching her in the past.

However, stimuli that exert antecedent control (A) are not restricted to events that occur solely outside the individual. Marie's experience demonstrates this:

Marie attends her company's monthly staff meeting. At these meetings, everyone is expected to brief the group about their progress in their respective projects. The fear is mounting inside of her as the meeting commences. These kinds of situations are the worst she knows: having to declare something you've done in front of a group and being held responsible for it. Sometimes this has been an absolute nightmare for her, even though her colleagues hardly comment on her work.

The critical thing here is not only the external situation itself. It is the external situation (the meeting) plus the fear it evokes. We could assume that fear is a response that has been associated with situations such as the meeting through respondent conditioning. This response can be said to have been established by experiences that Marie vividly remembers: when in high school, being paralyzed with fear while standing in front of her classmates and being unable to utter a single word; being made fun of when, as a teenager, she blushed; and being criticized by coworkers at her last job when she burst into tears. However, it is not only the external circumstances that have been aversive during these meetings. Actual aversive experiences, like someone criticizing her, are actually quite rare in her history. But numerous are the occasions when she has had the aversive experience of attending a meeting with an intense sense of anxiety, and this experience functions as a consequence of attending meetings.

Since approaching (B) these kind of situations (meetings = A) has previously been associated with aversive consequences in external as well as internal circumstances (C), the likelihood of approaching behaviors decreases. Marie also has had the experience that avoidance reduces the amount of contact she has with these aversive consequences, which poses a contingency of reinforcement. One could also say that antecedents "tell" the individual what historical relationship exists between behaviors and their consequences in the situations. It is in this way that antecedents influence behavior.

In a scenario such as the one described, it is not very meaningful to draw a sharp distinction between what happens externally and internally when we are trying to understand the behaving subject. Both areas essentially constitute the context within which humans act and react. In Marie's case, the context is the "fearsome meeting" (or the meeting she has experienced as fearsome). This example also illustrates the fact that respondent and operant learning are very often intertwined.

Generalization

Learning theory stresses the crucial role of the individual's historical experience in learning and the establishment of stimulus control. However, this does not imply that the individual will have to experience every unique situation and the consequences of each behavior in order to develop an adaptive behavioral repertoire. If this were true, then learning would be a hopelessly slow process. The reader is reminded, from the chapter on respondent conditioning, of the process of stimulus generalization. The same principle is at work in operant conditioning. The likelihood of emitting a behavior that has been reinforced under given circumstances increases also in situations similar to the original one (see fig. 6.1).

Figure 6.1 Generalization

In the presence of A (plus **A**, A, and @), B leads to C

When we as kids learn how to interact with a parent, the behavioral repertoire learned would have a circumscribed value if it were not for its ability to generalize to other interpersonal relationships. Learning how to ask for help, for example, generalizes to other people who are in one way or another similar enough to the parent. Generalization makes experience more effective, but it does so at a cost.

Discrimination Learning

"I'm not your mother!" is possibly one of the most common comments in relational disputes. This dilemma is merely an example of the cost of stimulus generalization. The opposite of generalization lies in discriminatory learning (see fig. 6.2).

Figure 6.2 Discrimination Learning

In the presence of A (but not @, **A**, or A), B leads to C

Most behaviors are only followed by reinforcement under certain circumstances. The critical thing for the process of learning is if I can discriminate, or separate out, these circumstances. If I do not perceive the difference between different antecedents, the behavior may well be emitted in the presence of all of them, even the ones where no reinforcement is available. This is certainly the case in social situations where our ability for discriminatory learning is vital. The concept of tactfulness, for example, relies on discriminatory learning. Attending a funeral calls for a certain subdued and dignified behavioral repertoire, even though the people who attend appear to be dressed for a party. If our behavior is under the control of a stimulus class that is too broad, we run the risk of behaving in socially inappropriate ways.

The concept of discriminatory learning points in the direction of another aspect that is of central concern for us. We are not consciously aware of all the stimuli that influence our behavior during our waking hours, and we should be thankful for that. If adaptive behavior required conscious control, we would have little time to consider anything else. It would be essentially nonadaptive! But this also means that I will behave in ways that I might not like, that might not be beneficial to me or that I do not understand, as when I obey a sudden command even though I don't want to and am under no obligation to do so. This makes the issue of discrimination of the contingencies that govern my behavior essentially a question of self-knowledge.

Under Stimulus Control

Control is a word that we, as humans, have a hard time with. It does not sound very tempting to identify ourselves as "organisms under stimulus control." The expression is associated with mindless automatons moving around like bouncing balls in the environment. We tend to associate the word "control" with something that inherently delimits us. This is one reason why it is easier to talk about being "influenced" by stimuli than being "controlled" by them.

Let us explain. Let's say you are walking and need to cross the street. When you are waiting at a red light at the intersection, the red light serves as a stimulus that influences the likelihood of you emitting different behaviors. It does so by signaling access to moving vehicles that potentially could hit you or run you over. You are not forced to stand there and wait in some absolute way, but the likelihood of you doing so is affected. Now, you could look around and find that there are no cars in sight and cross the road in spite of the red light. Your behavior is now influenced by another stimulus. What shows up in your visual field is a stimulus and this does not, to you, signal that cars may drive by and run you over. So you start crossing the street when you hear a woman and a child speaking. The child says, "Is it okay to go now?" "No," says the woman. "You must wait until it is green." You halt, because you know the importance of behaving in an exemplary manner in front of the younger generation. As time passes without either a green light or cars driving by, an increasing sense of restlessness starts to grow inside of you. Here we can identify yet another stimulus that influences you and will affect the likelihood of the behavior emitted.

The list of stimuli can, in a simple situation like this one, be long. We are under the control of a multitude of stimuli, but none of them forces us to behave in a certain manner. They influence us. We could experience waiting for the light to change as our being forced to stand there or that we choose to do it. But neither the statement "I must stand here" nor the statement "I stand here by free will" are adequate explanations as to why we behave as we do. This example demonstrates how different stimuli may compete in their potential influence and how they may be moderated when placed in relation to each other: red light in relation to a visual observation of the surrounding environment; in relation to auditory stimuli; in relation to morals; in relation to the physical experience of our internal processes in that very situation. The point of convergence in this complex situation is by necessity us, and the more we are in contact with these influencing stimuli, the greater the possibility of behaving in a way that will provide durable access to crucial valuables like good health or good relationships with our social surroundings—or stated differently, to make good choices in life.

Remote Control: Modeling

A special instance of operant behavior that has vast implications for the process of learning in life is that early on we learn to copy the behavior of others. There are indications that this is supported by inherited behavioral programs. We are biologically prepared to imitate our primary caregivers in life. In this way, "imitating" is reinforced as a general behavior. This early form of imitative behavior will evolve through life in the form of learning known as *modeling* (Bandura, 1977). As in the case of generalization, this is a way for us to avoid the inherently slow process of learning everything on every occasion by direct experience. Instead we learn by observing a person who models the behavior. This process of observing others will, in a vast range of situations, spare us the time and effort that individual exploration and experimentation requires. Instead, we just observe what the model does in order to contact reinforcing circumstances. From early on, we can see children, for example, "doing things like Dad." This way of learning will be present all through our lives. A great deal of our social behavioral repertoire is learned by modeling. We learn how to be social by observing and interacting with others. In the process of therapy, we find a relevant instance of modeling, where we can assume that one aspect of the learning process lies in the client's imitating the therapist in approaching different problems that are presented in therapy.

By modeling, we access a shortcut that increases the likelihood of performing certain behaviors, and in turn contact reinforcement that follows these behaviors. But modeling also establishes a special kind of reinforcer: behaving in accordance with a socially important model can be reinforcing in and of itself. For instance, how else could we understand the learning process behind the phenomenon of rock stars learning to behave like rock stars long before they are rock stars?

When developing self-harming behaviors, it is probable that modeling has a profound influence. Let's look at this in Jenny's situation:

> When Jenny was referred to the ward, she didn't have any known history of deliberate self-harm and more specifically had never deliberately cut herself. At this same time, however, one of the more experienced "self-harmers" in the clinic was receiving care on Jenny's ward. With her scarred forearms, she made a distinctive impression on the younger patients.

In this sequence, we could assume the presence of two simultaneous, but essentially different, contingencies of reinforcement. On the one hand, performing a behavior that bears similarity to that of socially important models is reinforcing in itself. On the other hand, by performing these behaviors, Jenny will contact the kind of reinforcers mentioned in an earlier chapter, such as attention from other people.

Through the process of modeling, we acquire greater autonomy in the surrounding environment as well as the ability to execute culturally transmitted behavioral practices. We no longer need to establish stimulus control of our entire behavioral repertoire in our own primary experience. It can be done by "remote control." But as always, when speaking of learning processes, this is a double-edged sword that also creates the possibility of establishing behaviors that are less benign. The possibility for autonomy in relation to the surrounding environment takes a huge leap forward through the verbal ability of the human subject. We will consider this in more detail in the next chapter, but a similarity with modeling should be pointed out in that it dramatically increases the ability of the organism to act under the influence of factors other than those that have been directly experienced.

RULE-GOVERNED BEHAVIOR

What has been described earlier in this and preceding chapters are processes of learning that are based on the actual historical experience of an individual. Through these processes, instances of stimulus control are established. We can understand our behavior as governed by a multitude of stimuli. When we approach the crosswalk, we stop and look for cars. But how did we learn that this was a proper behavior? Have we acquired the experience of walking straight out in the street, followed by the aversive event of nearly being run over? Has this preceded an actual experience of us later learning that our nearly being run over could have been neatly avoided by stopping and looking for cars? The probable answer is no. It is unlikely that I have had the experience of trying out different behaviors and discovering the appropriateness of certain functional behaviors.

We simply do not learn the kind of behavioral repertoires adequate for crossing the street through direct experience. It would mean certain death if we let small children learn to interact with the dangers of heavy traffic in order to develop a valid and experience-based knowledge of the proper way to cross a road. Instead we tell them how to do it and model an appropriate behavior in these situations. And here is an important component we have yet to discuss: we give rules such as "Stop and look both ways before crossing the street." This way of influencing, which is called *rule-governed behavior*, will have dramatic effects on what we can learn and how behavior can be governed.

But let's continue a little further with our example and illustrate how modeling and the establishment of rule-governed behavior co-occur. An event in childhood that is likely common in many people's experience is having had a police officer visit their elementary school to teach them how to cross a road at an intersection. First, the officer showed the correct behavior and all the children, waiting in line, observed this impressive figure first carefully look in both directions and then cross the road. And all the children, one at a time, were to approach the road, stop, and repeat this or a similar phrase: "Look to the left, to the right, and then again to the left!" Thereafter they were to cross the road. At the other side, the policeman waited and complimented the correct behavior. Then they were to wait in line again and repeat the procedure going back. And how do I behave when I cross a street today as an adult? I look to the left, to the right, and then again to the left in a predictable manner. Am I in a position to argue that this behavior has been beneficial for me or delivered me from harm? No, I am hardly in a position to do that with any firm evidential basis. Or have I, on some occasion, failed to perform this behavioral sequence in a proper way and nearly been run over as a natural punishing consequence on that behavior? No, I cannot remember any such experiences. I could have had them, but I probably did not. And yet this behavior is so consistent and predictable and occurs with remarkable stability. It would probably require a great deal of concentration to cross a road without performing this behavioral sequence before stepping off the curb. This is the way this kind of learning process works: I learn a rule-governed behavior that allows me never to make contact with the dangers that may be associated with situations such as crossing a road. We teach our children to be cautious and we do this in a safe situation so that they don't have to contact the aversive stimulus of being run over by a car. We do this both by modeling and by establishing rule-governed behavior.

In our next chapter, we will detail how rule-governed learning works. In particular, we will explore the basic behavioral principles that make this way of learning possible for humans.

CHAPTER 7

Learning by Relational Framing: Language and Cognition

Let's stop for a moment and consider the phenomena of thinking. How can we understand this from a learning perspective? Can we describe how it works and how it can be influenced? For an understanding of this, we'll have to take a closer look at human language.

HOW WE RELATE: LANGUAGING AND THINKING

Let's assume that I say to one of my neighbors: "Thursday I'm going away and I'll be gone for three weeks. If you water my plants, I'll take care of yours when you go abroad later this summer." This dialogue can take place without any direct contact with the plants. Maybe we talk as we meet in the supermarket. We use a number of sounds which in and of themselves are arbitrary. If we had grown up and lived in Turkey, the sounds we would use in our conversation would be quite different. It is through these series of sounds that the stimulus functions my house and my plants have for my neighbor will change. The probability increases that this exchange of sounds will change his behavior in the coming weeks. His house and his plants also will gain a controlling function over my behavior, even though this will not be apparent until I take care of his plants while he's abroad a few months later.

These are everyday experiences, known to all. But even in these ordinary events quite advanced processes can be hidden. Only a few more combinations of sounds are required for my behavior with the plants to be specified and made dependent on external variables that may be present a few months later. Maybe my neighbor will say, "If the sun is shining, you'll have to water the plants more often, especially the ones in the kitchen" or "Maybe my son will stay in my house then, in which case he'll take care of the plants."

All of these are what, in the previous chapter, we called "rules," and if we really do water each other's plants, this is an example of rule-governed or verbally controlled behavior (Hayes & Hayes, 1989). The actions of watering each other's plants are not controlled only by direct contingencies of reinforcement. Humans have the capability to give functions to any stimuli in the environment, functions that they don't have in and of themselves. We do this with each other, as in the example above when we ask each other to water plants while we're out of town, but we also do this with ourselves. The experience of "talking to ourselves" is as common to us as is talking to each other; we call it "thinking" when it is done internally. On the inside, we continuously deal with things that are going on, things that "have happened" and what we call "the future." We do all of this with the intent to control and influence events in our lives: "Not that way, that's not going to work ...," "If he says so, then I will ...," "Now remember this ...," and so on. This private behavior may include automatic short comments, prolonged monologues/dialogues, or even whole stories about what has been, what is going on, and what could happen.

Laboratory experiments have shown that verbally competent humans to some extent act differently than other animals and that this is due to the ability described above, what we call "human language" (Hayes, Brownstein, Zettle, Rosenfarb, & Korn, 1986). In the last ten to fifteen years, studies have detailed what humans do when "languaging," whether it is done with others or only with themselves (Hayes, Barnes-Holmes, & Roche, 2001). The central ability seems to be that we learn to relate different stimuli to one another, independent of their actual relations and/or of their formal characteristics. We learn to act or react on one stimulus in terms of another, depending on a relation arbitrarily established between the two. If someone says to us "Ken is not at all like Bill," these words will probably affect our thoughts and feelings toward Ken. If we meet Ken, we may act differently toward him than we would have if those words had not been uttered. This is so regardless of the fact that we have never met Ken before. At the same time, our response is due to our actual experience of Bill as well as the relation of Bill to Ken—that is, one of difference or of being opposites—that was established verbally.

RELATIONAL RESPONSES

We live in a world of actual relations. One thing comes before or after another, one object is bigger or warmer than another. That car is bigger than this one; this flower is the same red as that one; this bookshelf is situated below something else, and so on. In our earlier descriptions of operant and respondent conditioning, these relations have been central. A conditioned stimulus gains its function from its actual relation to an unconditioned stimulus. Operant behavior is controlled by the actual relations between a certain behavior and its consequences. However, through language, we humans learn to "sidetrack" this phenomenon. Or, more accurately, to a certain extent we can free ourselves of the grip of direct stimulus functions that are established by contingencies and "move around" and transform these functions by putting things in relation in a particular way.

We live within the context of these actual relations, together with all other animals on the planet. We all react to relations between stimuli in accordance with the principles of learning we have described. Many animals can also learn to react to an abstraction of such a relation. A rhesus monkey, for example, can learn to always take "the longest stick." If you reinforce this behavior, the monkey will learn to take a stick that it has never been reinforced to take, even though another stick is available and the monkey was reinforced to take that particular stick earlier in the experiment. The monkey acts on an "abstracted relation" between the sticks: it reacts to the relation between the sticks, which is that one stick is longer than the other. The monkey acts, so to speak, on "longer as such."

We are describing a *relational response*, that is, a response made to the relation. Note that this is an actual relation: one stick is longer than the other. Early on, however, humans learn something more: to react to relations that are not actual. We learn to react to relations that are established arbitrarily, not by actual relations between stimuli or their formal characteristics but by the whim of social context. We learn that, independent of the stimuli themselves, something else in the situation controls the relation between stimuli. The fact that the relations are independent of the stimuli implies that the social context can create these relations arbitrarily. Anything can be related to anything!

Let's say that @ is twice as much as #. We have established a relation between these stimuli that is independent of any actual relation between the two. Let's assume that # is ten thousand dollars. Notice that @ now acquires a new function—a function that would probably affect how you would act if you were asked to choose between @ and #. But what if # is a hard punch in the face? Are you still as attracted to @? We learn to react to one stimulus in terms of another, according to the arbitrarily established relation between the two.

Let's take another example: the written word "car." The fact that, as you look at the white page in front of you, you as a reader "understand" what these curving black lines—the letters c-a-r—mean is due to the fact that you relate these lines to an actual car in your history. Note that this relation of coordination—that is, one stands for the other—is arbitrary, established by a social context (see fig. 7.1). The relation is not established by any similarity or naturally given relation between the car and these letters (c-a-r). The relation is by social whim and does not exist outside of a specific context of people speaking (and/or reading) English.

Figure 7.1 Coordination

CAR

You easily neglect the fact that there is no naturally given relation between a real car and the letters c-a-r, or the sound "car" because your history naturally includes many instances of an actual relation between the two. The word "car" has been present many times when an actual car has also been present, as when you have seen an actual car and you or somebody else has used the word, or you have seen the letters at the same time as seeing the car. But note how flexible the system is and how human language is principally independent of such actual relations.

Let's do an experiment. We're going to give you a new word for car: *grado*. Imagine a grado and imagine yourself doing different things with it. Take some time!

What came to mind? Most of you probably visualized a picture of an actual car and the things you can do with it. Very few (if any) readers have in their history a relation between the word "grado" and a real car. The context above established a relation of coordination between the word "car" and the word "grado" (see fig. 7.2). Because the word "car" already was in a relation to a real car, grado acquired part of the functions of that real car—such as, for example, an image of a car. Anyone reading this book will now be able to discuss the advantages and the disadvantages of owning a grado. Different grados can be compared, and it is now meaningful to talk about a grado crash and a grado parking lot.

Figure 7.2 Coordination: New Word

As we saw in the examples above, we learn to put things in relation. By doing this, we're able to give anything in the phenomenological field a stimulus function that it does not have in and of itself, and that it might never have had before. In addition to doing this with objects such as cars, we're able to do this in relation to ourselves as well as in relation to others. We humans learn to do this successively; we learn it over a period of time during our early years (Lipkens, Hayes, & Hayes, 1993). We learn to act on and react to stimuli according to the relations thus established. Once again, we have described a relational response. However, these responses differ from what we described with the rhesus monkey. Humans can also respond in another way—with responses that can be applied arbitrarily, that is, they are independent of the actual relations between stimuli. Anything can be put in relation to anything, and through this process, the functions of the stimuli involved also are transformed. This way of relating is technically called *arbitrary applicable relational responding* (AARR), and it is the basic process of human language and thinking (cognition).

RELATIONAL FRAMING

Another, less technical, way of describing the phenomena we have just been discussing is to say that we *frame relationally*. Just as a picture can be put into many different frames, we put different stimuli into different relational frames. One basic "frame" is coordination (car = grado), another is opposition (car is not vrut), and a third is comparison (bigger than, smaller than, and so on). Other important frames are temporal (before/after), causal (If …, then …), and relations that establish perspective (here/there).

An important characteristic of these responses is that the great majority of them need not be directly trained. They can be derived. An established relation is *mutually entailed*, that is, one relation includes the other. If A is the same as B, we derive that B is the same as A (or, A is the same as B entails that B is the same as A). If A is bigger than B, we derive that B is smaller than A. If Peter is older than James and James is older than David, we derive that David is younger than James who is younger than Peter. But we may also derive that Peter is older than David and that David is younger than Peter. For each relation that is directly trained or learned by respondent and operant conditioning, many others are derived. Because the relation into which a stimulus is put changes the function of that stimulus, great changes can take place in the stimulus field of a particular individual through only one new relational framing. This can happen without any "real" change in what this individual is facing, as when the words "this is contaminated" change the way a person acts in relation to some food. Here you see an example of how the flexibility of human language and human thought is built up through these basic processes.

The Usefulness of Derived Relational Responding

If an organism that is not verbally competent (for example, a pigeon, a chimpanzee, or a small child) is offered a choice between an immediate reward and a reward that is delayed, the former will be chosen (Rachlin & Green, 1972). Given that we humans who are verbally competent have the ability to frame relationally, we can choose differently. This doesn't mean, of course, that we always do! Imagine, for example, that there is a piece of our favorite chocolate cake in front of us, perhaps one made with dark chocolate, almonds, and some whipped cream. We can have this piece of cake as an immediate reward. The fact that this direct contingency can control our behavior is clear to most of us: we take the cake, grab a fork, and dig in. But we don't have to do this. We can still abstain even when we feel the urge to eat the cake and even as we sense ourselves salivating. How do we do that? We can put the chocolate cake in relation to a picture appearing to our mind's eye: a picture of us in a swimsuit next summer on the beach. We can "see" our bellies, the size of our thighs, and maybe even other people around us. We can "see" all of this despite the fact that it's the middle of November, it's snowing outside, and everyone around us is fully—and warmly—dressed. As we "see" this, we put the chocolate cake in front of us into a relation of coordination with this imaginary future. This "future" is constructed through temporal (now/later) and causal (if … then) relational framing. "If I eat the cake, then I will look like this," so to speak. As this is taking place, the stimulus function of the piece of chocolate cake is transformed—and possibly also our behavior in the present moment, that is, we may decide not to eat the cake regardless of how tempting it is (see fig. 7.3).

Figure 7.3 Transformation of Stimulus Function: Chocolate Cake

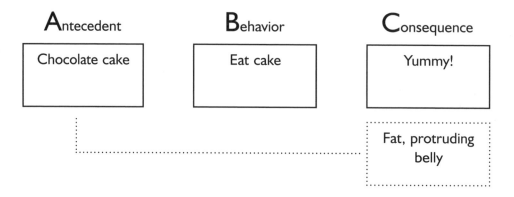

Our encounter with the chocolate cake implies that we human beings have the ability to abstain from immediate gratification. We can handle events "in advance," events that we do not have direct contact with. We usually call this basic ability "problem solving" and/or "planning." We can contact desired consequences that are far off in time or space (looking good in a bathing suit next summer), far off from the present context (a November day among fully, warmly clothed people), and these verbally constructed consequences can control our behavior in the present moment (we can abstain from eating the cake regardless of the fact that it is immediately rewarding). Using another example, we can submit to aversive experiences (study for an exam) and abstain from gratification that is at hand ("let's eat, drink, and be merry") for consequences that are far away (a degree, a desired profession). We verbally construct desired consequences and these then acquire a function of controlling our behavior.

(As a brief aside, the ability to frame relationally, unlike the abilities to learn by association and consequences, is not a given from birth but is learned early through operant conditioning. To give a fuller account of the theories and data that support this is beyond the scope of this book. However, we refer the interested reader to, for example, Healy, Barnes-Holmes, and Smeets [2000] for additional material on this topic.)

Our ability to frame things relationally means that we can "bring in" stimulus functions from events and phenomena that are far away from the present context. An organism that is not capable of this kind of relational responding can only act under the control of actual contingencies. Such an organism must, for example, have had actual contact with certain consequences in its history in order for these consequences to have a controlling function of the organism's behavior. Certain actions have led to certain consequences, as we have described in chapter 5 on operant conditioning. Stimuli have been associated with other stimuli, as in respondent conditioning in the example of Pavlov's dogs.

As humans, we have the added ability to act or react on arbitrarily established relations between stimuli. As a result, contingencies, which include private events such as thoughts and feelings, obtain functions that they don't have in and of themselves. These functions are "brought in" from events (stimuli) that are not present and which can also lack actual relations (in the individual's history) to what happens now, that is, to the present context. Functions can even be brought in from events that have never occurred but which "exist" in the "future," such as appearing slim and trim in a swimsuit next summer. As we have said earlier, the "future" does not exist in any actual way but is something that is created through our ability to frame things in our experience relationally. We can discriminate our experience now and frame this experience temporally: "now" and "then." By this very action, the verbally constructed "future" comes into existence (see fig. 7.4).

Figure 7.4 Temporal Framing

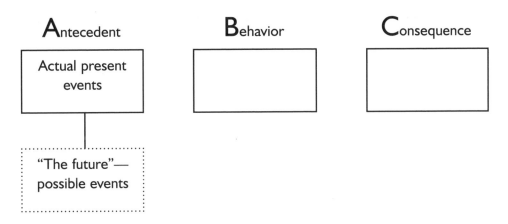

With temporal framing, planning becomes possible. When the actual future is at hand, it is no longer the future; neither is it identical to the constructed future to which we originally reacted. That our ability to do this helps us to relate to the actual contingencies as we meet them is obvious, but it also has complications. For example, we can become "disappointed." If we cannot verbally construct (frame relationally), we have nothing to "compare" to what is actually present and thus the possibility of disappointment is lost. You cannot be disappointed with how you actually look in a swimsuit if you cannot contact how you could have looked otherwise. The latter is only available to an organism that is capable of relational framing.

When a squirrel gathers food for the winter, we can see this as a kind of planning. In a superficial way, it looks a bit like our attempt not to gain weight. But the gathering behavior of squirrels and other hoarding animals is governed by genetics and is activated by actual contingencies such as the length of the day, the change of season, the rise and fall of temperature, and other factors in the natural context of the animal (Vander Wall, 1990). Compare this to the enormous complexity of and the adjustments to which humans are capable in relation to acquiring and keeping food. Just think, for example, how quickly change in our food supply can take place by our use of trade, refrigeration, genetic engineering, or agricultural development and innovation. In a way, of course, humans are also totally governed by contingencies in the present moment. The difference is that these contingencies, which can be both outside and inside the skin, obtain their functions from events that are far from being present, for example: "How it is in Russia," "How it will be in the future," "How we can get things to be the way they ought to be." The possibilities of relational framing are inexhaustible. We humans are fully capable of acting now from the point of how it would be if we moved to China in two years. Or, which can be a bit more complicated but still possible, we can act now in reaction to how we wish it had been at our family gathering last Christmas.

The Dark Side of Relational Framing

The ability to frame relationally has a dark side. One part of that dark side is that the ability to plan the future, gather food, and ensure safety for ourselves and others is the same ability, for example, used in fighting wars—the ability to plan battle strategies, gather armaments, and destroy the enemy. Problem solving can be used for different ends. But in addition to that, there is a more fundamental and pervasive dilemma that is built into relational framing itself.

Let's assume that you and your dog are out walking beside a lake on a cold winter day. For just a couple of days now, the lake has been frozen. The ice is shining, almost blue. You go out on the ice and there is a sense of freedom as you glide along. Suddenly the ice breaks, and you and your dog fall into the ice-cold water. Fear hits you like the slash of a scythe. Both you and your dog fight for your lives. One moment you're under the water, the next moment you surface long enough to catch some air. After a few minutes, both you and your dog are rescued by people passing by. They take you back home to warmth and safety.

If, several weeks later, you and your dog take another walk by the lake, close to where the accident took place, it's reasonable to expect that you'll both feel fearful, which will lessen the probability of your going out on the ice again. This is easy to understand from the perspective of respondent conditioning, both for you and your dog. But for you, there is an additional possibility: you can put "the outward threat" into relation with other things. For example, you can say to yourself, "Temperatures have been hovering around 5 degrees Fahrenheit for several weeks now. This is in contrast to the time when we ended up in the water; the ice then was only two days old." In this way, the ice on the lake, which is only a sign of danger to your dog, obtains other functions for you. This opens up a flexibility of behavior on your part. You can put yourself above your experience of danger by thinking that there is no danger now. In another way, though, this ability of yours gives you a problem your dog does not have. Let's assume that a few hours after you were saved from the water, you and your dog are sitting in front of the fireplace in your house. You have had enough to eat and to drink. What, then, is your dog experiencing? The cold water, fear that he or someone he cares about could end up in the lake again? Nothing we know about dogs would support that. What your dog experiences in this situation is the satisfaction of his present condition: he's safe, warm, and well-fed. It's probably not that simple for you, even though you're experiencing warmth and satisfaction too. A jumble of thoughts run through your mind: "How did that happen ...?" "Why didn't I realize ...?" "What if ...?" Suddenly you notice your daughter's jeans on the floor and remember that she went on a field trip with her class today—they were to visit the very area where you fell into the water ...

Verbal behavior, that is, relational framing, is a blessing for humans, but also, as we said earlier, has a dark side. It gives us an almost inexhaustible interface with pain. There is pain in the history of every organism. For a human, this pain is never only what it is "in and of itself." Let's take an example that is closer to our everyday experience of doing psychotherapy. A person has experienced contact with pain, such as bereavement or a panic attack. Our ability to put events into relations means that these experiences are easily put into temporal relations. They are framed as before/after, now/later. They are also easily put into comparative frames, for example, more/less. The experience of sadness now easily becomes, through temporal relational framing, more than it is in itself. It becomes "my experience now might last forever," creating a heavier burden for the person to carry.

A panic attack can, in and of itself, be a frightening experience, but through relational framing there is contact with the possibility of an even worse attack in the future. The formulation of this possibility is the result of both comparative (more/less) and temporal (now/later) framing. A symptom experienced in this attack—for example, a sensation of pressure in the chest—can become even more frightening with the thought that next time it could be even worse. Now I have more to fear than what I actually experienced. This relational framing can also give frightening qualities to what is only a small part of the experienced attack. A symptom, like feeling a bit unstable, can be related to totally losing control even though that has never happened, not even in the strongest attack that has been experienced (see fig. 7.5).

Figure 7.5 Relational Framing of Bodily Sensations

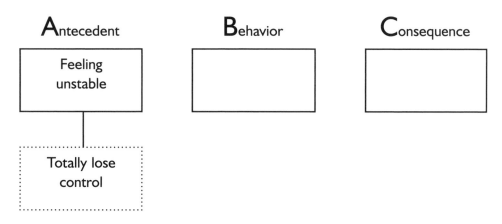

The Dominance of Relational Framing

Our ability to respond relationally can have the effect that the controlling functions of actual contingencies have changed. This has been described in a number of laboratory experiments (Hayes, Zettle, & Rosenfarb, 1989). Such an experiment might look something like this: You give a group of people a simple task such as pushing a button when a lamp is lit in a certain way but not if it is lit in another way. After dividing the group in two, one group is instructed specifically when to push the button ("to get the best result, push the button when the light is such and such"); the other group is given minimal instruction and must learn by trial and error. Both groups are allowed to practice pushing the button for a while. Both groups succeed in earning points by pushing the button in a way that works. After a while, however, the experimenters change the actual contingencies without either group knowing. Now they have to push the button in a slightly different way to continue to earn points. The group that learned the task by following a verbal rule ("push in such and such a way") has greater difficulty in shifting to what is actually working now. The instruction they received at the start now functions as a hindrance. The group that originally received the rule is less sensitive to the new contingencies. It is as if the verbal instruction has a life of its own and still controls the person, even though the actual contingencies it specifies have changed.

Doesn't this look a bit like what we see both in everyday and clinical situations? We continue to do things that do not work because "they should work" or we were told that's the way they worked. We continue to argue for our position because we "are right," even though the consequences of the argument are not what we want. We strive to forget what we cannot forget because "it is normal to forget things like that."

Examples of how our ability to frame things relationally dominates over actual contingencies can also be found in clinical situations. Here's an example from our client Leonard:

> Leonard is in therapy because he is often depressed and anxious. His problems
> started when his wife divorced him three years ago. He did not want the divorce.
> It was especially difficult because his wife took the kids with her and moved to
> another part of the country, so he does not see them as often as he wants to.
> The therapist has the impression that her relation to Leonard at this point is
> good. He has told her many things from his life, even deeply personal things. The
> therapist's position has been both accepting and encouraging. Leonard has often
> said that "it is good to come here to talk to someone who is not involved and
> who understands. It helps me feel like I'm not totally insane." So in therapy the
> actual contingencies for telling his story have been rewarding. Today the therapist
> asks him to tell her how it was the last time he met his kids, and something
> shifts. She asks Leonard about his kids, how they are, what they said, what
> they look like. All of these things are very important to Leonard, yet he avoids
> answering, letting the subject slide away. He seems uneasy and quickly starts to
> talk about something else.

The actual consequences of talking to the therapist about personal things have been reinforcing in Leonard's history so far with the therapist, as he also states himself in the example given above. In today's session, though, they lose their controlling function. Leonard reacts to something other than the actual contingency. How can we understand this? For Leonard, who can frame events relationally, telling the story of his children can put him in contact with both the pain he's experienced in the divorce and with pain about "how it could have been." This pain controls the avoidant behavior described above and alters the controlling function of the actual contingencies. Relational framing allows the same type of contact with pain in the general experience of sorrow after the loss of a close relative or friend. The pain can be greatest in a situation which in itself is good, such as a birthday party or some other kind of celebration. For example, a woman's husband died and years later their youngest child graduates from high school. In this moment of pride and joy, she can't help thinking, "What if Daddy could have been here to see you now?"

Another example of this same phenomenon can be seen in suicidality. When pain is great, a human can relate something of which she has no experience—her own death—to inner abstractions like "peace," "freedom from pain," or "it will be better." She can put this in a temporal relation (now/later) and, on the basis of these constructions, kill herself. Humans are the only species that commits suicide.

Humans no longer live in a world that is solely controlled by respondent and operant conditioning. Our capacity for arbitrary relational responding means that functions acquired through operant and/or respondent conditioning can change through relational framing. Something that up till now was neutral for an individual can, through relational responding, suddenly acquire a reinforcing function, or something reinforcing can acquire aversive functions. For example, a large glass of foamy beer will quickly change stimulus function even for a thirsty beer-loving person if the person's companion says, "The bartender put a small pill into your beer just before he gave it to you." This change of stimulus function will occur even though our beer lover has never been poisoned before and definitely has no experience with poisoned beer. Nevertheless, his thirst no longer has the same motivating quality after he's heard this remark.

The fact that we can put stimuli into arbitrary relations does not imply that we, by some inner power, can do as we like in a given situation. What is meant by "arbitrary" is that the relation is socially established; it is not there in any actual sense. The relation that is established is controlled by other factors in the situation than the actual properties of the stimuli that are related. What controls the beer lover's behavior in the example above is not any direct contact with changes in the beer. The relational responses are contextually controlled, in this case by arbitrary sounds of a speaker ("the bartender put a small pill ...").

Worry and Lack of Self-Confidence

The above throws some new light on Alice and her worrying. What happens when Alice gets so worried that she abstains from things that she was going to do? What happens when she won't go to work or to see friends by herself? In a certain situation, such as if her fiancé suggests that she should go to work tomorrow by herself, because he has to drive up north, momentarily certain associations and images turn up in Alice's mind. It might be a memory, some thoughts, or some bodily or emotional sensations. Some of this can be understood as respondent conditioning and generalization of these learned responses. But Alice's alarm system is not only sensitive to things she has actually encountered in her history. The different associations that were built by respondent conditioning can multiply through her ability of relational framing. Things that were painful can become "even worse." Alice can put her own fiancé in relation to a feature of the news program she just happened to hear in which they speak about an explosion on an oil platform out in the North Sea, even though her fiancé has nothing to do with oil platforms or similar situations. It's enough that they say on the news that "nobody had expected this; the platform was considered very safe." If that wasn't safe, what is safe? Accidents apparently can happen when you expect them the least!

Let's also give some thought to Marie's "lack of self-confidence." She regards this as a quality, something she "has" that is the cause of her difficulties to obtain things she wants. From this perspective, it is easy to understand that she wants to get rid of her lack of self-confidence. But how does she know if this "thing" is there or if it has disappeared? She probably does this by becoming aware of certain feelings, such as uncertainty and dysphoria, and certain thoughts, such as "This won't work …" or "I can't do this," that turn up in certain situations, such as when she needs to present a report at work. As long as these thoughts and feelings turn up, she still has her "lack of self-confidence." But if Marie has such thoughts often and if she often experiences situations that evoke such feelings, how can she stop this from happening again? For an organism that lacks the ability of relational responding (AARR), it is enough not to go to places similar to the places where these things have turned up before. This, of course, can be difficult in and of itself. For Marie, things are even more difficult. She also has to avoid everything that can be put in relation to such thoughts and feelings. These thoughts and feelings are what she has learned to call her "lack of self-confidence." How does she avoid those? It is an almost impossible task.

At the same time, it seems that Marie, in fact, struggles to do this "impossible task." Isolating herself at home and turning off the telephone can be understood as an effort to avoid her difficult thoughts and feelings. On Monday morning, when she remembers her lonely weekend, what feelings and thoughts turn up? What about her "lack of self-confidence"? Is it gone, or is it still there? It is still there. It is, at times, so hard to be a human!

HUMAN LANGUAGE AND PSYCHOPATHOLOGY

Human language has natural functions that contribute, in at least three ways, to the conditions that are usually labeled as psychopathology. The three ways are cognitive fusion, the difficulty of erasing established relations, and experiential avoidance.

Let's start with the concept of *cognitive fusion*. When we experience an event, we often do this without discriminating between stimulus functions of actual contingencies and stimulus functions due to our own relational responding. This is easy to see with evaluative and comparative framing. If we say an event is "bad," we mean that "bad" is a characteristic of the event as such. So if we say "the car is rusty" and "the car is bad," we construe both verbal events in the same way. "Rusty" and "bad" are characteristics of the car. We easily miss that "bad" is an evaluation that necessitates comparing the car to some kind of goal or standard. If all humans suddenly disappeared from the planet, the car would still be rusty. But in what sense would it be bad? For the car not to be rusty, it must change. We could sand the rust off or treat it in some other way. But notice that to change the car from being bad, we don't need to change the car. Instead we need to change the evaluation—that is, whoever evaluates it needs to evaluate it in a different way.

A depressed person who says "My life is meaningless" does not experience that statement as his own construction. It is more like a discovery, as if the lack of meaning is somewhere out there. A person with panic attacks may state that her "anxiety is unbearable." She sees the unbearability as a characteristic of anxiety, not as the result of her own relational responding. From this perspective, measures are needed to change the lack of meaning and the unbearability. And yet, since lack of meaning and unbearability are not "there" as objects, neither are they available for measures of change. However, believing that there is something out there that can change the meaninglessness and unbearability easily leads to fruitless efforts to achieve that change. The lack of change then ultimately leads to resignation.

Let's use this understanding of the problem of cognitive fusion to throw some light on Marie and her problems and her way of conceiving them, or rather their "causes." When she regards herself as having a lack of self-confidence, that sounds like a deficit and that is "bad." It is as if a part of her is bad.

In the examples of problematic comparative relational framing above, what is labeled "bad" is an object experienced by someone: a car, life as a whole, or certain painful sensations, for example. Taking the step from "that is bad" to "I am bad" is then a short one. What is needed, except for comparative framing as in the examples above, is the ability to experience yourself as an object. This ability is the result of relational framing of perspective (here/there), something every human learns early in language training. If I am bad, then I must change. If I try to change my behavior from the starting point of "I am bad," then I will have to check to see if I have succeeded. Am I good or bad now? Since a lot of what I then will evaluate—such as what I think, what I feel, and what has happened to me—is not under voluntary control, there usually will still be many good reasons to evaluate myself as "bad." To this, we easily add things like "I am only pretending" or "I am playing a role" and as I view these as actual characteristics of mine, they will have to change, and on and on it goes.

In this way, we don't discriminate our relational response as our own response but act on the basis of the functions with which that response puts us in contact. The technical term, then, for this is *cognitive fusion* or literalization: to confuse thoughts with what they are about, to act on or react to the language process as if what it says is identical to the things to which it refers. In other words, we take words literally, so to speak.

Second, we have the difficulty of erasing established relations. The networks of relations that are established by relational framing are insensitive to actual contingencies as we saw in the experiment we cited above where two groups were given the task of pushing a button when a lamp was lit in a certain way. In life, we can assume that relations, once established, remain. Relations change through the addition of new relations, but they don't go away. We know this from clinical experience, from experimental research (Wilson & Hayes, 1996), and also from everyday experience. Do you remember the new word for car that was used earlier in this chapter? Even if you don't, its function is not removed. If you were given a choice of words and "grado" was one of them, you would probably remember it when you saw it. Now, as you read this, it might even be hard to think of the word "car" without "grado" also turning up. Try it, to see for yourself. Let's assume that you have a week to get the word "grado" out of your mind. The goal is this: in a week's time, if someone would say "car," "grado" should not even cross your mind. Would you succeed? Most would agree that this would be difficult, though probably not totally impossible. After all, this new relation is not very well established. But even if you, through some powerful conditioning process, could make something else—such as a red rose—turn up instead of "grado" as a response to "car," the relation between the two stimuli would still not disappear. This could easily be demonstrated by responding to the question "Why did you think of a red rose?" or noticing what else comes to mind the next time you see a bouquet of red roses. One reason for this phenomenon is that once a specific network of relations is established, it consists of many derived relations that support the network as a whole. Grado is now not only in a relation with another word (car) but also with exhaust pipe, roads, gas stations, accidents, your work (if you drive to get there), the color red (if your car is red), and many other things. All of this occurs in the moment when you read: "In a few seconds, we'll give you a new word for car." Some of these relations are far-fetched, but they are still accessible to human beings. And the more important it is that you not think "grado," the more you attend to other stimuli in the network. These are the very relations you will have to watch out for!

Another factor that supports these networks is that we live in a linguistic context that continuously reinforces the maintenance of relational networks as such. In order for us to function in this verbally constructed world, we are taught that things should be coherent and "make sense." We talk so that others can understand us. This implies that being coherent or being "right" (which strengthens relational networks) functions as a powerful, generalized reinforcer. These networks can easily dominate over actual contingencies. As a result, dysfunctional verbal constructions continue to have controlling functions for the individual even if the resulting behavior has aversive consequences, as when Leonard isolates himself in spite of the effect this has on what he considers important in life, his relation to his children.

The third way that human language contributes to what is usually labeled psychopathology is *experiential avoidance*, which is an individual's attempt to eliminate or control negative or painful affects and any thoughts, memories, or bodily sensations that are related to them. For a languaging human being (in other words, someone capable of relational framing), it can be difficult to talk about a painful experience from his or her history. Telling someone about an experience can be painful for both the speaker and the listener, despite the fact that the painful circumstances are not being experienced at the moment or may never have been experienced directly. We are also able to construct a desirable future and compare it to an undesirable one. The result is often worry and sadness. Human language consists of extended relational networks, the result of which is that private events have stimulus functions that are "brought in" from events that are far off in our past or far ahead in a constructed future (see fig. 7.6).

Figure 7.6 Experiential Avoidance

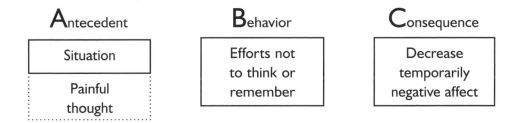

Let's return to Mirza to see what role experiential avoidance plays in his current situation:

> *Mirza is visiting some new friends. They met at a soccer match so they're chatting about the match and about soccer in general. The atmosphere is relaxed and calm. One of the fellows gets up and says he has to go. After he has left, Mirza asks if he was going home. "No," says one of the others, "he's going to pick up his brother at the railway station." Mirza senses a knot in his stomach, he has a flashback of the last time he saw his own brother, and it is as if a pall is cast over everyone and everything. Suddenly everything is just so heavy.*

Mirza contacts his painful history even in a situation where no pain is present through his ability to frame relationally. The points of contact are literally everywhere, wherever he is. For an organism without human language, it would be possible to avoid pain to a certain degree. This could be accomplished by simply not going to places where pain had been present in the past. The functions of language make this very difficult for humans, as is exemplified in Mirza's experience with his new friends. The network established through relational framing makes the instances of contact with pain innumerable and widespread. At the same time, most humans have been successful at controlling the outside environment, largely as a result of language itself. For example, if you need to remove the snow from your driveway, you can call and ask for someone to plow it for you. If you don't like the color of your walls, you can buy a can of paint and change it. The fact that we can control our environment to such a high degree is likely one of the reasons that humans put so much effort into trying to control and avoid painful thoughts and emotions. However, modern research shows that this very effort may be a crucial part of developing and maintaining psychopathology (Hayes, Wilson, Gifford, Follette, & Strosahl, 1996).

Cognitive Fusion and Language: Illusions of Hindrances and Causes

Cognitive fusion is very pervasive among human beings as a result of our use of language. One consequence is that private experiences easily obtain functions as if they were actual hindrances of and/or causes for other behavior. Here are some examples:

- "This morning I felt so bad that I didn't get out of bed."

- "I was so nervous that I didn't go out on that date."

- "I got so mad that I told him to go to hell."

We hear (and use) these kinds of statements quite often. Through relational framing, the experiences of nervousness and anger, for example, obtain functions that go far beyond what these sensations are in themselves. When these functions dominate, that is, when cognitive fusion occurs, the experience seems causal, as we see in the examples above. These functions thus become an explanation of our behavior, albeit an inaccurate one. But let's take a moment and see what's really going on. Each statement first indicates that the person making it is in an aversive emotional state and thus acts accordingly. But look at these statements once again—they actually convey two behavioral events:

- This morning I felt bad *and* I did not get out of bed.

- I was so nervous *and* I did not go out on that date.

- I got so mad *and* I told him to go to hell.

The word "and" used above makes the statements more accurate than the versions given earlier. We all have the tendency to explain one behavior as a cause for another. However, that there is no such necessary causal connection as the "but" version implies can be illustrated through a simple intellectual experiment:

- What if the "feeling bad" was experienced in the context of the bedroom being on fire? Would the "feeling bad" cause staying in bed? No.

- What if the nervousness was experienced in a situation in which not going out on the date would be followed by a heavy fine? Would the nervousness then cause not going? No.

- What if getting mad happened in the presence of the irascible karate master? Would "getting mad" then cause my telling him to go to hell? Most people would probably not even consider taking the risk of saying such a thing in that situation.

To notice feelings like the ones mentioned—feeling bad, nervous, mad—seems very reasonable and understandable, but the behavior to stay in bed, stand a date up, or tell someone to go to hell are not actions that are caused by those feelings and the behavior is not explained in any reasonable way by these internal states. As stated in the previous chapter, the actual behavior emitted is under the influence of a multitude of contextual factors. Internal states are one of them. However, in everyday language we often use them as if they were the exclusive explanation of a given behavior. We call this kind of explanation, where an internal experience is considered a cause of behavior, a *causal illusion*. This can easily become a part of vicious cycles in which clients try to solve problems by eliminating causes of their own behavior, causes that are not causes but only causal illusions. An example of this would be Marie trying to solve her problem of not going to certain social meetings by eliminating her feelings of nervousness.

Relational Framing and Change

That human language has such a central position in what we call psychopathology implies that working for change also should involve working with these relational framing processes. Can we help people to change their ways of framing relationally? Can we affect the negative consequences of relational framing? Can we counteract cognitive fusion, undermining factors that sustain relational networks and thereby facilitate release from the vicious cycle of experiential avoidance? We will address these issues in chapters 12 and 13 in which we deal with treatment principles. After deepening our understanding of the basic behavioral principles of respondent, operant, and relational conditioning, we now proceed to an enhanced and deepened version of an ABC analysis.

CHAPTER 8

Applying Your ABCs

After looking at the three main principles of learning—respondent conditioning, operant conditioning, and relational framing—we return to the foundation of our work: ABC analysis. How do the principles come into play in the various parts of the analysis? In many ways, it will become clear that operant learning (learning by consequences) is the foundation for an analysis. These three steps—analyzing A, B, and C—describe how consequences exert their influence: under specified conditions (A), a person does something (B), and certain consequences occur (C). These consequences increase or decrease the probability that the person in question, in similar circumstances, will behave in a similar fashion. Even if it is possible to untangle the separate principles of learning for purposes of illustration, in real life they are seldom separate but continually intertwine with each other.

We can see this complexity in a child's encounter with a dog. If little John is frightened by a dog, it is easy to understand, with the help of respondent conditioning, his fear of similar dogs. But if John refuses to visit Aunt Patty (where he's never seen a dog, much less been frightened by one) because someone said that her cat is like an old dog, then we need to use the principle of relational framing. This comment about the cat would not have provoked any anxiety if John hadn't been exposed to respondent conditioning in the first place. His declaration "I don't want to go to Aunt Patty's" is a result of his experience with an earlier consequence of expressing his wishes in this way, which affected the action of his parents in response to his wishes.

Let's return now to the clinical setting and to the cases of Mirza and Leonard. Here it will become more apparent how the principles of learning are interwoven.

ANALYZING MIRZA'S EXPERIENCES

Mirza has become accustomed to his new life in Sweden. Many of the practical issues that dominated his life when he arrived from Bosnia have been settled, but now other problems catch up with him.

Mirza says that lately his problems have been getting worse and he doesn't understand why. There were many problems when he lived in the refugee center, but he felt better then in spite of the problems. He was not sure he would be allowed to stay in Sweden and the struggle to achieve that goal (to be granted asylum) took all his time. Now he has been granted permission to stay. He even has his own apartment and has started studying at the university. Think of it! His own apartment after years of uncertainty!

If one of his fellow students says, "OK, let's go home," Mirza immediately feels a knot in his stomach. When he's alone in his apartment in the evening, it seems as if everything he does brings back memories of the war—not just TV programs about war or news from Bosnia. Looking out the window when it is dark makes him feel anxious. He often has the shades pulled down all day. He can't even boil water for tea without being reminded what it looked like in their kitchen in Bosnia. It's crazy! Now when he is free to live a new life, it's as if the old life crowds in around him, closer and closer. He prefers to eat in the school cafeteria instead of cooking for himself at home. In Bosnia, he used to like to help with the cooking. He tries to convince himself that everything is fine now, but he is not convinced. He has noticed that he feels good when he is busy with something that interests him, something that captures his attention for the moment—like when he went to the soccer game the other evening. But his anxiety caught up with him even there. Somebody mentioned his brother and that made Mirza think about his brother, Samir, and the last time he saw him. It's no use dwelling on him. He will never see his brother again. But he can't stop thinking about Samir, no matter how much he tries. And he can't always be on the run, away from his apartment. He should be able to be at home. Nowadays he has noticed that he avoids being at home whenever he has an excuse to be elsewhere.

What do we want to analyze? Where do we start? The above description contains respondent, operant, and relational framing responses. Mirza is most concerned with why his anxiety is getting worse. Readers will remember from earlier chapters that it is often advantageous to start the analysis with behavior (B)—what the person does. So, what are the central behaviors in Mirza's problems? Let's start there.

Looking More Closely at Behavior (B)

Since we know that avoidance plays a central role in maintaining and worsening anxiety, we look for actions that have this function. It is very easy to see that Mirza does several things that are functionally analogous:

- He avoids going home and avoids cooking.

- He pulls the shades down to avoid seeing that it is dark outside.

- He tries to reason with himself.

- He tries not to think about his brother.

What is common among these actions? Mirza is trying to avoid painful feelings, thoughts, and memories. This is a natural human reaction to disturbing private events, but it is also a source of problems.

It is important to look for more examples of actions that have this function of avoidance when the client describes his problems in the initial phases of the analysis since it helps us to locate patterns in his behavior. What may appear to be dissimilar actions at first glance (suppressing thoughts or pulling down a shade) can functionally be very similar. They belong to the same functional class. They are topographically different but functionally alike.

Starting our analysis with B is advantageous because B often has the greatest potential for change. When we change the way we behave, we increase our chances of coming in contact with other consequences and bringing the behavior under the control of other stimuli. However, it is often difficult to start our collaboration with the client by examining B for the simple reason that the client would rather talk about something else, which he sees as more important. Mirza, like many other clients with anxiety, focuses on his own experiences of anxiety: what might cause it and what can be done to remove it (see fig. 8.1). That's what he wants to talk about! This is another potential starting point for collaboration, since it means we can focus on A.

Figure 8.1 ABC Analysis: Mirza's Anxiety

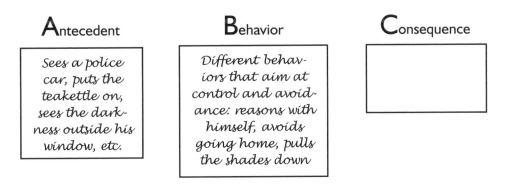

Antecedent	Behavior	Consequence
Sees a police car, puts the teakettle on, sees the darkness outside his window, etc.	Different behaviors that aim at control and avoidance: reasons with himself, avoids going home, pulls the shades down	

Looking More Closely at Antecedents (A)

Under what conditions does Mirza behave as described above? The simplest way to answer this question is to ask him what bothers him, how his anxiety manifests itself, and on what occasions it is present. It quickly becomes apparent that Mirza's problems turn up in a number of situations:

- When he sees the news from Bosnia

- When someone asks if he has any brothers and sisters

- When he hears a loud, unexpected noise

But his anxiety also appears in many other situations that are not so easily under-stood, even when we know his history:

- When he sees a police car

- When he sits down to have tea

- When he sees the darkness from his window

- When he sees a family with the children playing happily together

- When someone talks about a serious illness

- When he sees apple trees in bloom

This is a long list but by no means exhaustive. There are seemingly endless numbers of situations that can lead his thoughts to other thoughts that are more or less painful.

How should we analyze this collection of As? The list seems never-ending. It's important to realize that even when we examine A more closely, it is not necessary to minutely examine each condition in order to construct a clinically useful analysis of the problem. It is important, however, to identify the most central conditions, which turn up time after time. The external conditions that Mirza describes vary considerably. What keeps coming into the forefront is his focus on anxiety and the thoughts and memories associated with it. We could claim that the core of the problem is not the situations that generate anxiety. The analysis will show that an anxious reaction can be learned in response to any number of stimuli. The core of the problem is what Mirza does when anxiety is provoked. When Mirza experiences feelings, thoughts, and memories, he tries to avoid and/or control (B) this experience (A).

Respondent Aspects of Antecedents (A)

Mirza has been in a number of situations that have evoked strong fear and anxiety. His life has been threatened, he has been assaulted, and he lost his home and all his worldly possessions. All of these situations have elements of respondent conditioning. Sounds, smells, and sights have become conditioned stimuli (CS) that generate condi-tioned responses (CR) in the form of fear and strong negative emotions. A number of other stimuli are sufficiently similar to these CS to generate similar reactions through the process of generalization. A good example of this is the sight of police cars or uni-forms. Mirza no longer believes that he has anything to fear from the police. But the sudden appearance of a police officer in uniform outside his window is sufficient to elicit a fearful reaction through the principles of respondent conditioning. Other external stimuli can also lead to an automatic reaction beyond his volitional control. Another clear-cut example is darkness, which Mirza associates with painful memories (see fig. 8.2).

Figure 8.2 Antecedent: Respondent Function (CS–CR Relationship)

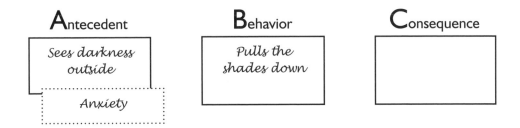

Relational Framing and Antecedents (A)

Some of the external signals that prompt Mirza to remember painful events are more difficult to explain by respondent processes. That the sight of a happy family in his new country of residence causes someone with Mirza's background to feel distress is not hard to understand from a commonsense perspective, but it is hard to explain how his reactions could be learned through respondent conditioning.

It's more likely that Mirza learned his reactions through another process by which even the most far-fetched reactions can be established with the speed of lightning. For a verbally competent person, relations among things are established not only because of some historical connection or mutual similarity. When learning language skills, the social context also establishes other kinds of relationships—for example, opposites. Happiness is in a relationship (relational frame) with unhappiness, black to white, life to death. New relations are continually established. Networks of relations emerge in a matter of seconds.

Consider the situation when a passing comment about someone's brother awakens traumatic memories for Mirza. When the trauma occurred, Mirza didn't know a word of Swedish. The sound of the Swedish word *bror* (brother) had no meaning for him. In all probability, he had never even heard the sound/word. But when the sound of *bror* entered into a relation with *brat* (brother, in Mirza's native language), which is in a relation with his brother, Samir, then the sound of *bror* is put into relationship with Mirza's long history of pain and suffering.

Mirza attends a multimedia course and has been assigned a group project about documenting a current social problem. His group is considering the topic of geriatric care. One of his classmates produces a picture from the newspaper showing an elderly person lying in bed. Mirza immediately feels that he doesn't want to work on such a project and quickly suggests something else.

Mirza explains to his therapist that he felt anxious in that classroom situation. The therapist takes note of the behavior when Mirza quickly suggested another topic to his classmates (B) as another example of avoidance. Yet geriatric care has nothing to do with Mirza's traumatic background. He has no memories of the war with content similar to the proposed class project. The only memory he has that might resemble this topic is of his grandparents who died before the war broke out, and he has only pleasant memories of his grandparents. For a verbally competent person, though, old age, illness, and insufficient care can easily connect with death. And for Mirza, death is associated with his memories of the war.

The same kind of connections can be made between other contexts and stimuli. If Mirza's anxiety only arose through respondent conditioning, then he would be able to get away from it in other contexts. But where can you go to escape the pain that comes to you through the vehicle of your own languaging?

When you analyze the behavior of nonhuman animals, years of research document the fact that A is always either something that the organism has actually been in contact with or the circumstances are similar enough to acquire their function through generalization. This is not the case for a languaging human being. The ability to frame relationally means that stimuli can acquire the function of A through a verbal connection. We each have our own personal history of relational framing. We can observe this when different individuals have different interpretations of the same event; each circumstance has a particular meaning for any given person. This is of great relevance when we attempt to analyze the specific circumstances (A) that precede what Mirza does (B). See figure 8.3.

Figure 8.3 Antecedent: Verbal Function (Established by Relational Framing)

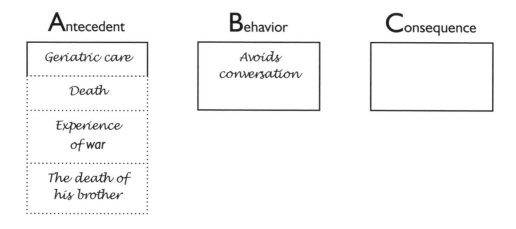

Looking More Closely at Consequences (C)

Which consequences control Mirza's behavior? How do the various principles of learning illuminate this process? When we attempt to survey the consequences that occur when Mirza avoids returning to his apartment or when he pulls the shades down when it is dark outside, we start by simply asking, "Then what happens?" What is the next event? What happens when he changes the subject in a conversation when he feels anxious? What follows his attempts to push aside any thoughts of his brother? Mirza's immediate reply is "it [my anxiety] just gets worse." How can we understand this chain of events? The consequences of Mirza's actions are aversive for him and he realizes it, yet he still persists with the same behavior. Mirza finds this bewildering.

I am not helping things by what I do. I get that. Things are only getting worse. It's as if I want to torment myself. It's crazy. Sometimes I think I don't deserve anything better.

Mirza's way of thinking is hardly unique. In fact, some psychological theories claim that humans actually want to hurt themselves. We prefer a different explanation and return now to what we find to be a more fruitful basis: the discussion of short- and long-term consequences.

When we say that Mirza's actions only make things worse in the long run, we are talking about long-term consequences. What are the short-term consequences of his behavior? When it is dark outside and Mirza feels his anxiety rising, he pulls down the shade. What happens to his anxiety? It subsides momentarily, and for a while he feels calmer. When a topic of conversation makes him feel anxious and Mirza successfully changes the subject, what happens to his anxiety? It decreases temporarily. When thoughts of his brother come up and Mirza can divert his attention by going out jogging, what happens to his anxiety? It becomes less intense for the moment. Jogging doesn't always work, but often it works well enough to give it a controlling function. Mirza's actions are governed by their consequences—or negative reinforcement, to be more precise. His behavior has reduced negative affect on a number of occasions, and as negative affect is distressing, its momentary decrease strengthens the behavior: the pushing away of thoughts, changing topics in a conversation, or pulling down the shade when it is dark outside.

Figure 8.4 Negative Reinforcement of Avoidance: Mirza

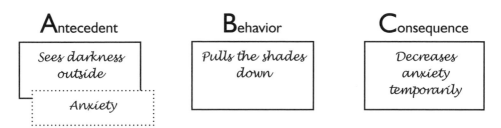

One explanation why Mirza's behaviors persist, despite the fact that they lead to aversive consequences, is the well-documented fact that was discussed earlier: short-term consequences have the upper hand. However, this is not an entirely satisfactory explanation, especially when looking at events over the course of time. Then the aversive consequences become more obvious. Many actions that once relieved anxiety lose their effect. The aversive consequences become more tangible. These consequences of increased anxiety are no longer long-term but are becoming short-term. It doesn't help to change the topic of conversation. Anxiety doesn't disappear when he pulls down the shade. Thoughts of his brother turn up even when he is out jogging. Yet these consequences do not terminate Mirza's avoidance. His actions remain firmly entrenched in his repertoire. In order to understand this process, we need to reconsider our abilities for relational framing.

Relational Framing and Consequences (C)

Earlier we described the principle from a lab experiment where two groups were given the task of pushing a button when a lamp was lit in a certain way. Their responses to a change in contingencies differed based on whether they had received instructions on pushing the button or no instructions. This illustrates how verbal constructions change the functions of consequences. Our ability to construct verbal rules and to follow these rules lessens the impact of the actual consequences. Remember the example of the chocolate cake and plans for the summer swimsuit season! That also illustrates how verbally established consequences block out the effect of direct contingencies.

This type of learning is very relevant in our analysis of Mirza's actions. He has a history of experiencing the direct consequences of avoidance as a means of avoiding anxiety (negative reinforcement) while at the same time acquiring a history of the consequences of rule-governed or verbal behavior. His actions in relation to anxiety are steered not only by the actual consequences he experiences but also by the rules that were established in the course of his social history. As previously described, antecedents (A) can be established through verbal learning, but this also applies to consequences (C). Our perception may be that avoiding anxiety is "what you have to do" or that it is "the only way to survive." This means that when Mirza exerts himself not to think about his brother or changes topics in a conversation, the consequences are not only a decrease in anxiety (negative reinforcement) but also a feeling of doing the "right" thing (positive reinforcement). He has acted in accordance with a verbally established rule: "I did what I had to do to survive" and/or "My anxiety didn't get any worse because of what I did" (see fig. 8.5).

These rules can supersede the actual consequences; in other words, rules replace them with other functions through relational framing. The actual consequences in a given situation are perhaps unchanged or may even result in increased anxiety. But the verbal construction dominates through "this is better than what would have happened if I hadn't acted at all." This consequence is a positive reinforcer, since "doing the right thing" is a powerful generalized reinforcer for humans.

Figure 8.5 Verbally Established Reinforcing Consequences: Mirza

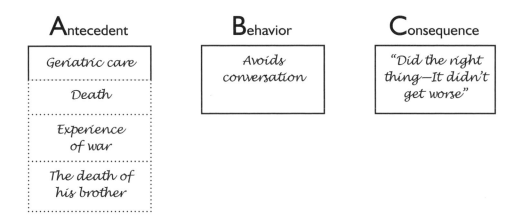

Antecedent	**B**ehavior	**C**onsequence
Geriatric care	Avoids conversation	"Did the right thing—It didn't get worse"
Death		
Experience of war		
The death of his brother		

Observing Establishing Operations

One day Mirza notices that being in the apartment leads to more anxiety than usual. Nothing distressing has occurred, at least not anything that has to do with his painful memories. The observant reader will remember that other factors may exert an influence and modulate the behavior in focus for our analysis. These factors can often be everyday events or variations in basic functions. A poor night's sleep or worrying about a coming exam can be enough to cause changes. It is as if anxiety is more easily aroused, despite the fact that it has nothing to do with Mirza's specific problems. In the same way that going without food changes the function of a hamburger for a given individual, so can lack of sleep facilitate certain emotional reactions.

ANALYZING LEONARD'S EXPERIENCES

Leonard's depressive state dominates his life more and more. He gives up activities that used to be rewarding to him, his sleeping problems increase, and he spends an increasing amount of time alone and ruminating.

> Leonard wakes up early. The first thing that pops into his head is how his children looked when they waved good-bye to him from the window of the train. Last night he drove them to the station and now they are back with their mother. He feels a pain in his stomach. A whole month until the next time he'll see them. How could things have turned out like this? He returns in his memory to one of the many arguments he had with Tina—when he came home late, when he didn't manage to do what he'd promised. If only he'd realized in time

that his work was his consuming interest and that she was getting tired of it all. How can one be tired of it all? Hadn't they promised one another "for better, for worse"? He remembered all too well that day when she came into the kitchen and said she was moving out and taking the children with her. That she wanted a divorce. How life became empty. Pointless—as it still is pointless. What could he have done? He can imagine himself having acted differently: Coming home in the evening and doing his share of the chores. Helping the children with their homework. Sitting in Alexander's room. If only he had it to do over again! He could have done it! If only ... After a while, Leonard looks at the clock. He's been awake for over an hour. The pain in his stomach is worse. He feels nauseated. How can he go to work? What's the point? It won't change anything. It will never bring back what he's lost. And all this brooding. What's the use of it? Yet he can't help himself. He's been awake half the night again ...

Rumination is something many of us have experienced at one point or another. For Leonard, it is part of what we usually call depression and it consumes most of his days. How do we perform an ABC analysis if we want to understand his behavior?

Looking More Closely at Behavior (B)

Rumination is a type of behavior that is only evident to the person performing it. It normally occurs inside the individual, although this is not always the case. One can ruminate out loud, such as when conversing with another person. Sometimes rumination is not noticeable for others, but the person doing it can behave in other ways that will indicate that he is ruminating. If Leonard paces back and forth across the floor and wrings his hands or sits silently without answering direct questions, these actions may indicate that he is engaged in ruminating. However, in this case described here, only Leonard really knows what's going on.

Examining the content of Leonard's rumination, we see that it is remarkably similar to what we call problem solving. He recalls images of things that have happened and tries to understand the reasons for what happened. He imagines alternative scenes, alternative actions in the past, and he tries to imagine what might happen in the future. He visualizes himself at work and staying at home. Leonard is able to imagine things the way they would have looked if he had been there in reality. He can see his son sitting at his desk, leaning over a book. It's very much like what he saw when he was actually sitting on his son's bed, watching him do his homework.

The ability to perform this operation is an extraordinary asset for us as humans. We can perform an operation internally in relation to external circumstances without actually being in the physical situation. We call this "planning ahead" or "thinking things through." For Leonard, however, this is problematic because it doesn't lead to what he wants and it only increases his feelings of hopelessness. Why does he do it? Under which circumstances does he do it and what does it lead to?

Looking More Closely at Antecedents (A)

The way Leonard spontaneously experiences rumination is not something he chooses to do. It is not an activity that is preceded by plans about how to do it. When his therapist asks him about it, he reports that it is something that occurs in a number of situations but is especially common when he wakes up early and can't go back to sleep. It can start when he remembers something in particular—in this case, the image of his children's departure on the previous evening. He wakes up and feels an immediate sinking feeling in his stomach, and he begins to ruminate: "How did things turn out like this? Why? What if …? There are times, however, when he wakes up without any particular thoughts. Once he is awake, then he starts thinking the thoughts he has thought a thousand times in bed, and he finds he can't go back to sleep. The memories come back, as does the sinking feeling that things will always be like this.

In addition to lying awake in bed, Leonard describes a number of situations that are likely to be associated with this way of thinking, for example: if someone criticizes him for something or if he himself thinks he has failed at some task; when the weekend is coming up and others start to talk about what they plan to do together with their families; when he reads in the paper how children are mistreated (see fig. 8.6). His therapist tries to find many examples to establish a reoccurring pattern. The common factor for Leonard's rumination seems to be situations that trigger painful memories or painful situations themselves. When these things occur, there is a strong possibility that he deliberately keeps these pictures and thoughts in his mind and tries to change them in various ways. In other words, he ruminates!

Figure 8.6 ABC Analysis: Leonard

Antecedent	**B**ehavior	**C**onsequence
Lies awake, receives criticism, experiences failure, thinks of upcoming weekend, etc.	*Ruminates*	

Looking More Closely at Consequences (C)

Leonard is painfully aware of the fact that his brooding won't solve his problems. Even though he knows that, it's still hard to stop doing it.

"What's done is done. However much I wish that things hadn't happened or words hadn't been said, it's too late to change things now. Digging around in the past won't bring my family back. But it's as if my brain can't process that."

This is a fairly typical statement that indicates that Leonard recognizes the futility of depressive rumination. Yet rumination is a behavior in which most of us are inclined to engage in moments of sorrow or grief. What are the maintaining consequences that steer this kind of behavior? One way to approach the answer to this question is to ask another question, as we observe Leonard's therapist doing in the following exchange:

Therapist: When you are lying awake in the middle of the night with these kinds of thoughts and memories going through your mind, what do you think would happen if you simply let them be? Let them turn up, bringing with them pain and agony, and do nothing about them.

Leonard: What do you mean? Let them be is exactly what I can't do. How can you do that? It seems impossible.

Therapist: Well, there are two parts of what's happening. First, things turn up. This is not something you choose to happen. It's almost like a reflex. You remember what happened yesterday: you noticed that you woke up earlier than usual, you felt a pain in your stomach. Isn't there more to this sequence when you deliberately let your thoughts wander? Think about what you should have done? Try to remember some of the hazy details, decide what to say to Tina next time you talk with her?

Leonard: Yes, that's what happens. I have never thought about how it happens, but when you describe it in those words, I can see that's what happens. Some thoughts appear automatically; others I get involved with and try to think them through.

Therapist: What would happen if some of these automatic thoughts turned up and you didn't try to think them through?

Leonard: (*after some time of silence*) That would be like giving up somehow. How can I get on with things if I haven't figured out what to do?

Therapist: Okay, let's describe what happens: Something turns up on the inside, something difficult or distressing, and the next step is that you try to figure out what to do about it. You remember something hard that has to do with Tina and the children. So you try to keep thinking about what happened, what you could do, how you could solve the problem. Is that what you do?

Leonard:	Yes, but it's not only that. I also try and figure out how it could have turned out so badly. I try to understand.
Therapist:	So that's something else you try to do when thoughts pop up, you try to understand what caused the problems with your family. Have I got that right?
Leonard:	That's exactly what happens. The whole time I keep thinking in circles around the question "Why?"

What consequences is this behavior under the control of? Leonard describes what happens when certain recurrent painful thoughts turn up (A). He tries to think things through, over and over again (B). He doesn't achieve what he is striving for: to come to some reasonable conclusion. He has also noticed that, after a while, he feels worse than before he started. But he still keeps going over the questions, again and again. How is this possible? What are the consequences (C) that steer his actions?

In the dialogue with his therapist above, we can see that Leonard's rumination has an indirect function for him. While he is ruminating, he is avoiding something that, to his way of thinking, is worse—the feeling of giving up. If he didn't keep thinking it through, he would get stuck in something that scares him. By going over these questions, time and time again, he lessens the unpleasant feeling of giving up. Once again we have an example of negative reinforcement. Ruminative behavior reduces certain aversive consequences.

Therapist:	So the question "Why?" pops up and you try to find an answer to it. What do you think would happen if you simply noticed the question and tried not to answer?
Leonard:	That would be weird, like giving up. That would make things worse. At least I am trying to do something. It sounds so strange when you say that. If I didn't try to answer all those questions, then it feels as if everything is over.

What we see here is another example of how behavior that is rule-governed or verbal can become a problem. Leonard, like all of us, has a long history of trying to think things through, of examining problems and threats and looking for different courses of action. This behavior has been reinforced, over and over again, for most of his life. We can also assume that Leonard has successfully used this strategy for solving problems in the world outside. This means that the behavior we are trying to analyze is an example of "doing what you do to solve problems." This feels like the right course of action. Thus the verbally constructed consequence functions as positive reinforcement and changes the effects of the actual consequences of his behavior (feeling worse, not solving the problem) and keeps them from controlling his behavior (see fig. 8.7).

Figure 8.7 Dominance of a Verbally Established Reinforcer: Leonard

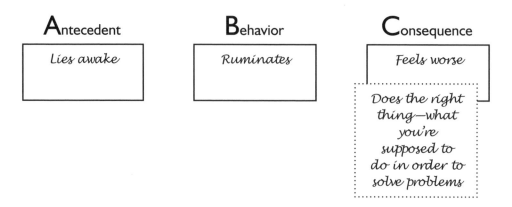

Back to Behavior (B)

Describing inner behavior is often difficult. We have never been able to observe other people's inner behavior in the same way we can often see their external behavior. We can watch people walking every day and can reliably observe how they do it. Based on our common experiences, we can also discuss what we have seen. But how often have we seen what other people do when they think? As a result, we have not learned much about how to talk about this behavior with others or even with ourselves. Thus we can never describe with any degree of detail how other people think or even how we ourselves think when engaging in this kind of private behavior. In order for us to help Leonard express something of what happens internally, it is helpful to discriminate between A and C. The momentary thoughts and memories that turn up prior to his rumination are painful. By walking him through what might happen if he didn't ruminate, it is possible to delineate what he does in fact do. When B is vague, as is often the case with inner behavior, it is often helpful to obtain a description of A and C in order to arrive at a useful description of B.

An inner behavior such as ruminating leads to questions of how it persists. We have seen that it can be reinforced, which increases the probability of it occurring in the future. This in turn influences the total behavioral repertoire. In clinical work, it is common to find that worrying and ruminating compete with more constructive responses for influencing the course of events. Ruminating in and of itself tends to interfere with falling asleep and more functional problem-solving skills. Ruminating for longer periods of time is also a tiresome activity that can lead to fatigue and increased negative emotion.

Observing Establishing Operations

As we saw with Mirza, Leonard's behavior was influenced by establishing operations that had no direct connection to the presenting problem. Nonetheless these conditions influence his actions and indirectly his problem, which we can define as depression. For example, when Leonard has things to do at work that are hanging over his head and which take some time to do, he then becomes frustrated and feels inadequate. When this happens, not only does he wake up early in the morning but he is also more likely to move through the whole rumination sequence, despite the fact that his difficult thoughts are not work related. In the same way, fatigue increases the probability that he will succumb to moodiness and that he will be more devastated by it, which in turn makes him persevere in his search for "solutions."

ABCS IN SUMMARY

In both of these examples, we can see how antecedents are established when an individual goes through something that is painful. The problem is not, however, that the individual has a history but rather that this history establishes stimulus functions which continually remind the person of the pain within that history. In and of itself, this is an adaptive feature. We should learn from experience. It would seem wise for us to remember where painful experiences may be lurking and to be on the lookout for this danger, based on history.

We can see how both Mirza and Leonard act to reduce the presence of this pain. Mirza avoids a number of situations; Leonard has a different strategy—he ruminates. It may seem far-fetched to see rumination as avoidance since Leonard is anything but avoidant of his problems in his thoughts. As we learned in the dialogue, though, this activity can serve the function of not having to come in contact with something worse. Ruminating functions as an attempt to keep these more unpleasant experiences at bay. Thus it belongs in the functional class of avoidance.

Now the time has come to turn our attention to more specific clinical attempts to assist clients in changing what they want to change. Thus we move into part 3, Changing Behavior.

PART 3

Changing Behavior

CHAPTER 9

Functional Knowledge

From a pragmatic point of view, psychological knowledge is a practical form of knowledge. When we have gained understanding of the way an individual's behavior varies with the antecedents and consequences that we can identify, this potentially opens up ways to influence this behavior.

In some ways, evolution has not been all that advantageous to us humans. We are not brilliant swimmers or adapted to stay under water. Neither can we, by using our mere bodies, fly south and escape the cold winters up north. And as carnivores, we are hopelessly slow and are not equipped with any claws worth mentioning. But evolution allowed us to develop other abilities to master these shortcomings. Evolution allowed us to develop language, and through language abstract problem solving became possible. Furthermore, language made science possible and thus opened an array of possibilities. From an evolutionary point of view, the ultimate purpose of science is to aid the task of survival. And it is within this agenda of survival that theories of learning fall into place. Knowledge of human behavior is also knowledge of behavioral change—change that should not only help humans to survive but also hopefully to thrive.

BEHAVIOR ANALYSIS: FOCUSING ON THE FUNCTIONS OF BEHAVIOR

If we return to the topographical analysis of behavior, we remember that problematic behaviors can be defined as excesses or deficits. This logic readily transfers to behavioral change. The process of change can be aimed at decreasing the frequency of certain behaviors or at increasing the frequency of other behaviors. These two principal ways of changing behavior translate into a vast range of different treatment methods, so we will only give examples to illustrate the basic principles (see chapters 12 and 13 where we describe treatment techniques).

Once again, let us stress that it is always the function rather than form or frequency of singular behaviors that is the focus of our interest. Identifying function is vital because it concerns what consequences clients make contact with—or stated differently, what kind of lives our clients live.

This means that different aspects of the theoretical understanding of learning processes will be stressed in different treatments or during different phases in the same treatment. In some cases, the exploration of antecedents and the understanding of stimulus control will be the primary focus. In other cases, the focus will be on expanding the behavioral repertoire or influencing the maintaining consequences of the problematic behavior. This calls for a different analysis than in the first case. The kind of analysis we describe here is not limited to determining the content of specific psychotherapies. The analysis, and with it the possible strategies for behavioral change, could apply equally well when working with the environmental factors surrounding the client. It could, for example, be used to understand why interventions do not achieve the desired effects or to analyze the possibility that different interventions might counteract the purpose of each other.

Establishing the Length of Behavior Analysis

How long should a proper behavior analysis be? This question is probably one of the most frequently asked by students undergoing clinical training. Any attempt to answer it would essentially be arbitrary. In principle, every single analysis could be infinite. There is no fixed point where it is absolutely clear that the analysis is beyond dispute. The aspects of a single individual's life that could be included in a behavior analysis are in principle, as we just said, infinite. But richness in detail is not an objective in itself. If you regard the theoretical analysis of behavior as an attempt to create an approximation of reality, then the level of detail gets an illusory mark of quality. It is as if mere quantity of descriptive statements gets you closer to truth in an absolute sense.

A pragmatic perspective, however, emphasizes functional knowledge, which does not necessarily increase with the level of detail. So the answer to the question of how long a proper behavior analysis should be is fairly simple: it is sufficient when the things we do as clinicians work! A proper clinical behavior analysis guides the clinician to effective actions. It is thus "analyzing" as behavior and as antecedent for the clinician's behavior that matters in clinical settings rather than some kind of final conclusions that are stated with certainty about a given client.

This implies that behavior analyses may be done in different ways, not only depending on with whom—that is, which client—it is done, but also with who is doing it, in what context it is done, and when it is done. It also implies that a behavior analysis should not extend toward infinity. It can be long and "correct"—that is, functional for the clinician—but it can also be short and correct.

Inherent in the process of analyzing human behavior is the understanding that it will be based on a selection of observations. As clinicians, we need to circumscribe or delimit the observational field. This is really a matter of course, but in the field of psychotherapy it is commonplace to endorse statements that suggest that humans should be assessed within a "holistic perspective." These words often evoke positive associations but don't necessarily say much about the perspective taken. Rather, we should be grateful for the fact that evolution made us capable of responding selectively to the surrounding environment and spared us the perceptual overload that is implied in the concept of a "holistic perspective."

Determining Clinical Priority

In clinical situations, we are confronted with the question of therapeutic priorities. We will supply some principles for this process of prioritizing below, but we would like to stress that these are just principles. They are not founded in empirical research, nor are they rules based on any official or general agreement. Instead, they are factors to help guide clinical decisions—that is, why we should give more priority to one area and less to another. Please note that the priorities below are not necessarily given in order of importance.

Danger to self or others. Behaviors that pose an immediate threat to the life and health of the client or others in proximity to the client should usually be attended to first. Such behaviors include, but certainly are not limited to, suicidality, self-destructive acts, and violence. As clinicians we are bound ethically and legally to attend to these behaviors; we are not allowed to disregard them in the process of clinical assessment. It should be noted, however, that our obligation to attend to these drastic behaviors does not per se inform us about the proper measures to be taken in their treatment. If a client commits suicide or a serious offense against someone close to him or her, for example, we cannot claim as extenuating circumstances that other issues were the focus of attention in therapy. But neither do these grounds for prioritization oblige us to be successful with our interventions or to predict every possible behavioral event. Clients will, in many cases, continue with behaviors that are destructive. We are obliged, however, not to disregard these aspects of client behavior when they reasonably should be taken into consideration in the task of behavioral assessment.

Centrality. Behaviors are given priority because they pose a central part of the total clinical picture that the client presents. These behaviors influence a wide range of areas in the clients' lives, and substantial change is not likely to occur without changing these behaviors.

Reproduction. Behaviors are given priority because we as clinicians can reasonably assume that an intervention in one area could reproduce and make way for change in other areas as well.

Necessary prerequisite. Treating areas in which change is a necessary prerequisite for change in other areas is a priority. Suicidal behaviors, for example, tend to paralyze the social context of a client. Therefore, the control of such behaviors may be a necessary prerequisite for establishing a meaningful treatment program. Being able to attend therapy sessions is another necessary prerequisite—it's just as basic as being able to open your mouth when you go to the dentist.

High likelihood of success. As clinicians, we may give priority to an area because we assume we can influence that area with the treatment methods we know. We might, for example, consider the possibility of rapid change in one area—something that in itself could provide the client with an experience of successful behavioral change which then motivates the client for attempting change in other, perhaps more difficult, areas.

Clients' explicit requests. It might seem strange that we have not mentioned clients' explicit requests until now, but please remember that these points are not presented in order of importance. Clients' explicit requests about the areas in which they seek help are crucial to formulating an agenda for therapeutic work. These requests, however, should always be considered in conjunction with all other therapeutic priorities.

Suffering. Areas that are a source of considerable suffering for the client can be given priority, though they may not necessarily be considered top priority. We want to stress that areas that cause suffering should not automatically be considered the most important areas to work with in an attempt to immediately alleviate the suffering. It may be more important to focus on effecting long-term change rather than on what hurts most at the moment.

Long-term change. We give priority to an area because it is assumed to be of vital importance for long-term change in clients' lives. That area might also constitute an essential prerequisite for continuing client change beyond the temporal limitations of therapy.

Preventing deterioration. An area may also be prioritized because if it is not treated, the client's overall well-being will be compromised.

BEHAVIOR ANALYSIS AND PRIORITIZATION

The list above is not exhaustive. We could easily identify further aspects of assessment that could serve as a basis for assigning clinical priority. We want to emphasize, however, that the process of prioritization is an essential part of doing clinical behavior analyses.

Some areas will be considered to be of greater therapeutic concern, and others will be considered more marginal and thus receive less attention. This, however, is not a characteristic solely of clinical behavior analysis. It is a characteristic of any clinical assessment process, regardless of theory or ideology. By focusing our attention on fewer areas, we increase the potential for client learning. Learning new behaviors, as we all know from our own experience, takes much greater effort and much more time if we try to cover too much at once. Prioritization, therefore, is essential for efficient and effective therapeutic intervention.

CHAPTER 10

Dialogue Toward Change

As we mentioned in the introduction, our intention is not to supply a treatment manual. We still want, however, to give some practical guidelines that we think grow out of the perspective on treatment presented so far. So with this in mind, we once again turn to Alice and her problems.

During a session with her therapist, Alice describes her uneasiness and tendency to worry:

> *"I don't understand how things have gotten this way. It's true that I have always been a bit of a worrywart, but it used to seem more normal. These days, it's totally out of control. Could it be because of work? It has been a little hectic lately. But I'd been able to cope with that earlier without feeling this way. What am I supposed to do? I remember that my mother often worried a lot when I was a child, especially when she thought I was going to get sick. Am I having these problems today because of what it was like when I was young? But I actually think things were rather secure for me then, weren't they? Just think of what some people go through; their parents are drug addicts, or they have other kinds of difficulties. I can't really see why I should feel this way. What's wrong with me?"*

THERAPY THROUGH TALKING—AND ITS DILEMMA

The therapist meets with Alice once or maybe twice a week during a limited period of time. This means that most conditions that govern and affect Alice's life exist in a place where the treating therapist does not. How, then, are we to make a difference in a way that helps Alice?

You might say that all psychotherapy is performed in two separate arenas. The first arena is the time during which therapists and clients actually meet, and the second arena is made up of those situations in the clients' ordinary lives when they are confronted with the difficulties that made them seek help. Therapists become acquainted with the latter arena through what the clients relate. Only in the first arena can a therapist be present and have an impact, and yet it is the second arena that is important to the clients seeking help. This is the arena that makes up their lives outside of the limited time in therapy. As a result, there are some important prerequisites for dialogues that are meant to lead to change.

Problems must be made present. In order for the therapist to be of support, the client's problems need to be brought up or "made present" in one way or another during therapy sessions. This seems to come naturally in Alice's case. She expresses that her problem "out there" is that she worries about things, and she does so while seeing the therapist as well. This means the therapist is present at the same time as the problematic behavior, and her chances of having some influence increase. However, the problem being made present is not always something that happens this naturally. It may call for a conscious strategy on the part of the therapist. If the case were that Alice only struggles with uneasiness when asked to take a stand on some issue, then this is not likely to come up during her time with the therapist. It is possible, however, for the therapist to deliberately act in a way that makes the problem present—in this case by demanding Alice take some kind of stand during their dialogue.

"Help to self-help" is crucial. Therapy needs to give as much "help to self-help" as possible. Even if a client's problems are available in the interplay with the therapist, it is not enough to be able to solve the problems there in the presence of the therapist. If therapy is to benefit a client, new behavior must be performed or replayed in "the other arena," out there in the client's life. What the client learns in therapy needs to be generalized. Psychotherapy, therefore, is always a collaboration between the therapist and the client. Its aim is for the client to learn something that can be taken back into "real" life and used there, outside of therapy.

SOCIALIZING THE CLIENT TO THE THERAPY MODEL

The first step in the therapy dialogue is establishing a partnership or collaboration. Since psychotherapy involves a model meant to enable clients to change something in their lives, this model is to be introduced to the clients. This means making the general framework known—for example, that you will meet for sessions once a week for a certain length of time—as well as sharing more specific details on what therapy consists of.

There are two ways of introducing this to clients. The first method is simply for you to explain it. You can describe "the two arenas" and how the purpose of therapy sessions is to create a learning situation where clients can attain something that will be of use out there in "real" life. Based on this perspective on therapy, you can explain that to facilitate this, there will be homework assignments between sessions. You might want to stress that the focus will be on present-day situations where the clients' problems become apparent. You may also mention at the very beginning that should issues arise between the therapist and the client that bring the client's difficulties to the fore, they may serve as golden opportunities to talk about precisely these difficulties.

The second method of introducing the therapy model is by exemplifying the method. The therapist holds on to something the client relates about his or her difficulties, and, by acting on it, displays how therapy works. This type of introduction is especially suitable for sharing how to perform an ABC analysis. This is central to the therapeutic task, and it is the foundation for all other work you do. Seeing psychotherapy precisely as a collaborative project and an occasion for learning, this analysis is not just something therapists perform but rather what therapy is meant to teach clients to do by themselves. If Alice, for example, knows how to analyze what she is doing (B) in connection with what she feels is difficult or painful, if she notices under which circumstances (A) she does this, and what the consequences are (C), then her possibilities of making changes will increase.

Alice:	You see, I often find myself worrying that something's wrong with my heart or something.
Therapist:	Has this happened recently?
Alice:	Yes, almost every night.
Therapist:	Can you tell me about the last time you felt this way?
Alice:	Yes, it was just last night. When I was watching TV.
Therapist:	What was the first thing you noticed that worried you? [looking for A]
Alice:	I felt my heart beat really violently … and kind of irregularly.
Therapist:	In what way did you worry?
Alice:	How do you mean? I worried!
Therapist:	Exactly! But there are many different ways we can worry, and I'd like to know in what way you were worrying yesterday. [looking for B]
Alice:	Well, I guess I'm trying to find out what's wrong. Or that maybe they overlooked something at the doctor's office. Then I try to tell myself I'm only imagining things.
Therapist:	Did that work? Do you think you found out what was wrong? [looking for C]

Alice:	No, that's not how it works, you know. It just makes me feel really desperate that I keep doing this. Then I called Bob, but you know, he's so tired of hearing all this. He does try to comfort me the best he can.

When this is done at the beginning of therapy, as a part of socializing the client to the therapy model, you want to avoid going into too much detail. The main thing is finding relevant answers for each part respectively, and then to point out that this was, in fact, an example of the method.

Therapist:	This is how I thought we could approach things that are painful to you and try to see what is going on. Once we have a better understanding of that, our chances of finding alternatives for you will be better.

This way we introduce an important method to work by, while at the same time our focus is clearly turned to specific events and episodes. In doing this, we have already launched an active therapeutic procedure called *self-monitoring* (Korotitsch & Nelson-Grey, 1999) in which clients observe and monitor their behavior, including what activates it and what the consequences of the behavior are.

Asking Questions

Early on, during the phase of socialization, it is clear that asking questions is an indispensable tool to the therapist while in session. The reason is simple: the therapist is unacquainted with a number of things concerning the client, and he or she needs to become informed. The therapist only has immediate access to a very small part of the client's life (the first arena, which the therapist and client share in session) and all else is dependent on what the client tells him or her. This state of affairs motivates a humble attitude on the part of the therapist. For the most part, the client—not the therapist—witnesses firsthand what happens outside their sessions. This not only means what takes place "out there" in the client's regular life but also what takes place "in there," that is, the thoughts, physical sensations, recollections, and feelings that only the client can observe. These private events (as we described them earlier) are often crucial to the problems that make people seek psychotherapy and therefore need to be surveyed.

When attempting to perform an ABC analysis, we direct questions to the different parts. The central question is always this: what is the function of the behavior (B)? Initially, however, questions such as these are posed to collect general data: "When was this?" "Was there anything else earlier that you think may have had an effect on events?" "Who was present?" "What did he say then?" "How did that make you feel?" "How did your thoughts run then?" "What did you do?" "Did you notice any physical reactions?" "Then what happened?" "Did it turn out the way you wanted it to?" In collaboration with the client, you try to outline the events as an ABC sequence: antecedent, behavior, consequence. In attempting to find things of general validity to the client, you ask for more examples of similar situations: "Could you give any more examples of when you've felt increasing uneasiness this past week?" You then go through this new example in the same way, looking for A, B, and C as described above.

While these are open-ended questions that are built around the client as a firsthand witness, they are not haphazardly posed. The therapist bases them on an understanding of how a process of worrying usually evolves. There are models available to guide the therapist here. The knowledge that anxiety complexes often consist of futile attempts to gain control of private events makes the therapist ask for such things as momentary thoughts, feelings, or physical sensations, as these are important components of A, that is, the things that trigger the client's actions. B and C are subject to questions in the same way so that it becomes clear whether the function is precisely to avoid personal events. In questioning Alice, her therapist may ask, "When you check your pulse, what is the point of that?" or, the same question in a slightly different way, "What are you trying to attain as you see it?" "If the pulse check goes really well, how would that strike you?" and "Does it turn out the way you want it to?"

You run greater risk of misunderstandings while trying to map out internal phenomena than you do with external events. Therefore the therapist needs to pay close attention to the client's account of the events and his or her expression. While external behavior could be verified by an independent observer, private events can only be verified by the holder of these events. It is important to summarize the client's account like this: "Let me see if I got this right. When you heard Larry say this, you felt all empty and you thought to yourself, 'He's going to leave me.' Then you left the room. Did I get that right?"

It is not always easy to elicit thoughts that emerge instantaneously in a certain situation. From our experience, the question "What were your thoughts about that?" is rarely fruitful. The answer is often "I wasn't thinking at all." Though this is seldom true, the question easily leads clients in the wrong direction. Most people associate the word "thought" with something that has been pondered and reflected upon. An expression like "What went through your head right then?" is more likely to lead clients in the right direction. It's important to formulate the question in a way that emphasizes the spontaneous character of momentary thoughts. You might use metaphors, for instance: "If you had a teleprinter connected to everything that passed through your head at that very moment, what would the printout of that be?" When using metaphors, however, you do need to make sure that they seem natural to the person in session at the time. Not everyone, for example, is familiar with teleprinters. (We'll explore the use of metaphors further a bit later in this chapter.)

It is essential as a therapist to keep in mind that the purpose of these questions is to shape an analysis that will function as a foundation for a process of transformation. The analysis needs to be detailed enough that it doesn't leave out anything crucial for this process. This doesn't imply "knowing all there is to know." A fully comprehensive understanding of a course of events is not possible in this context, and neither is it necessary for change to take place.

One important aspect of the questions posed by the therapist is how he or she then shapes observations of certain parts of the stimulus field, such as things the client hasn't noticed earlier. These observations may address the consequences of the client's actions or the circumstances under which the client behaves in a certain way. If the therapist, by way of these questions, introduces the client to parts of the available stimulus field that were not previously known or recognized (for example, what feelings arise in a certain situation), two things may happen. First, a change becomes possible for the client in situations of this type, and, second, the client may acquire a general ability, such as asking himself what he feels with a wider function.

Validation

In a therapeutic conversation, asking questions that show a genuine interest in what clients are experiencing and how they view what goes on will usually lead to yet another result. This gives clients a sense of acceptance and recognition, and thereby creates a working alliance. The reader needs only refer to his or her own experience. When someone asks for your opinion or about your inner experiences in a way that suggests genuine interest, how does that affect you? And if, in addition, this person summarizes the things you've said and asks if this was how you meant it all, what does that do for you? For most people, this is a rewarding experience. In a therapeutic setting, the therapist thus uses validation for a specific purpose: to reinforce a wide array of behavioral classes, such as coming to therapy to work on one's problems, to share some things about one's life, and to relate personal events. The therapeutic conversation becomes a place where these types of behavior are accompanied by the consequences of feeling understood and of feeling someone's involvement in the conditions of one's own life.

We can usually describe the person seeking psychotherapy as a person with two problems. The first is the problem for which the person seeks therapy. This might be constant worrying, as in Alice's case, or depression, as in Leonard's case. The second problem is the condition of being a person with a problem like this: "What's wrong with me when I'm in this state and I can't seem to change it?" The latter is particularly evident with people who have struggled with their difficulties for a long time. The behavioral point of view assumes that all human behavior is essentially comprehensible when taking into account the individual human being's learning history and current circumstances. A client's experiences are in line with the principles that apply for other human experiences, and they are not signs that something is "wrong" with the client. On the contrary, they imply that what the client is experiencing is valid when seen in the light of personal experiences in the past. It is a fundamental therapeutic mission to communicate this to the client. This takes the sting out of futile attempts to "find what's wrong" and helps clients to trust their own experience. Learning to trust and explore one's own factual experiences is an important basis for working on change, and therefore something that the therapist wishes to encourage. Let's look at an example of this as Leonard shares what happened last night:

Leonard:	I was leaving to go out with my colleagues from work. I went through my mail and found a travel brochure on Crete. It made me think of when I was there with Tina and the kids. Those times are gone. I felt like there was no use in going out. The rest have their families, but what have I got? So I never got around to leaving. Just sat there, watching TV all night. Sure it is crazy. Why is everything such a burden? Looks as if I'll be afraid of stepping outside my door soon.
Therapist:	So you get home and something reminds you of things that bring back painful thoughts and feelings, that you are not living with your family any longer. And it strikes you that you're liable to be reminded even more this evening, since your colleagues from work have their families at home and will probably talk about them. I can see why that would feel difficult. I mean, you can't govern what you'll be reminded of. You see a brochure on Crete, and if your brain is healthy, it carries out its task to remind you of your own history with Crete. And that makes you remember your family and all the grief there is in living by yourself. That makes sense to me.
Leonard:	Well, I guess that's a way of looking at it, once you say it. I have not thought of it that way. But I can't go on like this—all alone in an apartment, just watching TV. That's not a life.
Therapist:	Okay, so while it's natural for you to feel what you feel when you're reminded of difficult things, what you do in this situation is not working very well. That's how it seems.

Questions as a Means of Change

During initial therapy sessions, you ask questions mainly to elicit data. The quest is to describe—in collaboration with the client—important variables in the client's behavior and the circumstances that precede and succeed this behavior. It is also possible, however, to ask questions with a different intention, that is, with a more direct purpose to have an influence on your client's behavior, to trigger change. The dividing line between these two is hardly precise, but it is useful nevertheless.

Let's return to Alice and her constant worrying. Let us suppose that the initial ABC analysis describes the typical sequence as follows: Something that happens evokes certain unpleasant thoughts, feelings, or images for Alice. What this "something" is varies. It can be something in a TV broadcast ("heart attacks are increasingly common in women," "road conditions along the coast are extremely hazardous"), something her fiancé mentions ("I'm driving up north tomorrow"), something she feels in her chest (her heart is beating faster), or being back in a place where she didn't feel well before.

What these things (and a large number of other possible circumstances) all have in common is they awaken thoughts and/or inner images related to a "catastrophe" or "danger" theme as well as the affective components connected with it. All of these are examples of A, according to our analysis. Alice's typical response to this (B) is to try, in different ways, to change or control these thoughts and emotions. She tries "not to think about it," or she thinks more about it in an effort to make herself "realize that it's not that serious." Topographically these actions are different, but functionally they are very similar. The purpose is to "calm down." As for the consequences (C), Alice describes how she sometimes achieves what she wants (she feels calmer), but that many times it's just the opposite—she worries even more. Furthermore, she can see that in the long run her worrying is increasing. Despite this, her comment "if I could only have some peace and quiet sometime" displays how natural she finds her own behavior. Let's return to Alice's session with her therapist:

Therapist:	How did you feel when you heard that heart attacks are increasing in women?
Alice:	There's so much spinning around in my head. I can't stop myself, it's just spinning ...
Therapist:	What is spinning?
Alice:	Well, you know, I see myself being taken to the emergency room, with lots of tubes and everything ... (*shudders*)
Therapist:	How about the road conditions along the coast?
Alice:	Same thing there, I guess. Except then it's a call from the emergency room and I have to go there, and there's Bob. And all the tubes again ...
Therapist:	How do you act when all this pops up?
Alice:	Well, of course, I try to get it out of my head and tell myself that it's not going to happen. You know, I try to convince myself that things aren't that critical, that it's just my weak nerves ... But that's not easy to do.
Therapist:	You're not successful?
Alice:	Sometimes I am, but it's like there's a rubber band attached to these thoughts. They just keep coming back. And it's weird somehow. When I've managed to convince myself that Bob is a safe driver, then the idea pops up that a drunken driver could run into him or something. Like what happened last week that was in the paper. That's so terrible!

Therapist:	So it doesn't get any better?
Alice:	No, it's like it gets worse!
Therapist:	Then what is the point in doing this? Trying to get these thoughts out of your head?
Alice:	Well, I have to calm down somehow. I just want some peace. It's like that's my only way of making it, right then. Becoming calm …

How can questions from the therapist help to change this? From a behavioral perspective, change has to take place by Alice doing something different than what she has been doing so far. She will thereby get to experience new consequences. In accordance with what we've written earlier about "the dark side of language," we may assume that, in many cases, the consequences that could control better functioning behavior are already present in Alice's experience. However, the mechanisms of language cause them to lose their influence on Alice's behavior. By posing questions, the therapist tries to undo this "blocking" effect of language and to put Alice in touch with the consequences of her actions. The unwanted consequences are present: Alice feels even more worried when she focuses her actions on "calming down." But those unwanted consequences do not decrease the likelihood of her worrying behavior. This may have to do with the fact that the short-term consequences of "calming down" actually—at least some of the time—bring about a certain temporary feeling of more composure. This experience then functions as a reinforcer. Likewise, this may also have to do with the verbal construction "my only way of making it" being in coordination with the behavior of "calming down." This in itself reinforces the act of worrying.

These two factors of negative and positive reinforcement respectively make it difficult for the client to make the connection between her actions and the painful consequences. When the therapist, by way of his or her questions, points to this connection, the stimulus function of the act ("calming down") can change from "what is my only way of making it" to "what makes things worse." This enhances the prospect that Alice will act differently, and that she will thereby experience new consequences. A promising side of this is that just as Alice has "an enemy" in her verbal process, she has "a friend" in her own experience. The experience of her behavior not getting her where she wants to be (become calm) is something that the therapist can help her get in touch with through questions, as we see in this exchange:

Therapist:	So you try to calm down? That's the only way you can make it, you say. How do you think that is working?
Alice:	No, I just can't do it, not when it gets that intense.
Therapist:	What if that very experience is your friend, showing you that this "calming down" strategy leads to a dead end?

The primary purpose of questions like these is to increase flexibility in Alice's behavioral repertoire. When something crops up that rouses thoughts and feelings of danger, Alice's behavioral repertoire narrows down to a single behavior: "act to become calm." She has different ways of doing this, but they all aim at this one thing: "becoming calm." The consequences of this have long been evident, and they are not likely to change as long as she acts in the same way in these types of situations. If the therapist, through his or her questions, can boost flexibility in Alice's actions, there is a greater chance that she will in fact encounter different consequences with new behavior as a result. This may take place during the therapy session when the therapist asks, "Is it possible that anxiety, as a rule, does not lessen when you try to control it, but rather increases?" Speaking about things results in the speakers being in contact with parts of the stimulus functions connected to the things they speak about. Because of this, the question above to Alice means that she is put in contact with parts of "anxiety" and parts of "try to control." Now suppose that Alice feels this is new to her—that is, the question brings out the possibility that "trying to control" is something that increases anxiety rather than something that reduces it, which till now has been an integrated part of her actions. If this is the case, it may then result in a change in Alice's behavior. Surprised and suddenly attentive, she may say, "You mean I could handle this some other way than trying to calm myself down?" At this moment, during the session, her behavioral repertoire has broadened. Faced with anxiety and the behavior that she formerly connected with it—what she called the "natural thing to do"—she now displays interest in investigating an alternative behavior.

This may lead to two new types of consequences. First, an investigative attitude may lead Alice to discover potentially new relations between what she fears, on the one hand, and how she acts in response to her fear, on the other. Since, to a verbally competent person, the experience of coherence, or "how it all fits together," is rewarding in itself, a new way of thinking is formed. Concerning feelings of anxiety about, for example, her heart or hazardous road conditions, Alice may find herself thinking something new like "somehow that isn't as dangerous as it feels." Concerning her attempts to gain control, she may begin to think those attempts aren't worthwhile. Whether this experience in itself is enough for Alice to change her actions the next time she feels worried is an open question. It may do so, if this precise way of thinking has a sufficiently governing function. However, that is not certain. It may be that factors that are not under verbal control carry more weight. This leads us to yet another possible consequence for the therapy sessions.

The second new type of consequences may grow out of the first. The fresh investigative attitude we discussed above may make it feasible to deliberately approach nonverbal parts of the anxiety during the therapy session and to develop a different way of handling them. The new element of verbal control (the new way of thinking) that has been established as a result of the therapist's questions may not be enough for Alice to establish new behavior a few days later on her own, but it might allow her to try out new behavior right now in the session. For example, the therapist can ask Alice to evoke anxious and worrying thoughts on purpose, and then to note how her body reacts, what else emerges, what she is tempted to do. The therapist can also help Alice refrain from "soothing measures." If this approach is successful—that is, if Alice feels anxious but manages to broaden her behavioral repertoire so that the consequences are different than usual—then chances increase that Alice's new behavior will be generalized to contexts outside the therapy situation.

Naturally this example is limited, and the crucial question is how Alice will respond the next time she experiences anxiety in "real" life. Will her experience in the therapy session be sufficient to enable her to change her behavioral repertoire? Will the repertoire become more open and flexible, which would allow her to function better in the face of her anxiety? As talking about something is not the same as doing what you talk about, this is the weak spot of therapy through talking. The heart of the matter, as we've said above, is to what extent the newly attained behavioral repertoire is generalized to situations in the client's life outside therapy sessions. But Alice's experience shows us how a client's behavior can be influenced in the therapeutic session itself, thus setting the stage for fresh prospects to take shape.

CHOOSING A DIRECTION FOR THERAPY

It is well known that psychotherapeutic work shows better results when directed toward goals that have been mutually expressed and agreed upon (Tryon & Winograd, 2002). What does the client want to achieve by therapy? Speaking about this early on also gives the therapist a better chance of evaluating means of helping the client reach this goal.

Here are some points to consider when establishing goals for therapy:

■ Have the client determine the goals. Since this is "help to self-help," it is absolutely essential that the client determine what the goals are. What does the client feel is important to achieve?

■ Decide, as the therapist, if these are goals that you want to work toward and feel able to help the client attain.

■ Help the client to describe goals in terms of desired behavior, such as "I would like to do/make/act …"

■ Help the client reformulate goals, if stated in terms of lack of symptoms, to specify desired behavior. For example, if the client wants to "get rid of anxiety," ask what she would do then—that is, what would getting rid of anxiety make it possible for her to do? This may require additional discussion in order to clarify the goals. When tormented by anxiety, it's natural to want to escape it. But making a lack of symptoms (usually synonymous with negative affect) a goal creates a goal that is difficult to aim at in a direct way. People have poor tools for exercising direct control over emotional conditions, and if this becomes the expressed goal, you easily end up in the kind of vicious circle that the client is already caught in. Establishing goals that are thoroughly the client's own, on one hand, and within reach of the therapeutic process, on the other, is important for successful therapy.

■ Outline concrete steps that lead to the desired goals.

One difficulty in working toward goals is they often feel too distant. This is especially true for people with substantial and long-standing problems. If clients formulate goals that feel urgent and important, the actual wording itself can be very painful as it shows how far they are from what they desire. Far-off goals can emphasize perceived deficiencies and shortcomings, thus causing the client to once again say, "There is something wrong with me." One way of emphasizing the possibilities of constructive action instead is to formulate goals that are immediately accessible. Steps toward these goals can be taken immediately and clients can experience the reward of reaching goals close at hand. These are goals that are consistent with the client's own values. What is important in the client's life? Try asking your clients these questions: "If you could have it your way, what would life be all about?" "If you could make the choice, what would you like your colleagues at work (your children? your partner?) to remember about you?" Identifying actions that are in accord with client values is one way of formulating goals that are immediately accessible. To many of those who seek help, "a mutually satisfying, working marriage" is a far-off goal, even if they are currently in a relationship. If, instead, they want to be supportive spouses to their partners, actions that match that goal are often within reach. Another example could be to contribute as a colleague in your work situation or to develop your own creativity. Identifying these actions enables clients to move in a valued direction with their lives right now. Here's an example from a session with Leonard:

Therapist:	Something that often seems to crop up when things get difficult for you is thoughts that revolve around your family. I guess that shows us that there is something important here, something that means a lot to you. What would you say is the most important?
Leonard:	How do you mean, the most important? No doubt the family is important.
Therapist:	Exactly. What I mean is—in a world where you were free to choose how things are with you and your family, what would you choose?
Leonard:	That we were living together. That things were like they used to be. That all the things that happened had never happened. But that's impossible, I know that. What's done is done. I just don't understand how I'm supposed to go on from here.

Therapist:	It's true that we can't relive or change the past. But the desire to be living together—what do you think is the most important about that for you?
Leonard:	Being with the kids, being able to give them my support, to see how they are doing. I don't know—just having someone care about me. But what's the use of talking about this? Things will never be the same again.
Therapist:	Yes, but here's what I'm thinking: Doesn't what you're saying show us that the most important thing to you is not exactly living together? Even if that is part of it, there are other issues here: being a supportive dad, caring about each other, and so on. I mean, if you were living together and your kids thought you were a jerk, and you were never involved with them, would that be fine?
Leonard:	No, of course not. It's not just about living under the same roof. There has to be something inside. You want to be something to your kids.
Therapist:	Exactly. And what is there inside that is important to you? What do you want to be to your kids?
Leonard:	I want to be a dad who can give support, I want to be involved, and I want us to have a relationship that works well. There hasn't been much of that lately.
Therapist:	What has kept you from these things?
Leonard:	This bad shape I'm in. There I am, in front of the TV, my thoughts just going over the same thing over and over. Not much of a dad exactly.
Therapist:	Okay, so we have two things here. First, the things that are important to you in connection with your family—things like being a dad who is involved and supportive to his kids. And second, the things that are in your way: The shape you're in. All the difficult thoughts and feelings that things are so burdensome for you. There are things that want to get in your way. And at the same time there are these things you're telling me about: what kind of a dad you would like to be. What do you think—is this something we could work toward here in therapy?
Leonard:	If I could change in this area, that would be great. But I feel like that's a long way off. We're not living in the same city anymore.

Therapist:	No, it's hard to know exactly what you can accomplish, how things will turn out in the future. But this is how my thoughts run: all this about being a dad who gets involved and who cares, that's certainly something you value, something that matters to you. Are there things you can do at this time that work in that direction? Can you do some things here and now that allow you to stay faithful to what you feel is important, although you don't know exactly what the result will be in the future?
Leonard:	Well, yes, I suppose I can. Though, it feels difficult.
Therapist:	Okay, what would they be? What would you do then?

A client who is going to stop avoiding pain and begin doing something different from what he or she has done so far needs something that brings purpose to it all. Making clear what a client values and focusing on those values is one of the most powerful motivating factors we can apply when we're working on change.

THE USE OF METAPHORS

Metaphors are at the core of human language. Many are so well established that we don't immediately think of them as actual metaphors but rather as proper descriptions. Language that describes inner conditions, in particular, is often of this kind. I feel "worked up," "dull," "run-down," "empty," "high-spirited" are all examples of this.

Metaphoric language transfers functions from one experiential field to another. Anyone reading "My neighbor Evelyn is a lioness" transfers functions from lioness to Evelyn. This transfer is based on certain likenesses between Evelyn and a lioness, and these very likenesses in Evelyn are enhanced and developed by way of the metaphor. Once this is said, the listener's actions in relation to Evelyn are likely to change in some respect. But there are only certain functions that are transferred from a lioness to Evelyn. No reader believes that what we intend to say is that Evelyn has a tail, or that she is in the habit of hunting and bringing in prey for dinner. The metaphorical meaning of "my neighbor Evelyn is a lioness" is usually clear to the reader, who automatically also makes distinctions between "Evelyn" and "lioness."

The point in using expressions like these is that a number of functions are very rapidly transferred from one verbal stimulus to another, and to the external stimuli that are put in relation to the verbal stimulus—in this case, the real person Evelyn. You might say that when you use a metaphor, you link (X is like Y) a network of connections with another network.

This way of speaking has essentially the same function in psychotherapy as it has in ordinary life. By using a metaphor, the functions belonging to one experiential network are transferred to another, which swiftly opens up new possibilities, both internal ("thinking in a different way") and external ("acting differently than usual"). This can be important for several reasons in therapy. You may want to bring the client into contact with something that is next to impossible to describe in more matter-of-fact language. Often private or inner behaviors are of this type. And even if it is possible to describe something in a more factual way, it may work better by using a metaphor. Think, for example, of what you would have to say in order to portray Evelyn in a way that matches "lioness" if you tried to express this without using a metaphor.

Research also indicates that the use of metaphors in psychotherapy is positively related to both the therapist's and the client's experience that the therapy in question is beneficial (Clarke, 1996). Let's look at a clinical example in an area of general importance that may help us see the benefit of using metaphors. You are working with a client who has some kind of anxiety problem, and the analysis so far shows that certain types of situations trigger a negative affect (fear), physical uneasiness, and certain typical thoughts of catastrophes ("I think I'm going insane," "What if they notice that I'm nervous?" "I just can't handle this …"). In different ways, the client acts to withdraw from or to somehow clear away the peril he experiences in these situations. Since these reactions are predictable to some extent (certain situations make them more likely), the client refrains from doing certain things or going to certain places. The client has two problems here: first, anxiety still crops up, and second, avoidance has a high price. His life is narrowed down, and there's so much he can't do (things he'd like to do) under these conditions. This is what it looks like from your perspective. Now you want to describe this to the client, and show him why things turn out as they do, as well as introduce him to an alternative attitude that you think could be part of a solution. This could be done as follows:

Therapist: You experience how all this pain emerges in certain situations that you have described. Let's suppose (and here's a somewhat silly example) that I experience this pain every time I walk on a blue-colored floor. Other than this, things are pretty good, but if I step on a blue floor, all this pops up—panic, fear, strange physical sensations that I can't control, and so on. How am I going to solve this? Wouldn't it be pretty much the natural thing for me to solve it by not stepping on blue floors? If I have reason to believe that there's going to be a blue-colored floor in my way, I try to take a different route, and if I end up on one anyway, I try to get away from there as quickly as possible. That's natural. But there might be problems. What if there are things I want that are placed on a blue floor? What if they renovate my workplace and the new floor turns out to be blue? What if my daughter moves to a house with blue floors? I can still avoid going there, but there is a price to pay. The price is high. And then there's one more problem. I don't know in advance where all the blue floors are. What am I supposed to do when some people invite me to their home for the first time? Ask them if their floors are blue? Ask someone who knows them if their floors are blue? The problem is that I have to be on guard so much of the time, that is, I have to do a lot of thinking about blue floors. I can't avoid blue floors without thinking about them. This means that in my very attempts to keep blue floors away from my life, thoughts of blue floors are going to take up an increasingly large space. And since the thought of blue floors to some extent brings on a feeling of blue floors, my fear will not be far away, even when I'm far away from those actual blue floors.

At this point it may be important to get feedback from the client's experience. Does he recognize anything like this in his own life? If so, you can proceed:

Therapist: I can live like this, but the price is high. And I still haven't gotten rid of what I wanted to get rid of. What if the only way to change this—to take control of my life—is to actually venture out on blue floors? If this resembles your problem, what would it involve for you to venture out there?

It is often useful to keep metaphors for common dilemmas at hand and ready to use. It's also important to be sensitive to metaphors that clients use as they describe their difficulties. These can be used in a similar way in therapy. Alice's metaphor of her thoughts having a rubber band attached, for example, could be a valuable tool to incorporate into her therapy sessions.

Before we move further into practical applications of a functional perspective on behavior change, let's take a short look at the interaction between the different principles of learning.

CHAPTER 11

Principles and Practices

Behavioral psychology is not just a system for understanding how something might originally have been learned and how it continues to live on in the life of the learner. Behavioral psychology also deals with processes of change, since these too involve learning. Because of this, let's briefly review our three basic principles for learning—respondent conditioning, operant conditioning, and relational framing—and see how they interact in different interventions that grow out of a theoretical analysis of behavior.

RESPONDENT CONDITIONING

Respondent conditioning can make a number of internal phenomena (such as negative affect, painful physical reactions, and flashbacks) surface and become a part of the problems for which the client seeks help. Earlier in this book, we described a natural extinction process that involved repeated contact with the conditioned stimulus (heights) without occurrence of the unconditioned stimulus (falling) that originally provoked fear. If this repeated contact continues over time, the conditioned response (fear) will gradually decrease. This basic principle lies behind *exposure* as a treatment strategy. It is one of the most essential principles behind a number of behavioral treatment methods. Though not used exclusively in treating phobia, it is most easily recognized there.

OPERANT CONDITIONING

This is the fundamental principle of operant conditioning: actions are governed by the consequences that have followed similar actions taken at an earlier time. Seen from this perspective, we may assume that a client's problem might, at least partly, be due to poorly functioning actions. These actions are nevertheless maintained because of the consequences that follow. When we say that an action functions poorly, we are also saying that there are consequences that follow upon the behavior emitted which the individual regards as undesirable or that the behavior emitted is insufficient for contacting vital consequences. We stated earlier that actions can have different consequences —some short-term, some long-term—and the consequences that are closer in time to these actions usually have a more powerful governing effect. It is essential, from our knowledge of operant conditioning, for the therapist to keep in mind that when certain actions occur, there are consequences that govern them.

All behavior has "a point" or a function. The following practices guide work toward change:

- Work to reinforce behavior that is defined as desirable (where there is a deficit).

- Try to obstruct reinforcement of actions for which there are good reasons to reduce (where there is an excess).

- Establish conditions that increase the likelihood that the client will come into contact with naturally occurring reinforcers in ordinary life outside the framework of therapy.

- Help the client practice the ability to discriminate contingencies that govern his or her behavior as well as that of others.

- Work toward generalization of behavior that exists in the client's repertoire but which isn't occurring in situations where it might be beneficial.

- Work to develop the behavioral repertoire where adequate skills are partly or completely missing in order to increase the chances of contacting potential reinforcers.

RELATIONAL FRAMING

This behavioral principle is crucial because of how rapidly it can create considerable changes in the functions of specific contingencies. Something that is neutral per se in the client's personal history can instantly become reinforcing or punishing by way of thoughts or utterances. Something that arouses a certain emotion, based on factual experience, can swiftly, through a complex chain of relations, stir up a different emotion.

It is bewildering to see a depressed person withdraw at home, despite the very real, painful consequences experienced because of this behavior. It's as if he doesn't "take these in" in a way that leads to change. The capacity for relational framing lies at the root of this behavior. As human beings, we can construct consequences that we have never been in contact with ("how things could have been") and then relate them to "it's no use trying." So on top of the pain that is already present, the depressed person carries the additional pain that arises from how he views his situation.

It is just as bewildering to see the anxiety-ridden person continue to worry endlessly. She thinks of what might happen, what people might say, where this might lead in the future, and wonders how she could possibly manage. She does this even when her misgivings aren't justified and despite the pain the worrying causes her.

This "insensitivity" to actual circumstances is the curse as well as the blessing of relational framing. The principles of treatment grow out of this and take both the blessing and the curse into account. On one hand, the therapist works to remove obstacles composed of verbal functions, thereby putting the client into contact with actual contingencies. On the other hand, the same verbal functions are used to formulate a direction for therapy, naming things that are essential for the client to achieve. Here are some points of guidance:

- Change the content in relational framing ("think differently").

- Change the governing function that thoughts and other internal phenomena have over the person's actions.

- Establish increased verbal control in areas where this seems functional, such as when describing desirable consequences and the actions that lead to them.

INTERACTION

It serves us well to consider learning from the perspective of respondent conditioning, operant conditioning, and relational framing. Each provides a viewpoint that is valuable as we work with our clients. But these three principles do not stand alone. In real life, they all overlap and intertwine. We can rarely influence behavior by a practice based on one principle of learning alone without simultaneously influencing behavior that is governed by other principles. Methods that are based on operant theory, for example, also bring about changes in how something makes a person feel, which is a respondent function. And treatments that originate in respondent theory (for example, exposure) change the cognitive content associated with the disorders treated (Arntz, 2002; Öst, Thulin, & Ramnerö, 2004).

Learning theory describes relations between events that occur and that are susceptible to influences in accordance with certain predictable patterns. A treatment method connected with a particular principle, such as respondent or operant conditioning or relational framing, focuses on the relation it is primarily meant to influence. Most of the time that treatment method simultaneously influences relations based on the other principles as well. In practice, therapeutic processes will differ from one another depending both on where we work—mental health facility, public clinic, private practice—and with whom we work—a group of people who work together, a family, a couple, or an individual. Of practical significance is the degree to which the therapist can influence those consequences that have a governing function in the client's behavior.

In the next two chapters, we will illustrate how these principles, when put into practice, guide our work with the different people with whom we have become acquainted in this book. We will begin by describing situations and interventions in therapy where the therapist to a greater degree can exert influence on the external environment of what we have called "the second arena," that is, in the client's daily life. A great deal of the research done on therapy in the wake of functional analysis has been carried out in this type of therapeutic setting.

After this, we will take a closer look at the therapeutic setting usually referred to as psychotherapy, where the therapist is involved in the client's life outside the therapy session only to a slight degree (if at all). Certainly therapy of this kind can involve sessions at locations other than a consulting room, as occurs in certain types of exposure therapy. Yet even here the therapist can only affect the circumstances or context surrounding the client. Psychological therapies provide no tools for exerting a direct influence on "the internal level." All influence on the client's "internal level" occurs in an indirect way, by changing what takes place in the external environment. When the therapist speaks, looks the client in the eye, or nods in agreement, this is still all taking place in the context, as seen from the client's perspective.

The private therapeutic conversation is a trivially small part of the client's daily life timewise. But, like all environments, the psychotherapeutic setting does supply consequences, and therefore provides a platform for experiential learning and change.

CHAPTER 12

Principles of Treatment: One

In some cases, we as therapists have access to a number of external contingencies surrounding the person or persons we are working with, and it is possible for us to influence these. This obviously applies in an institution or in a person's work environment. These are social settings where our work involves more than just a therapist and a client. In cases where one or several therapists work with a couple, a family, or a group of some kind, you have an intermediate situation. On one hand, the therapist is in the same situation as she would be in an individual therapy setting, that is, she is not involved in or a part of the client's ordinary life. Yet, on the other hand, several of the other participants (for example, in a family) may be involved in each other's lives, thereby giving them the possibility (and the need) to regularly contribute actual consequences in different ways.

A therapy setting of this kind contains opportunities as well as difficulties. There's a good chance you can have an impact on several governing factors. The difficulties lie in making several different persons work together toward the goals and measures involved in therapy. This calls for a solid functional analysis on which to base therapy work, on one hand, and on the other, all those involved need to be guided by that analysis.

PROVIDING AN ENVIRONMENT

When we meet with Jenny, it's at the request of the care staff around her. She is rather hesitant herself about seeing a therapist as she doesn't think it helps to talk. Several earlier attempts were made, but none led to a good working relationship. We're faced with a rather typical clinical priority issue. Jenny's self-injuring behavior is potentially dangerous, and there are immediate as well as long-term risks. When Jenny harms herself, there are often acute measures taken, and sudden changes in her care plan as well, which in turn interfere with long-term treatment goals. This means we need to intervene here in order to make way for other efforts as well. At the same time, this must be done in collaboration with her.

We have established that Jenny's self-injuring behavior occurs in two circumstances, leading us to two hypotheses about what governs her:

- It takes place in the presence of adults with potential control over her life. In this case, the behavior has the function of giving access to reinforcers such as concern, care, and increased influence.

- It takes place in the presence of inner painful experiences, like flashbacks, in which case the behavior has the function of distracting her from, and pushing aside, these painful emotions.

These two different circumstances will require different paths toward change. In particular, our work with the second function (avoiding painful inner experiences) will require establishing the kind of working alliance that defines therapeutic work. ("Alliance" is usually defined as the degree of mutual agreement on goals, methods, and the emotional bond between therapist and client. The actual agreement is "to watch, learn, and do therapy" [Gelso & Hayes, 1998].)

> When we talk to Jenny, she has two wishes concerning her situation. She wants to be discharged from the ward, and she doesn't want everyone to always be deciding things for and about her. Her foster family is doubtful, however, about her desire to be discharged, due to events that have occurred lately.

We'll have to begin here. We can see that Jenny's self-injuring behavior doesn't benefit her first wish; however, it probably has a function when it comes to her second one. Harming herself gives her some means of controlling those around her to a degree. This will be the starting point for our therapy strategy.

Jenny's behavior is governed by the reception and the reactions from those around her. These are meeting basic human needs in the environment she is in. It is our responsibility to shape, as far as possible, the patient's surroundings in a way that they don't have such toxic effects on the individual. The first important objective is to find the reinforcers in the care environment and to try to reduce these. This is easy to say but often very hard to do. The second thing we need to do is shape the environment so that it supplies the best conditions for a working alliance with Jenny. We will need an alliance with her in order to work together on developing a skill repertoire that can replace the self-injuring acts that have been there to soothe the pain she feels—a skill repertoire that is more fitting for living a life with her specific past experiences (see fig. 12.1).

MANAGING CONTINGENCIES

Theoretically one might think we should extinguish Jenny's behavior by holding back the consequences that govern it. This means her self-injuring behavior would be responded to in a way that does not include concern, attention, and an increased influence on

Figure 12.1 Altered Contingencies: New Paths of Behavior for Jenny

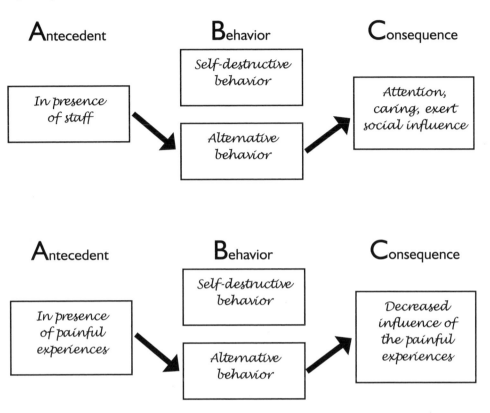

her own situation. The behavior would then lose its basic function. Experience shows us this can be extremely difficult to achieve. We risk causing an extinction burst, that is, the behavior initially intensifies as the reinforcers are withdrawn. Also, many times care wards or environments offer amazing opportunities for finding social reinforcers for unhealthy behaviors. In order to counter this, you would need nearly completely uniform responses from all those involved. If this isn't accomplished, the risk is that the behavior escalates to the next, and more dangerous, level. Jenny will have to make a deeper cut to make it work.

You will notice that the behavior isn't governed by some odd or extraordinary reinforcers. The common expression "just to get some attention" may mislead us into thinking that is the case. On the contrary, Jenny's expectations of basic reinforcers, such as concern and influence, are legitimate expectations. Her self-injuring behavior, however, is a drastic and perilous course to achieving this. We can see the same thing when looking at the second contingency. Being able to influence one's own pain is of basic interest to a person. Yet again, self-injuring behavior is a drastic and perilous course by which to get there.

Another problem with focusing therapy strictly on extinction is that this won't help Jenny discover the alternative behavior that could lead to the consequences she's aiming for. We make the assumption that her learning history has not allowed her to develop certain adequate social skills nor skills in handling unexpected, sudden affects. Concerning social skills, we can think of a number of alternative behaviors that could serve precisely the same function, and so put her in contact with the desired consequences. Three alternative behaviors that Jenny could do are:

- Telling those around her that she needs help.

- Sharing her opinion, clearly and plainly.

- Expressing wishes in words, and waiting for an answer.

These are behaviors where Jenny shows a deficiency in her repertoire. The purpose of *social skills training* is to develop these types of general skills (Lieberman, DeRiel, & Meuser, 1989; Linehan, 1993).

> Jenny has agreed to join the rehabilitation ward's "Girls' Group" on a trial basis. There are six young girls in the group—all different from one another and with different problems. What they have in common, however, is difficulty asserting themselves in social relationships. In the Girls' Group, they work through short sequences of role playing. They often start out from an example—something a group member has experienced, or something people find difficult in general. Role playing gives them the chance to try alternative behaviors. They switch roles in order to learn from one another. Sometimes they work in front of the video camera so that they get feedback right away on how they act. The group members get homework assignments between sessions that encourage them to practice their skills outside the group.

This training rests on social modeling to a high degree. You observe each other and give different approaches a try. Social modeling is facilitated by social similarities between the person modeling and the person watching. The group is unique in how it can offer models that are usually easier to identify with, compared to professional staff in the care environment. Studies have also indicated that modeling, rather than instruction, is the most important element in this type of training (Rosenberg, Hayes, & Linehan, 1989).

In addition, training of this kind can be significant in therapy work with the second circumstance where Jenny cuts herself (to control painful flashbacks and emotions). The skills Jenny learns can make it easier to approach these difficulties without her regularly harming herself. This more classic individual therapy work will be brought up and expounded in the next chapter.

But let us return to how the people in Jenny's environment act in connection with her self-injuring behavior. In cases of self-injury, there is a risk that precisely the dramatic measures taken by those around the indivudual can prove to be reinforcers that in the long run make the situation grow worse. It may therefore be important to do as little as possible, except for any medical measures that are necessary, in order not to reinforce the behavior.

How, then, should we act? These are some principles for measures that focus on the behavior of those in the surroundings, that is, what we call *managing contingencies* (Boyce & Roman, 2003):

- The attention from those in the environment should be distributed in such a way that it isn't expressed too much following self-injuring behavior. Self-injuring behavior should be followed by neutral responses. Vital functions should be secured, but in other respects the level of attention should be kept down. On these occasions, drastic measures and reconsiderations of care plans should be avoided.

- You should give Jenny attention in an evenly distributed manner, without clearly following upon a certain behavior. In this way, Jenny will contact concern and encouragement at intervals, just by the behavior of her being present, not by behaving in drastic ways.

- You can strive for differential reinforcement of certain behavior, that is, you define a number of Jenny's behaviors that will be reinforced in a selective way.

DIFFERENTIATING REINFORCERS

Reinforcing behaviors is one of our most essential tools in a therapeutic situation. When Jenny expresses wishes concerning her own situation in the ward, this should be received with interest and respect, and also by a readiness to make changes. Those are natural reinforcers in this context. Those around Jenny need to be attentive to any behaviors that can be seen as gradual steps toward what she needs to learn. The whole care environment should, as much as possible, support the skills training that takes place. Bad as it may be from many points of view, we cannot disregard the fact that in some regards self-injury works. When, for the first time, Jenny is standing by the ward office with something she wants to say, that is not the right time to say, "You'll have to wait!" Jenny, after all, knows a way of not having to wait!

We can also make agreements with Jenny that certain behaviors will be followed by consequences that are desirable to her. "If you do this, we'll do this." The agreements should be worded in a positive manner. "Not run away" or "not nag" are examples of expressing behavior in a negative way and should be avoided. In addition to this, the "dead man's rule" applies. This rule states that behavior that can be executed by the dead is unworthy as a goal for the living. "Sit still," "be quiet," and "stay in your room" are all examples of behavior that can be executed by a dead person.

In its most elaborate form, we call this a *token economy* (Ghezzi, Wilson, Tarbox, & MacAleese, 2003). This stands for a system of reinforcers that accompany specific behaviors that are mutually agreed upon. Specific behaviors are compensated for by some kind of symbolic reinforcer (token) that can subsequently be traded for concrete reinforcers or reinforcers of some other type—in short, a system that resembles the system of labor and wages.

This description of therapeutic work sometimes causes objections of the type we mentioned earlier. Isn't this manipulation? It is a form of manipulation, in the sense that it is influence. We are trying, in collaboration with the client, to influence the way she acts. We do this with an explicit and well-reasoned aim of achieving goals that are important to the client's well-being.

The object of this type of work must always be to provide a setting that does not reinforce destructive behaviors and that reduces those already established. The purpose is, moreover, to create a platform for learning skills that can benefit the individual in different situations, both in and outside of the institution. It is important to recognize that the essence of this is not a matter of taking over other people's responsibility for their behavior. It is, above all, about taking responsibility for one's own behavior and the consequences this might have on those around us.

PROGRESSING TOWARD CHANGE BY INFLUENCING THE ESTABLISHING OPERATIONS

Moving on to Peter and Anna, we find a rather typical example of how an establishing operation is influencing the problem for which they are seeking help. In their own problem definition, they particularly point to their quarrels and that they don't talk to each other. Our analysis shows that alcohol is one of the establishing operations. When Peter has been drinking, the conditions that easily lead to an argument increase in both frequency and intensity. But an establishing operation influences several levels, and alcohol is characteristic of this. It lowers the natural threshold of behaviors that are socially undesirable. Alcohol also has the effect of alleviating the normally aversive consequences after, for example, having said something offensive or menacing. The guilty conscience isn't aroused as promptly as it would have been when sober. Notice, however, that Peter doesn't end up arguing with just anyone when he is drunk. The antecedents of the problematic behavior are always present in relation to Anna.

At this point, the therapist makes the assessment that it should be highly essential to influence Peter's drinking habits. This is not a way of stating what the problem "really" is. This is not a statement of whether it is found in their relationship, in his drinking habits, or in Peter's situation at work (as he offers as a reason for his heavy drinking lately). The priority rests on the assessment that drinking is a problem that may make other problems grow worse over time (centrality, long-term change) and that as long as this problem persists, the problems in the relationship, as well as any problems

Peter has in his work, will be considerably less accessible to interventions (necessary prerequisite).

Theoretically we can expect a number of effects if we are able to eliminate this establishing condition:

- A = If Peter doesn't come home drunk or doesn't stay around the house drinking on weekends and in the evenings, this means there are fewer occasions that provoke annoyance.

- B = Better command of behavior and ability to reflect on different alternatives then and there.

- C = Easier to contact natural punishers at the same moment, like feelings of remorse when having said something bad, or feelings of guilt and shame for not having kept an agreement.

Restricting the effect of alcohol has motivated the use of blocking drugs in working with alcohol addicts precisely to attain effects that we can understand from a behavioral viewpoint. The object is to establish a negative reinforcer for staying sober and to provide conditions for alternative behavior in the presence of this soberness. But there are other reasons to change the circumstances of Peter's drinking habits as well.

> Peter tells us that he has been called to a "health issues talk" at the company health service, since he has had repeated short-term sick leaves. These have usually occurred after weekends, and he hasn't managed to keep them within the flextime balance. He brings this up with the therapist, who encourages him to bring up his work situation, so that they, jointly with his employer, can look over his fluctuating workload. The therapist also brings up that Peter should think about sharing that drinking has become a problem—a problem that he is now trying to deal with. Peter is very hesitant, as he is worried about what they'll say. He knows that they value him at work.

What would happen if Peter stated that drinking has become a problem that he intends to do something about? Those who have held a dinner where one of the guests has told you in advance that he is a "sober alcoholic" know that this affects the way you act toward this person. It establishes a new context around drinking. If you are the sober alcoholic, the number of times you are offered alcohol is fewer. Nonalcoholic drinks will be served without you having to ask specifically for an alternative. The responses from those around you will most likely change from puzzled or coaxing to signs of respect. If you were to drink, it would probably attract attention in a negative way. There probably won't be any encouraging and affirmative responses to something like "Well, I guess a nip wouldn't hurt!" as is common otherwise. A new context has been established around drinking.

If Peter were to share with his colleagues at work his efforts to cope with his drinking problem, it would be likely to influence their reactions to some of his behaviors:

drinking mineral water at Friday's after-work beer party, not taking part in their wine lottery, and saying "no thanks" when invited to go barhopping with his buddies.

Do Less or Do More?

A good and fulfilling relationship cannot be defined as the absence of quarrels. If that were true, it would mean that the dead, too, could have good relationships. They're not likely to be quarreling. Furthermore, the instruction "fight less" doesn't really tell Peter and Anna much about how they can manage this. It is probably more fruitful to try to increase a low-frequency behavior—something that is in line with what they hope to attain. Therefore, they are assigned the task of doing something together the day after the therapy session. The result is discussed in the following therapy session:

Therapist: So how did things work out last Friday? What did you do?

Peter: We went bowling! All three of us.

Anna: Mmmhmm.

Therapist: That was a good idea! How did you decide on that?

Peter: I guess that was the only thing we thought of. We used to do that sometimes earlier, before Lisa was born.

Therapist: So how was it?

Peter: Well, it was okay, I guess. It's kind of weird to do it like this. It's like it's phony.

Anna: You know, it's like we're watching each other a bit. So it's not really spontaneous.

The therapist notes a common tendency in their behavior: to turn what happens into a problem. This is a verbal behavior that lessens their contact with rewarding consequences that occur in the moment. The therapist tries to establish contact with natural reinforcers instead:

Therapist: Tell me more! What went well that evening?

Peter: Lisa had lots of fun; she was really having a ball. And she still talks about it every day.

Anna: Yeah, and that was worth a lot, right there (*starts to cry*). She hasn't had a lot of these times, when the three of us do something together.

Peter: (*swallows, tears in his eyes*) No ... there hasn't been much of that.

Therapist: It must have been great to see her that happy.

Peter:　　　　Mmmhmm …

The therapist makes the assessment that the two of them are in touch with an important reinforcer. They are emotionally touched in a positive way by what they've experienced together. This is an essential reinforcer that they have had a hard time contacting for a long time.

It's important to see this behavior as valuable in its own right. If we view Peter's and Anna's activities only as a way of reaching long-term goals (turning their relationship into a good one), we can easily lose focus on the reinforcing experience in itself. To always be assessing whether "it will be better if I do this" is a verbal behavior that weakens contact with the reinforcer in the experience. Instead we want the frequency of these events to increase, since they are valuable in themselves. They also define a good relationship per se.

It's common to hear people say it feels staged, when you work to change specific behaviors. The client as well as the therapist can sometimes take this to mean it isn't very good. And, yes, it is staged, in a way, when you go to a therapist and discuss what activities define a well-functioning family relationship and in addition to that account for performances the following week. It seems like this is exactly the type of staged situation that this couple needs, considering that their ad hoc solutions don't carry them forward anymore.

Therapist:　　It looks like you'll just want to think of more things to do together.

Anna:　　　　We have already talked about going to a spa.

Peter:　　　　They have family hours on the weekends—that's what I heard at work.

Solving Problems

Most people who seek psychological help do so because they want help in solving problems. From a behavioral point of view, the act of problem solving is precisely what is essential (Nezu, Nezu, & Lombardo, 2003). Next, Peter and Anna are encouraged to pin down things that frequently turn into problems in their relationship:

Anna:　　　　I never know what time Peter is going to get back from work in the evenings, so I'm totally tied down. Last Wednesday I missed my workout at the gym because Peter didn't get home until after eight o'clock. That happens all the time.

Peter:　　　　That's how it is; you have to work overtime now and then. It's the same for everyone. That's a part of working there.

Anna:　　　　I know, but it makes your work seem so much more important than we are.

Peter:	What do you mean? Do you want me to stop working? What about the house? We couldn't have afforded it if I had stayed at my last job. But I hardly ever see you two, because you just take Lisa along to your sister's house as soon as the weekend comes. And if we've had a fight, you're off to her place in a flash …
Anna:	Yeah, I don't want Lisa to have to be around the lousy atmosphere then. But it's like you don't want me to spend time with my sister, like we're not supposed to be in touch …
Peter:	Yeah, but sometimes you just get hung up on something I say, and the next thing I know, you'll be in the hall, ready to leave …

The discussion that takes place before the therapist is probably rather typical of what it sounds like in their relationship. It has a few characteristics: they are dealing with several problems at the same time, they speak in terms of generalized issues, and they focus on finding out whose fault it is. Furthermore, the discussion doesn't seem to lead to a solution to any of their everyday problems.

You start by defining what the problems are. This should be done as specifically as possible, as we see here:

Therapist:	Just to be clear on what problems we are discussing—I understand that you, Anna, get tied down because you don't know what time Peter is going to be home in the evening. Am I right?
Anna:	Yes.
Therapist:	So it's not about whether Peter should be working where he is or not?
Anna:	No, not if we can solve it.
Therapist:	And you, Peter, have brought up the problem that you don't see each other during the weekends since Anna often goes to visit her sister.
Peter:	Yes, that's the time of the week when I could spend more time with Lisa.
Therapist:	So it's not about whether Anna should be in touch with her sister?
Peter:	No, it's fine with me that they spend time with each other.
Therapist:	Good! Just so we all agree what problems we are discussing right now.

The therapist goes on to encourage both of them respectively to look for any opportunities they have to change their own behavior. Attempts to exert control over the other person's behavior evoke aversion per se. It constitutes a stimulus for *counter-control*, that is, behaviors that oppose the other person's attempts to exert control. These behaviors, in turn, easily turn into an antecedent for the other person to try to increase control. This spiral is often devastating in relationships.

Therapist: Okay, Peter, what do you think you could do to make Anna less tied down in the evenings?

Peter: Well, I think that may be resolved now that we're going to have this talk about my situation at work.

Therapist: That's one alternative—to discuss it with your manager. Are there any more?

Peter: I can't quit work, can I?

Therapist: Theoretically you could, and that would solve this problem too. But that's probably not a good option since it would lead to a lot of other consequences. But let's put that down on the list.

Anna: You could at least call and let me know that you're going to be late. Then I wouldn't have to do all this waiting.

Peter: I could devote one night a week to working late in order to get some work off my hands when things are piling up.

Therapist: We're beginning to see different alternatives. Would you be able to just say you have to leave if you knew Anna had something that evening?

Peter: Don't know what they'd say, but in theory I could. Sure I could.

This is another aspect of problem-solving skills: producing different options and not immediately getting hung up on one single alternative—and not constantly criticizing suggestions, as so often happens when they seem like attempts to exert control. Here you want them to be brought to the table more openly. The therapist can likewise produce poor options (like quitting work) in order to show that these too are alternatives that can be evaluated in terms of pros and cons. Not until a number of alternatives are produced do you start to evaluate them in order to decide which you want to stick to. Then you go on to the second problem: the fact that Anna goes off to her sister's, taking Lisa along. This results in two things: first, leaving has begun to function as escape behavior, and second, Peter's time with Lisa is minimized.

Keep in mind that learning to solve problems is not only important in order to solve the specific problem of the day. What is important is to help Anna and Peter to practice and develop mutual problem-solving skills that work well for these types of problems in their everyday life. In other words, it is the behavior we want to develop. That's why this procedure is repeated over and over. It is used on new problems during the therapy session, and simultaneously more work is gradually left for the couple themselves to do on their own.

USING CONTRACTS TO CHANGE THE CONTEXT

In the Jenny case example, we have described how in institutions it can be useful to make certain consequences accompany certain behaviors in a well-considered way, and that this should be based on mutual agreement. The same thing works in many other therapeutic settings. You draw up a behavioral contract.

Let's take a closer look at Peter and Anna's conflict. Peter is disappointed that his work is always questioned, and he thinks he deserves some recognition for giving the family financial security instead of having to hear that he's never home on time. Anna's free time is curtailed, and her evenings are padlocked. When Anna lays claim to Peter's time, he acts on this as an attempt to exert control over his behavior—an aversive stimulus to him. He can escape this by avoiding giving straight answers and by "taking things as they come." The result of these behaviors is that their mutual relationship is weakened.

Anna goes over to her sister's place when there has been an argument. Consequently this doesn't only have the function of maintaining a relationship with her sister. It is also an escape from Peter and an avoidance of situations that could lead to clashes. The result of these behaviors is that their mutual relationship is weakened.

Notice how both Peter and Anna are acting from a desire to see their relationship grow stronger. This is an example of when ad hoc solutions don't work. Intuitive solutions to problems within intimate relationships often include a condition: first the other person has to change and then you'll be ready to change your own behavior. And in intricate contingencies of control and counter-control, the relationship just gets more problematic.

A *behavioral contract* is based on four general conditions (Houmanfar, Maglieri, & Roman, 2003):

1. It contains a clear agreement on goals.

2. It makes sure that all involved can access and follow the process toward these goals as well as evaluate success.

3. It describes what is required of those who are embraced by it.

4. When the contract is drawn up, it needs to be clear that all those involved are to be active in how it is formulated.

One way of making sure all are participating in an active way is making a written contract that is signed by each of those involved. It can also be agreed on verbally, but it has to be plain and clear. A nod in agreement to someone's suggestion is not sufficient. Any situation like this is very susceptible to control–counter-control, and that is what you want to get past by establishing mutual responsibilities in the way the contract is drawn up (see fig. 12.2).

Figure 12.2 Behavioral Contract: Anna and Peter

Contract

Goals

- To take greater mutual responsibility for familial concerns
- To be better at resolving the controversies that come up between us

Short-Term Goals

- Anna will be able to attend exercise class or some other regular activity in the evening during the week
- Peter will be able to spend more time with Lisa as well as with Anna on the weekends

Peter will:

- Discuss with his employer how his irregular and unpredictable office hours are incompatible with a well-functioning family life
- At least once a week, on a day agreed upon in advance, be home no later than 6:00 p.m.
- Call or in some other way leave a message specifying when he is likely to be home in case of having to do unexpected overtime at work

Anna will:

- Give notice at least one day ahead if she is going to visit her sister when this coincides with Peter's free time
- Remain at home if there's been a quarrel and she hasn't planned in advance to visit her sister and given her sister notice of these plans

We will:

- Sit down once a week and go over the upcoming week's schedule and plan ahead in order to increase the likelihood that these stated goals will be achieved

---

We can think of the contract as a pedagogically clear way of trying to change a context that is dissatisfying for those involved and where ad hoc solutions aren't leading to any change. It contains some of the basic mechanisms that we assume are central to psychotherapy as well. A verbally constructed stimulus—"Our relationship as we would like it to be"—is the starting point for behavioral change that aims to contact precisely these desirable consequences.

So, is it going to work? The answer to that question can only be "We don't know!" The crucial issue is being ready to try it. We are seeking to attain flexibility and variation in the behavior, and so, by trial and error, find something workable. What we can't do, however, is prescribe a number of predefined behaviors with a function warranty!

We have described principles for two strategies toward change that have this in common: we try to change C in a direct way, in order to influence a behavior that has undesirable consequences. We try to influence the behavioral repertoire (B) so it will open up contact with a wider field of consequences. The measures taken have been clearly focused on factors that are external to the individual. In the next chapter, we will continue illustrating learning principles applied in therapy in the setting where a therapist and a single client meet for scheduled appointments in the way we assume most people associate with the word "psychotherapy."

CHAPTER 13

Principles of Treatment: Two

To understand the conditions of psychotherapeutic interventions, it is vital to return to what we have said earlier about "the two arenas." The therapist is only in touch with the client during a very small part of his or her daily life, and only has very limited access to the actual contingencies that govern the client's behavior. Forty-five minutes of therapy per week means there are 10,035 minutes of "remaining time"! It is in this remaining time that changes need to take place, and the work that client and therapist perform during sessions is meant to help the client to achieve these changes. This is help to self-help! As therapists, the only thing we can influence directly is the context, the situation present while we and the client meet.

GENERALIZATION: THE ALPHA AND OMEGA OF THERAPY

The fact that the client makes changes while the therapist is present is, quite obviously, not an adequate goal for therapy. Therapy can be said to be successful when a new behavior is generalized to life outside therapy sessions in "the other arena." How is this brought about? It can only take place if life out there contains consequences that, if the client were to contact these, could govern new behavior. This is why the therapist, when seeing the client, should reinforce behaviors that would put the client in touch with naturally occurring reinforcement if the client were to act in similar ways in every-day life. Of course, the client's daily context can be different in many respects. It is a prerequisite for psychotherapy, however, that the client's context does, in fact, contain potential natural reinforcers. Psychotherapy, too, has its limits, and cannot solve all problems. The fact that psychotherapy often can contribute constructively to problem solving shows us that in most cases there are naturally occurring reinforcers available. As we like to say, reality is the therapist's best friend.

At the same time, it is precisely in this process of contacting naturally occurring reinforcement contingencies that our capability for relational framing can cause problems for us as humans. Let's take Leonard as an example. If he were to give up his isolation, it would be possible for naturally occurring reinforcers to govern more well-functioning actions. And yet his verbal behavior could thwart this effect in different ways. He could, despite having had these new experiences, keep his main focus on "how things were" or "how things should have been." There is a risk that, through relational framing, he changes the function of the actual consequences so that they no longer govern well-functioning actions, even if he were to go out and see other people.

USING THERAPEUTIC INTERACTION

There is an important interpersonal element present in many cases where people seek psychological help for their problems. In problems with relationships, for instance, this element can be clearly defined as difficulties in establishing intimacy with others or issues of aggressiveness. But the interpersonal element is also often involved in cases where it is not, at least at the beginning of therapy, the focus of attention. Clients seeking help for other specific problems often find they also have problems in how they interact with people. This is hardly surprising as human beings are essentially group beings. If this is a core issue, it would also seem evident that these behaviors can be triggered in the relationship with the therapist. This likewise makes them available for therapeutic work. This approach has traditionally had little influence on behavioral therapy, but from our perspective it unquestionably has an important place here, especially if we hope to understand the operant aspects of psychotherapy as a learning situation.

If, for example, Leonard has difficulties in maintaining his own opinion when someone significant has a different view, then it is possible that this problem will be triggered in his dialogue with the therapist. The way the therapist acts on these occasions can either reinforce Leonard's problematic behavior (to fall silent, to think "no use trying"), or it can reinforce different, better functioning behavior.

If you find yourself in a similar situation and catch something in the interaction that is relevant to the client's problem, simply try to perform an ABC analysis of the client's actions in the matter. Use these questions to guide your analysis:

- What is the client doing (B)? Looking down, becoming silent? Starting to talk about something else in a way that interrupts the dialogue?

- Under what circumstances does this behavior occur (A)? When you bring up something in particular? When you disagree? When you switch topics?

- What are the consequences (C)? Does it make you more unyielding? Is there a weakened sense of alliance in the dialogue?

The first step for making use of what happens in the dialogue is to discriminate that something significant is taking place. You, the therapist, can do this within yourself, but it is also possible to invite the client to take part in making an analysis, as we see here:

Therapist: Are you sure this is what she meant?

Leonard: (*breaking eye contact, looking down, taking a deep breath*) No … maybe she didn't. I guess that's just the way I interpreted it. I can't even talk about something as simple as that … I keep getting it wrong.

Therapist: (*who finds something important is taking place*) Mmmhmm … tell me … just now, when you told me what Tina said and I asked if you were sure that's what she meant, how did you feel about that?

Leonard: (*looks up, hesitant*) How do you mean that?

Therapist: Well, I mean, I kind of disagreed with you somehow, and I was wondering how that made you feel.

There are actually two types of behavior that the therapist needs to practice observing: first, the problematic behavior, and, second, any alternative behavior that might occur. Apart from perhaps leading to a dialogue about how the client acts, under what conditions he does this, and what the consequences are, something new or different may be brought into the dialogue itself. The therapist's actions offer new consequences that, first of all, interrupt a problematic behavior, and then, second, can make the client try a new way of behaving, like (in this case with Leonard) making his opinion known. Here are two important guidelines for the therapist:

1. Reinforce what you perceive as an alternative, desirable behavior—the kind of behavior that is in line with the defined goals of this therapeutic work. It is important to offer reinforcement in an unconstrained and natural way. In order for the behavior to be generalized to situations outside the therapy setting, it is fundamental to give the type of reinforcement that you would expect to find in ordinary life. Responding to the client's self-assertion by saying something like "I'm glad you're really raising your voice and disagreeing!" probably isn't very fruitful. That's hardly something the client will hear from colleagues at work or from his partner. The fact that the therapist actually listens and reflects on what he is saying is a more natural way of giving reinforcement. It is vital for us as therapists to practice and develop our ability to discriminate our own behavior as well as to see what is actually functioning as reinforcement of desirable behavior in the dialogue. We need to do this with regard to the client in question and so make use of it in working with this specific person.

2. Discriminate behavior on your own part that has a punishing function to the client, and try to refrain from this. It is important to understand that punishing functions are not restricted to situations where we show our dissatisfaction, irritation, or the like. They could just as well involve, for example, turning obstinate, withdrawing, or questioning the client's motives. Interventions that function as openings to discrimination skills training for one client can have a punishing function for another. An analysis must always be made for the individual person, and relationship-oriented interventions should never be performed in a stereotypical way.

SELF-OBSERVATION AS A GENERAL SKILL

In working toward change, we as therapists can also reinforce skills of general significance within the framework of therapy sessions. One such important skill is self-observation.

In the therapy model we have outlined, this partly takes place automatically. The kind of observation tasks we engage in when studying behavior—for example, behavior tests and registration assignments—are not just a way of collecting data. They are potential methods of consistently practicing self-observation. When we invite clients to take part in performing an ABC analysis, this presupposes that the clients are observing their actions and reactions during therapy as well as on their own in between sessions. We therapists are continually taking different actions to reinforce this. We ask for the clients' observations and repeatedly emphasize their role as a "firsthand witness." Interest of this kind in what clients can observe probably does not correspond to life outside therapy sessions. Instead the naturally occurring reinforcers we depend on for generalization here are different consequences, for example, when clients discover new options, manage to do things that work out better, or experience changes in affect.

EXPOSURE

At this point, we are stepping inside behavioral therapy's "golden grounds." No other principle of therapy has such strong empirical support as exposure does (Barlow, 2002). Neither has any other therapeutic principle been found useful in as many different areas.

Exposure is most readily described from work with specific phobias, for example, spider phobia: it involves making the client gradually approach what provokes anxiety or other conditions of negative affect, and to remain there long enough for extinction to take place. The client's strategy up until this point has been to take action(s) that will reduce or fully steer him or her away from anxiety each time it is awakened. This way a natural extinction process cannot take place. Notice how behavior that is governed by consequences (operant) plays a crucial role here. Avoidance is maintained by negative reinforcement, since it leads to reduced anxiety. Exposure entails breaking off avoidance behavior and approaching what provokes the negative affect (for example, a spider) in a way that allows for an extinction process to take place. This makes behavioral relearning possible, a process that makes anxiety subside. Another classic example is treatment of obsessive-compulsive disorders. In a certain context (such as finishing washing hands after a visit to the bathroom), anxiety is provoked and the client does something that (at least temporarily) reduces it (repeats the hand wash). In this case, exposure means the client is made to expose him- or herself to this very context and this time to refrain from performing the anxiety-reducing measure; this is called *exposure with response prevention*.

But exposure is a therapeutic principle that has a much broader area of application than these classic examples. Take, for example, Alice and her tendency to constantly worry. It can be illuminating to discern between "worrying thoughts" (for example, something might happen to her fiancé or there's something wrong with her heart) and what she does to relieve them or to "calm down." Having the courage to let these thoughts exist (although they provoke anxiety) and not give in to "comforting reasoning," such as assuring herself that nothing has happened to Bob or that her heart is alright because the doctor said so, involves exposure both to the thoughts per se and to the affective components they arouse. To refrain from "calming down" (response prevention) means there is an opportunity of extinction on one hand and of contacting new consequences that enlarge the behavioral repertoire (*response extension*) on the other.

The What and How of Exposure

All exposure should be preceded by an ABC analysis, where B is the behavior that is seen as avoidance. You are to expose the client to relevant elements of A. What, then, are these?

In cases of specific phobias, the answer is often simple enough. A spider phobic will be exposed to spiders, and an acrophobic to heights. When taking a closer look, however, we find that relevant elements of A are often affects and other internal conditions. Let us consider a woman troubled by panic attacks. The circumstances where the client experiences panic and resorts to diverting maneuvers usually have some similarities—crowds, waiting in line, movie theaters. But off and on, the same client also has a problem with being alone. Of course, you could say that the client should be exposed to all of these kinds of situations. Yet these varying situations often have an element in common, namely, different phenomena such as affects and physical sensations. The awareness that these are often fundamental in the contexts to which the client is to be exposed has led to the concept of *interoceptive exposure* (Barlow, 2002). This means that a client might be exposed to physical phenomena that she is afraid of (for example, dizziness and feelings of unreality), or to thoughts that she tries to avoid because they make her feel uneasy. In any case, it is essential to be able to make clear precisely what is relevant for each person individually, based on the analysis. You can then determine what kind of context needs to be established in order to perform exposure in the most favorable way.

Exposure can take place as a part of the client's everyday life situation, as when a client with social anxiety chooses to share something in front of a group of people at work. Many times, however, it is necessary to arrange a situation together with the therapist, as when a spider phobic gets to handle a spider that the therapist has brought to the session. A good rule of thumb is to make the exposure process gradual, prolonged, and repeated. There are a number of different ways of doing this. Let's return to Alice's situation:

> *Alice and her therapist have agreed that the most common difficulty in her everyday life is her fear of and avoidance of doing things on her own. This is one part of her difficulties as a whole where the therapist believes that therapy has a particularly good chance of being successful.*

To begin this process, the therapist may use a list of several of the situations that Alice avoids. In order to make a strategy for the exposure procedure, these are arranged progressively (with input from Alice), beginning with the situations connected with the least fear and ending with those connected with the most. In doing this, Alice and her therapist have sketched a fear and avoidance hierarchy (see fig. 13.1).

Figure 13.1 Fear and Avoidance Hierarchy: Alice

100	*Take the train to another city*
95	*Take the bus to another city*
85	*Go by car with someone I don't know*
80	*Walk in places where I don't see anyone living*
70	*Take the bus for a shorter ride*
65	*Take a cab*
55	*Go to the shopping mall*
45	*Walk all the way to work*
40	*Stand in line at the shopping mall*
35	*Shop in any larger store*

Exposure can then be pursued with the therapist's assistance, or by way of homework assignments that Alice is to do on her own, or by a combination of both. Whatever the case, thorough work with home assignments is the be-all and end-all of accomplishing generalization. To make the fear extinction possible, several conditions need to be met:

First of all, there must be enough time to stay in the situation for fear to begin to wane naturally and not as a result of escape. Second, the procedure needs to be repeated within a short time. In Alice's case, she would have to practice this several days a week. Third, another important aspect is having exposure performed in a sufficient number of different situations that are relevant to Alice's problem. This is because extinction is not necessarily generalized across different contexts in the same simple way that fear is when originally learned; consequently, the process of extinction is frequently referred to as *context-bound* (Bouton & Nelson, 1998).

Exposure—Not Just Extinction

Exposure is also a therapeutic principle that displays how the three principles of behavioral learning work together, even in therapy. In exposure, we make use of extinction, a natural process connected with respondent conditioning. At the same time, working with exposure is connected with operant conditioning, since it is intended to interrupt a behavior that is governed by its consequences, namely avoidance. To illustrate this, let us return to Jenny and the fact that she cuts her wrists.

It is obvious that cutting oneself in this way has negative consequences. This is something Jenny experiences on a daily basis. The consequences torment her in different ways. She sees the connection between her cutting herself and the undesirable pain, but, as Jenny puts it, "I just don't know what to do." What consequences are maintaining her acts of cutting herself, a behavior that persists despite the fact that Jenny clearly sees and experiences those negative consequences? The reasons may be of several different natures, but let's look at one possibility. In certain situations, Jenny has a strong feeling of despair. She feels as if she is "going to fall apart." That's when she cuts herself, which gives her a distraction in relation to her despair. This occurs through negative reinforcement (the feeling of despair is reduced), and positive reinforcement (other people care and get involved) may also play a role.

Now let's take a look at feasible therapy interventions. We have already noted how the care staff around her should tune their approach so that it minimizes reinforcement of the self-destructive behavior while increasing reinforcement of alternative behaviors.

Exposure will also play an important role in Jenny's individual therapy. Jenny's avoidance of "the feeling of despair" seems to be central to her problem of cutting herself. She cuts herself (B) under the condition of "feeling despair" (A), and the result is less negative affect (C), at least for the time being.

If Jenny can be persuaded to refrain from cutting herself, she would inevitably be confronted with her negative affect, and the different thoughts, sensations, and perhaps flashbacks associated with it. If her ability to contain the affect grows stronger, her cutting herself would decrease, provided our analysis is correct. If she could be made to step closer to "her feelings of despair," much like someone whose negative affect is provoked by the presence of a spider does, then a respondent extinction could take place. The feeling would no longer be the same. Note that if this were to happen, more things would take place than what we associate with respondent conditioning. Remaining with her feelings of despair rather than avoiding them by cutting herself is an operant behavior, as we know. What would the consequences be? Well, they would at least be different from those that follow if she cuts herself. Jenny would contact new consequences, and new behaviors would emerge. The therapist can coach Jenny in alternative behaviors, like noticing what is happening, using alternative diverting actions, or endeavoring to reach what is important to her. Notice that exposure in this case has a clearly operant side. What we are seeking to attain is not just extinction through response prevention but also by response extension, which, as we mentioned above, means contacting new consequences that enlarge the behavioral repertoire. Jenny would be put in contact with a new context that in turn would govern new behaviors. This would be a new context to her, since earlier she had always done something (cut herself) that she now refrains from doing.

Relational framing, too, is of great significance in this process. The feelings of despair that Jenny shields herself from are not just affect, physical sensations, and flashbacks. All of these are there and play an important part. But another essential element is what Jenny makes of all of this, revealed in a comment such as "I can't cope, I'm going crazy." Exposure will change this. Maybe Jenny will be able to move from seeing her feelings of despair as "what makes me fall apart" to "something I can handle."

Trauma Processing

Another example of exposure to personal events is the work that needs to be done together with Mirza. A number of everyday occurrences—like seeing a police car downtown, a TV episode that shows a person who is hurt, or hearing someone mention Bosnia—provoke anxiety, nausea, painful memories, and physical discomfort. He has, over time, gotten used to trying to act so that these won't be aroused. For a while, he can lessen his pain this way. However, besides not working very well in the long run, the price he pays is high. His life is greatly restricted. Working with exposure here has two sides: First, Mirza is encouraged to actually expose himself in his daily life to what frightens him, and, second, the therapist uses staged opportunities of exposure. The latter can involve asking Mirza to close his eyes and picture the things he has been avoiding, such as a specific recollection. Remaining in what provokes anxiety increases possibilities of extinction, and expanding the behavioral repertoire enhances Mirza's chances of facing new consequences.

Therapist:	What are you picturing?
Mirza:	(*anguished*) I see a car, and a pair of legs sticking out at the side.
Therapist:	Could you take a couple of steps forward and see if you can see anything else? You can step forward slowly …

Mirza:	(tense) I see the rest of the body ... it's terrible ... just blood all over. How could they do something like this? (crying) How can anyone do something like this ... ?
Therapist:	Yes, it's like ... it's something you just can't grasp. Can you stay there and just keep gazing at what you see?
Mirza:	It's so awful ...
Therapist:	(who is trying to expand Mirza's repertoire in relation to his inner experience) I'm asking you now to stay where you are, but for a short while take a look around in the picture you're seeing. Can you see what clothes the person lying there is wearing? Are there any other people around that you can see? Can you see the color of the car?
Mirza:	I can't see his clothes ... oh, yes ... I can see that he is wearing a pair of brown boots. I've never thought about that before. The car is blue; it's some kind of van.
Therapist:	Can you see what the weather is like?
Mirza:	Yes, the sun is shining. It's cold. It's strange that I remember it this clearly.
Therapist:	See if you can take another brief look at the man lying on the ground.

Notice that the dialogue is carried out in the present tense; the client is encouraged to "be there now." A different approach is to ask the client to leave the specific recollection and focus on his own physical sensations in the present so that he can register himself "in the here and now," and then in different ways allow him to describe the physical phenomena from different angles. It is important to understand that the point is not to endure the pain but to be able to observe and handle the feelings and recollections that crop up in a more flexible way. That's why Mirza is encouraged to take a look around rather than to keep staring at what frightens him.

BEHAVIORAL ACTIVATION

If exposure is the therapy associated with conditions of anxiety, then behavioral activation has the corresponding position in connection with depression (Martell et al., 2001). Depression is a state of withdrawal and passivity. This means that many mechanisms of reinforcement that normally govern a person's life are not functioning. By persuading a client to be more active, possible consequences that would be rewarding to the individual may regain their function.

In many ways, activation is the same process as exposure. Passivity isn't really "not doing anything." Being passive is a behavior. Let's return to Leonard when he withdraws instead of going out with his colleagues from work.

Leonard had agreed with his colleagues to get together one evening. Just before leaving home, he is reminded of the fact that he no longer lives with the rest of his family. He thinks that talking with his colleagues during the evening will probably stir up the pain he feels around that. They usually end up talking about how the kids have grown and what they're doing, so Leonard stays at home. The ABC analysis concludes that when Leonard thinks of what could happen during the get-together that evening (A), he chooses to do without this social contact (B). The short-term consequence is that he doesn't have to think about "what might have made him feel bad during the evening" (C). This behavior has other very obvious results, however, like increased loneliness and isolation.

Activation means breaking these types of vicious circles. Doing so is based on the conviction that reality is the therapist's best friend. If Leonard could be made to seek more social contact, then he would contact consequences that govern better functioning actions. We are talking about an operant process here. But note that here, too, is a clear element of exposure. If Leonard, in a new similar situation, would choose to join the get-together with his colleagues, the same kinds of thoughts and feelings might arise. His willingness to expose himself to this is an important part of a new behavior. And here, too, one can expect his feelings of grief and dejection to change as he exposes himself to these thoughts and feelings.

It's important not to use activation haphazardly but instead to connect it with things that are essential to the client; this is similar to what we said earlier about the importance of connecting goals for therapy to what the client values in life. Going out to see his colleagues from work just because he'll "have something to do" is nowhere as positive for Leonard as doing it because he enjoys his colleagues and spending social time with them is a part of the life he wants to be living.

CHANGING THE CONTENT OF THOUGHTS

We have emphasized throughout our discussion that relational framing is a very flexible behavioral principle that can rapidly change the function of what we encounter. It therefore seems reasonable that working directly with this principle is important in psychological therapies. If, in addition, the very way we interrelate things has the side effect of easily making us insensitive to actual contingencies, then there are strong reasons to work on changing this. Studies show, however, that attempts to disconnect already established relations are rarely fruitful (Wilson & Hayes, 1996). Relational responses do not change by subtraction but by addition. The task is to help the client to think in new ways, not to abolish old ways of thinking. We cannot erase experience. What we can do, though, is develop our way of thinking, just as we can develop other things we do.

One generalized reinforcer of great importance in this work is experiencing coherence. By *coherence*, we're referring to the fact that at an early age we are taught that things should make sense and add up. It's easy to illustrate how important this is: If you first announce that you are a teetotaler and shortly thereafter tell people about a fine-tasting whiskey you tried last weekend, people will be perplexed and are likely to say, "That doesn't make sense!" We humans want coherence, so it should add up. If someone points out the incoherence in your comments, there's a fair chance that you—a whiskey-sampling teetotaler—will say something else so that it will add up. You try to explain that, just for this past weekend, you weren't a teetotaler. But that still doesn't make sense. Or you may try to explain that, except for when specifically offered some fine whiskey, you really are a teetotaler. But that doesn't add up either—and it should. This isn't just for the sake of appearances with regard to what others will think. If something doesn't add up, we try to make it add up, even if only inside ourselves. The generalized reinforcer of experiencing coherence is established early on in our language training.

Our need for coherence means that questioning existing verbal constructions (thoughts) and how they square with other verbal constructions and other phenomena is a powerful way of helping people think in new ways. Let's go back to Jenny and a dialogue she has with her therapist about something that happened in relation to Larry, a friend of hers:

Jenny: Larry promised to be there, and then he just didn't bother to come! It's always the same! Nobody cares, regardless. I might as well end it all.

Therapist: Yes, it must be difficult to be let down in that way ... but is it really true that no one cares?

Jenny: Yes, he said he would be there ... !

Therapist: Well, it does seem like Larry didn't care enough to be there. But I was thinking, for instance, of what you told me about Lisa calling yesterday. How does that add up with saying nobody cares?

Jenny: Okay, I see what you're saying. I guess even if Larry doesn't care there are others who do.

Different types of educative components in psychotherapy, too, are based on this therapeutic principle. Information on what happens in your body when you're frightened can, for example, be important when talking to a client like Alice. This may make her think differently about her palpitations, and that in turn can help to make her stop her dysfunctional behavioral pattern.

Alice: It's a darned nasty feeling when my heart beats that hard and irregularly. It makes me afraid of going out all alone. I feel like there must be something wrong.

Therapist:	You describe how you feel this way when you're at the breakfast table and getting ready to leave. Do you remember what we said about anxiety? How does that affect the heart?
Alice:	Well, that can make it beat hard too—that's something you know from when you feel nervous …
Therapist:	How about heart disease—when do you notice this most?
Alice:	Well, it's supposed to be worse when you're exhausting yourself. I read that when I looked it up in a medical handbook. Bob's dad had some kind of a heart condition, you know. It acted up when he did something stressful.
Therapist:	How do you feel when you do something that's stressful? Does it get any worse?
Alice:	Well, I usually avoid doing things when I feel that way, but sometimes the pounding has actually gotten better when I take off on a walk—and I do walk quite fast then!
Therapist:	So your experience tells you some important things here, concerning your thoughts when you worry about having a problem with your heart. You're troubled by palpitations when you're inactive, and it gets better when you're active. That's often the case with anxiety. In connection with heart disease, it's usually the other way around.

CHANGING THE FUNCTION OF THOUGHTS

In the chapter on relational framing, we stressed that the power of thoughts is dependent on being related to something else, and a thought gets its function from what it is related to. The thought that we're leaving for a vacation on the Mediterranean Sea holds some of the stimulus functions that actually being on the Mediterranean entails, like seeing the sea in front of us. This means that it can be very useful to act based on one's thoughts in order to, for instance, achieve certain desirable consequences. But it also means that we easily get caught in "the illusion of language." This means that we don't see that thoughts are what they are in themselves—that is, a type of internal response—but instead we take them to be "what they pose as" and act as if they actually were that even when this leads to consequences we do not desire. We have previously referred to this as "cognitive fusion."

Let's look at how this operates in Marie's life. For many years now, Marie has been increasingly dominated by her feelings of anxiety and shame. In many different situations, she totally focuses on avoiding other people's attention so that they won't notice her uneasiness. When going over a sociophobic situation, Marie again describes how she feels about this, and how she struggles to rid herself of these feelings:

Marie: *(desperate)* It's so unfair. It's not natural! Becoming nervous and turning flaming red just because someone looks at you. What will people think? It's like I can't think of anything else. All that's in my head is I have to get away, just get away … I can't live with this …

If the therapist were to work to change the contents in the inner dialogue Marie describes, he might question parts of it. How much do people look at Marie? Will people really think badly of her? A problem with this approach is that it just serves to further strengthen the control that verbal responses have on Marie's actions. In one way, this is the agenda she already has—control of internal events, like what she thinks and feels. A different strategy would be to leave the contents of these responses aside, and instead focus on the precise function these responses have, which could help Marie to act independently of them. This approach involves accepting painful inner experiences (Hayes, Strosahl, & Wilson, 1999). The first step toward this is to discriminate these responses precisely as what they are in themselves, that is, to see thoughts as thoughts as opposed to acting on their indirect functions, that is, functions contacted through relational framing. One way of doing this is for the therapist to point them out precisely as responses, as we see here:

Therapist: So one thing that happens is, when you're standing there, you think about what other people will think, that you have to get away, that you just can't keep coping with this.

Marie: Yes, well, that's how it is!

Therapist: Okay, so right here and now you have the thought that "that's how it is."

Marie: But that's how it is, I don't understand what you mean … You mean people don't see how nervous I am and how I'm blushing? I know they do!

Therapist: I don't mean anything concerning if the thought is correct or not. What I mean is this: true or false, what you actually have and what you notice right now is—a thought.

If Marie can be made to observe her thoughts in this way (without being absorbed by what they contain), it will be easier to explore with her what the function of these inner responses usually is, what Marie does (B) under the conditions of such a thought (A), and what the consequences (C) usually are.

Therapist: When you have a thought like that, what do you usually do?

Marie:	I always try to think of what to do.
Therapist:	What to do? What to do about what?
Marie:	About making it go away. I don't want to think and feel that way!
Therapist:	In all these years, have you found out what to do about it? What are you supposed to do in order not to think and feel that way?
Marie:	No, nothing works. I think it just keeps getting worse.
Therapist:	What if this experience is accurate, that it doesn't work to try to maneuver your feelings and thoughts in that situation? What if you were just to have that thought? Have it and let it be?
Marie:	How do you mean?
Therapist:	You know, the thought that is so painful. The thought that people see how you turn red, that you can't live with this, and so on. What if you were to just have that thought as it is in itself. As a thought! And at the same time try to find your way to something that works.

Here the therapist is working to establish a different kind of verbal context than what Marie is usually surrounded by. Like Marie, we are trained to act on thoughts based on their content. We see thoughts and feelings as instructions for our behavior and as something we should follow. An alternative context is being established here, one in which thoughts are something you can observe and then act independently of. Seeing thoughts and emotions for what they are—inner events that occur in the moment—is a way of practicing our acceptance of them and of focusing our actions on other objectives. The point of this is precisely to thereby cut off the blocking effect that verbal behaviors can have. In this way, direct contingencies ("what works") can take over.

As you can see, the dilemma of generalization is once again apparent. The kind of context that is established together with the therapist is unusual, to say the least. How can this be generalized? The answer is the same as what we pointed out in the description of self-observation above. If, in this way, the client acts independently of some of her verbal responses, her life out there will offer natural reinforcement in the shape of increased contact with things that she sees as desirable. This is a process that aims at making the person take the path she wants to take (B), rather than avoid the paths that her thoughts and feelings (A) warn her of. This opens opportunities for her to contact these new consequences (C). Thus, as we said earlier, reality is the therapist's best friend—and ultimately the client's too!

Afterword

Behavior is what the organism is doing.
—B. F. Skinner, 1938

What happens after reading this book? For verbal organisms such as we humans are, a book can control our behavior in situations far from the situation where it is read. So writing a book is about changing behavior. Our hope, of course, is that for you who have just read this book as a part of (or in preparation for) your work with clients, the book will function as an antecedent (A) for useful therapeutic work (B). We hope that you have found it—and will continue to find it—useful in several ways: useful for understanding what is happening on the therapeutic "playing field"; useful in broadening your own behavioral repertoire when you are doing psychotherapy; and useful in being of assistance to people like Jenny, Mirza, Anna, Peter, Marie, Alice, and Leonard. We hope this usefulness, for example, means that someone like Jenny stops cutting herself, is discharged from the psychiatric ward, and involves herself in relationships that are meaningful to her; that someone like Mirza wholeheartedly creates a new life in his new country and reestablishes healthy contacts with his old country, both in his mind and in reality; and that someone like Alice learns to live a life out of what she wants rather than in response to her fears. To our thinking at least, these are objectives that clients like these might have. Surely the reader, in a similar fashion, can imagine change that would be valuable for the other people we have followed throughout this book. To facilitate such change is one of the desirable consequences that motivated us to write this book.

Desirable consequences, however, are not necessarily the same as actual consequences. As we draw this writing project to a close, we're experiencing the satisfaction of accomplishment as an actual consequence. What other actual consequences will follow as you and others read this book, we do not know. We only know what has been stated before: the one who lives will get to C.

Suggested Reading

We have written a book on clinical assessment and psychotherapy. It includes guidelines for treatment—guidelines that can be developed and deepened in different ways. With that in mind, we offer this list of books, which, in our opinion, can assist in developing and deepening an understanding of the clinical and therapeutic field from a functional contextualistic perspective. Of many excellent books from the whole field of behavioral and cognitive therapies, we have chosen ones that clearly stand in the behavioral tradition from which we have written. For readers who want to deepen their knowledge of psychotherapy from this perspective, we believe you will find these books valuable.

Dougher, M. (Ed.). (2000). *Clinical Behavior Analysis*. Reno, NV: Context Press.
   This book includes several very interesting chapters on both theoretical and practical questions regarding psychotherapy from a behavioral point of view. One is an overview on the history of different directions within behavior therapy, and there are several chapters on the position of verbal behavior. One chapter includes a short but very good introduction to relational frame theory.

Hayes, S. C., & Strosahl, K. (eds.). (2004). *A Practical Guide to Acceptance and Commitment Therapy*. New York: Plenum.
   This book gives a general introduction to ACT (acceptance and commitment therapy) and then describes in different chapters how this way of working can be applied to different problems. ACT has a special interest in understanding a behavioral perspective for how to work with thoughts, feelings, and other internal phenomena.

Kohlenberg, R. J., & Tsai, M. (1991). *Functional Analytic Psychotherapy*. New York: Plenum.
   This book shows how classical learning theory can be applied when working in intense therapeutic relationships. Also presented is a behavioral perspective on phenomena that in a psychoanalytical context usually would be referred to as "transference."

Linehan, M. (1993). *Cognitive-Behavioral Treatment of Borderline Personality Disorder*. New York: Guilford Press.

This book presents dialectical behavior therapy (DBT), the most widely known of "the new behavioral therapies." It describes therapeutic techniques for a particular problem area—borderline personality disorder—but also includes much general material that is useful for a behavioral psychotherapy.

Martell, C. R., Addis, M. E., & Jacobson, N. S. (2001). *Depression in Context*. New York: Norton.

This book gives a very readable and clear presentation of a functional contextual perspective on psychological treatment. It also includes practical guidelines on how to apply this to the treatment of depression.

O'Donohue, W. (Ed.). (1998). *Learning and Behavior Therapy*. Needham Heights, MA: Allyn & Bacon.

This is a very comprehensive anthology and is recommended for anyone who has a serious interest in understanding basic experimental psychology of learning and its relevance for clinical work.

O'Donohue, W., Fisher, J. E., & Hayes, S. C. (Eds.). (2003). *Cognitive Behavior Therapy: Applying Empirically Supported Techniques in Your Practice*. New York: Wiley.

This is a "cookbook" of techniques, sixty chapters long. Each chapter presents one empirically validated therapeutic technique as well as when and how it should be applied. The book covers a wide field, from how teachers can solve problems in the classroom to treatment of complicated psychiatric syndromes.

Rachlin, H. (1991). *Introduction to Modern Behaviorism*. New York: W. H. Freeman.

This is a somewhat easier book on experimental basics than the anthology edited by O'Donohue. Nevertheless you get a good introduction to respondent and operant conditioning and also an introduction to the history of ideas that forms the background of behaviorism.

Skinner, B. F. (1974). *About Behaviorism*. New York: Knopf.

For anyone who wants to read an original text by Skinner, this is a good first choice. It gives an especially good overview of Skinner's basic position regarding the philosophy of science.

References

Arntz, A. (2002). Cognitive therapy versus interoceptive exposure as treatment of panic disorder without agoraphobia. *Behaviour Research and Therapy, 40,* 325–341.

Bandura, A. (1977). *Social learning theory.* Englewood Cliffs, NJ: Prentice-Hall.

Barlow, D. H. (2002). *Anxiety and its disorders: The nature and treatment of anxiety and panic* (2nd ed.). New York: Guilford Press.

Bouton, M. E., Mineka, S., & Barlow, D. H. (2001). A modern learning theory perspective on the etiology of panic disorder. *Psychological Review, 108,* 4–32.

Bouton, M. E., & Nelson, J. (1998). The role of context in classical conditioning: Some implications for cognitive behavior therapy. In W. O'Donohue (Ed.), *Learning and behavior therapy* (pp. 59–84). Needham Heights, MA: Allyn & Bacon.

Bower, T. G. R. (1977). *A primer of infant development.* San Francisco: W. H. Freeman.

Boyce, T. E., & Roman, H. R. (2003). Contingency management interventions. In W. O'Donohue, J. E. Fisher, & S. C. Hayes (Eds.), *Cognitive behavior therapy: Applying empirically supported techniques in your practice* (pp. 109–113). New York: Wiley.

Clarke, K. (1996). Change processes in a creation of meaning event. *Journal of Consulting and Clinical Psychology, 64,* 465–470.

Darwin, C. (1872). *The expression of the emotions in man and animals.* Chicago: University of Chicago Press. (New edition published 1965)

Ekman, P. (1992). An argument for basic emotions. *Cognition and Emotion, 6,* 169–200.

Gelso, C. J., & Hayes, J. A. (1998). *The psychotherapy relationship: Theory, research, and practice.* New York: Wiley.

Ghezzi, P. M., Wilson, G. R., Tarbox, R. S. F., & MacAleese, K. R. (2003). Token economy. In W. O'Donohue, J. E. Fisher, & S. C. Hayes (Eds.), *Cognitive behavior* therapy: Applying empirically supported techniques in your practice (pp. 436–441). New York: Wiley.

Hayes, S. C. (1981). Single case experimental design and empirical clinical practice. *Journal of Consulting and Clinical Psychology, 49,* 193–211.

Hayes, S. C. (1992). Verbal relations, time, and suicide. In S. C. Hayes & L. J. Hayes (Eds.), *Understanding verbal relations* (pp. 109–118). Reno, NV: Context Press.

Hayes, S. C. (1993). Analytic goals and the varieties of scientific contextualism. In S. C. Hayes, L. J. Hayes, H. W. Reese, & T. R. Sarbin (Eds.), *Varieties of scientific contextualism* (pp. 11–27). Reno, NV: Context Press.

Hayes, S. C., Barnes-Holmes, D., & Roche, B. (2001). *Relational frame theory: A post-Skinnerian account of human language and cognition.* New York: Plenum/Kluwer.

Hayes, S. C., Brownstein, A. J., Zettle, R. D., Rosenfarb, I., & Korn, Z. (1986). Rule-governed behavior and sensitivity to changing consequences of responding. *Journal of the Experimental Analysis of Behavior, 45,* 237–256.

Hayes, L. J., & Hayes, S. C. (Eds.). (1989). *Rule-governed behavior: Cognition, contingencies, and instructional control.* New York: Plenum Press.

Hayes, S. C., Strosahl, K., & Wilson, K. G. (1999). *Acceptance and commitment therapy: An experiential approach to behavior change.* New York: Guilford Press.

Hayes, S. C., Wilson, K. G., Gifford, E. V., Follette, V. M., & Strosahl, K. (1996). Experiential avoidance and behavioral disorders: A functional dimensional approach to diagnosis and treatment. *Journal of Consulting and Clinical Psychology, 64,* 1152–1168.

Hayes, S. C., Zettle, R. D., & Rosenfarb, I. (1989). Rule following. In L. J. Hayes & S. C. Hayes (Eds.), *Rule-governed behavior: Cognition, contingencies, and instructional control.* New York: Plenum Press.

Healy, O., Barnes-Holmes, D., & Smeets, P. M. (2000). Derived relational responding as generalized operant behavior. *Journal of the Experimental Analysis of Behavior, 74,* 207–227.

Heidt, J. M., & Marx, B. P. (2003). Self-monitoring as a treatment vehicle. In W. O'Donohue, J. E. Fisher, & S. C. Hayes (Eds.), *Cognitive behavior therapy: Applying empirically supported techniques in your practice* (pp. 40–45). New York: Wiley.

Hersen, M., & Barlow, D. H. (1976). *Single case experimental designs: Strategies for studying behavior change.* New York: Pergamon Press.

Houmanfar, R., Maglieri, K. A., & Roman, H. R. (2003). Behavioral contracting. In W. O'Donohue, J. E. Fisher, & S. C. Hayes (Eds.), *Cognitive behavior therapy: Applying empirically supported techniques in your practice* (pp. 361–367). New York: Wiley.

Kanfer, F. H., & Saslow, G. (1969). Behavioral diagnosis. In C. M. Franks (Ed.), *Behavioural therapy: Appraisal and status*. New York: McGraw-Hill.

Kazdin, A. E. (1981). Drawing valid inferences from case studies. *Journal of Consulting and Clinical Psychology, 49*, 183–192.

Korotitsch, W. J., & Nelson-Grey, R. O. (1999). An overview of self-monitoring research in assessment and treatment. *Psychological Assessment, 11*, 415–425.

LeDoux, J. (1996). *The emotional brain: The mysterious underpinnings of emotional life*. New York: Simon & Schuster.

Lieberman, R. P., DeRiel, W. J., & Meuser, K. T. (1989). *Social skills training for psychiatric patients*. New York: Pergamon Press.

Linehan, M. (1993). *Skills training manual for treating borderline personality disorder*. New York: Guilford Press.

Lipkens, R., Hayes, S. C., & Hayes, L. J. (1993). Longitudinal study of the development of derived relations in an infant. *Journal of Experimental Child Psychology, 56*, 201–239.

Martell, C. R., Addis, M. E., & Jacobson, N. S. (2001). *Depression in context*. New York: Norton.

Michael, J. (1993). Establishing operations. *The Behavior Analyst, 16*, 191–206.

Nezu, A. M., Nezu, C. M., & Lombardo, E. (2003). Problem-solving therapy. In W. O'Donohue, J. E. Fisher, & S. C. Hayes (Eds.), *Cognitive behavior therapy: Applying empirically supported techniques in your practice* (pp. 301–307). New York: Wiley.

Novak, G. (1996). *Developmental psychology: Dynamic systems and behavior analysis*. Reno, NV: Context Press.

O'Donohue, W. (1998). Conditioning and third generation behavior therapy. In W. O'Donohue (Ed.), *Learning and behavior therapy* (pp. 1–14). Needham Heights, MA: Allyn & Bacon.

Öhman, A. (1994). *Ångest, rädsla, fobi* [Anxiety, fear, phobia]. Lund, Sweden: Scandinavian University Press.

Öhman, A. (2002). Automaticity and the amygdala: Nonconscious responses to emotional faces. *Current Directions in Psychological Science, 11*, 62–66.

Öhman, A., & Mineka, S. (2003). The malicious serpent: Snakes as a prototypical stimulus for an evolved module of fear. *Current Directions in Psychological Science, 12*, 5–8.

Öst, L.-G., Thulin, U., & Ramnerö, J. (2004). Cognitive behavior therapy vs. exposure in vivo in the treatment of panic disorder with agoraphobia. *Behaviour Research and Therapy, 42,* 1105–1127.

Power, M., & Dalgleish, T. (1997). *Cognition and emotion: From order to disorder.* London: Psychology Press.

Rachlin, H. (1991). *Introduction to modern behaviorism.* New York: W. H. Freeman.

Rachlin, H., & Green, L. (1972). Commitment, choice, and self-control. *Journal of the Experimental Analysis of Behavior, 17,* 15–22.

Razran, G. (1961). The observable unconscious and the inferable conscious in current Soviet psychophysiology: Interoceptive conditioning, semantic conditioning, and the orienting reflex. *Psychological Review, 68,* 81–147.

Rescorla, R. (1988). Pavlovian conditioning: It's not what you think it is. *American Psychologist, 43,* 151–160.

Rosenberg, I. R., Hayes, S. C., & Linehan, M. M. (1989). Instructions and experiential feedback in the treatment of social skills deficits in adults. *Psychotherapy, 26,* 242–251.

Sheldon, B. (1995). *Cognitive-behavioral therapy: Research, practice, and philosophy.* London: Routledge.

Skinner, B. F. (1938). *Behavior of organisms.* New York: Appleton-Century-Crofts.

Skinner, B. F. (1945). The operational analysis of psychological events. *Psychological Review, 52,* 270-277.

Skinner, B. F. (1953). *Science and human behavior.* New York: Macmillan.

Sturmey, P. (1996). *Functional analysis in clinical psychology.* New York: Wiley.

Tomkins, S. S. (1982). Affect theory. In P. Ekman (Ed.), *Emotion in the human face* (pp. 353–395). New York: Cambridge University Press.

Tryon, G. S., & Winograd, G. (2002). Goal consensus and collaboration. In J. C. Norcross (Ed.), *Psychotherapy relationships that work* (pp. 109–125). New York: Oxford University Press.

Vander Wall, S. (1990). *Food hoarding in animals.* Chicago: University of Chicago Press.

Williams, J. M. G. (1992). *The psychological treatment of depression.* London: Routledge.

Wilson, K. G., & Hayes, S. C. (1996). Resurgence of derived stimulus relations. *Journal of the Experimental Analysis of Behavior, 66,* 267–281.

Jonas Ramnerö, Ph.D., has worked as a licensed psychologist since 1989. He earned his license as a psychotherapist in 1995. He is currently assistant professor in the Department of Psychology at Stockholm University in Stockholm, Sweden. He has extensive clinical experience, mainly in the treatment of anxiety and mood disorders, an experience that stems both from general psychiatry and private practice. Since 1998 he has served as a clinical supervisor, both for students and trained psychologists, and as a regular lecturer in clinical psychology at the university. Ramnerö earned his Ph.D in 2005 with the thesis *Behavioral Treatments of Panic Disorder with Agoraphobia: Treatment Process and Determinants of Change.*

Niklas Törneke, MD, is a psychiatrist and has worked as a senior psychiatrist in the department of general psychiatry in his hometown Kalmar (in the southeast of Sweden) from 1991 until he started private practice 1998. He earned license as a psychotherapist in 1996 and was originally trained as a cognitive therapist. Since 1998 he has worked mainly with acceptance and commitment therapy, both in his own practice and as a teacher and clinical supervisor. His clinical experience ranges from psychiatric disorders such as schizophrenia to common anxiety and mood disorders with high prevalence in the general population.

Index

29-30; evaluation of, 39-40; functional
classes of, 91-92; imitative, 87, 104-105;
influencing, 11; monitoring, 32-39;
observing, 16, 31-45; rule-governed,
106-107, 110; self-destructive, 38-39;
topographical aspects of, 15-30
behavior therapy, 1, 3
behavioral activation (BA), 3, 193-194
behavioral approach test (BAT), 37-38
behavioral contracts, 182-184
behavioral deficits, 22-27; categorizing, 25;
distinguishing from excesses, 25-26;
examples of, 22; relating to excesses, 26-27
behavioral excesses, 22-27; categorizing,
24-25; distinguishing from deficits, 25-26;
examples of, 21-22; relating to deficits,
26-27
behavioral psychotherapy, 3
behaviorism: explanation of, 5;
misconceptions about, v; origins of, 68;
overview of, 1-2
biologically prepared learning, 68-69
bodily sensations: interoceptive conditioning
and, 74-75; relational framing of, 117
books, recommended, 201-202
Boring, E. G., v

C

case examples, 6-7
causal illusions, 125
causes of behavior, 10, 124-125
centrality of behaviors, 147
change process, 145-146; clinical priority and,
147-148; content of thoughts and, 194-196;
dialog toward change and, 151-166;
establishing operations and, 176-181;
function of thoughts and, 196-198;
relational framing and, 125; triggering by
asking questions, 157-161
classical learning theory, 1-2
clients: asking questions of, 154-156, 157-161;
establishing goals with, 161-162; explicit
requests by, 148; socializing, 152-161;
validating, 156-157
Clinical Behavior Analysis (Dougher), 201

clinical contexts: case examples in, 6-7;
evaluation in, 41-45; punishment in,
96-98; reinforcement in, 88-94; stimulus
control in, 101-105
clinical priority, 147-149
*Cognitive Behavior Therapy: Applying
Empirically Supported Techniques in Your
Practice* (O'Donohue, Fisher, and Hayes),
202
cognitive behavioral therapy (CBT), 1-2
cognitive fusion, 121-122, 124-125, 196
cognitive therapy, 1
*Cognitive-Behavioral Treatment of Borderline
Personality Disorder* (Linehan), 202
coherence, 160, 195
collaboration, 152
comparison, 113
conditioned reinforcers, 86
conditioned response (CR), 63; basic affects
and, 66-69; relationship to UCR, 65
conditioned stimulus (CS), 63
conditioning: interoceptive, 68, 74-75;
operant, 79-98, 167-168; respondent,
63-78, 167; second-order, 70; traumatic, 73
consequences, 48-49; analysis of, 133-134,
137-140; context for, 52-53; learning by,
79-98; long-term, 52, 53, 133; observation
of, 49-52; relational framing and, 134-135;
short-term, 52, 133-134
content of thoughts, 194-196
context-bound extinction, 191
contexts: for ABC analysis, 52-53, 56-59;
contracts for changing, 182-184. *See also*
clinical contexts
contingencies: altered, 173; managing,
172-175
contracts, 182-184
control: counter-, 180-181; remote, 105;
stimulus, 99-107
coordination, 111, 113
counter-control, 180-181
covert behavior: explanation of, 18-19;
observation of, 35-37

D

danger to self/others, 147

Darwin, Charles, 66
deficits. *See* behavioral deficits
depression: adaptive actions and, 97;
    behavioral activation and, 193-194;
    rumination and, 136-141
Depression in Context (Martell, Addis, and
    Jacobson), 202
detailed descriptions, 28-29
deterioration prevention, 148
diagnosis, 20
dialectical behavior therapy (DBT), 2, 202
differentiating reinforcers, 175-176
direct contingencies, 198
discrimination, 59, 71
discrimination learning, 103
discriminative stimulus, 100
disgust: basic affect of, 66, 67; facilitation of,
    70
dog salivation experiment, 63, 65

E

elderly patients, 53-54
emotions: basic affects as, 66-69; external/
    internal stimuli and, 68; observation of,
    28; unconditioned responses and, 67-68
environmental provisions, 171-172
escape behaviors: operant conditioning and,
    91-92; respondent conditioning and, 75-76.
    See also avoidance
establishing operations (EOs), 53-56, 135,
    141; ABC analysis and function of, 55;
    change through influencing, 176-181
etiology, 20
evaluation: of clinical problems, 41-45; rating
    scales for, 39-40
excesses. *See* behavioral excesses
experiential avoidance, 123-124
experimental designs, 45
exposure, 167, 188-193; extinction
    and, 190-191; how to use, 189-191;
    interoceptive, 189; operant conditioning
    and, 191-192; relational framing and, 192;
    with response prevention, 189; trauma
    processing and, 192-193
external stimuli, 68

extinction: exposure and, 190-191; operant
    conditioning and, 92-94; respondent
    conditioning and, 71-72, 75
extinction burst, 94, 173
eyeblinking, 64, 68

F

fear: basic affect of, 66-67; behavioral
    approach test and, 38; exposure therapy
    and, 188-193; hierarchy of avoidance and,
    190; traumatic conditioning and, 73
feelings. *See* emotions
flexibility, increasing, 160
framing: relational, 113-120, 168-169;
    temporal, 115
function of thoughts, 196-198
Functional Analytic Psychotherapy
    (Kohlenberg and Tsai), 201
functional analytical psychotherapy (FAP), 3
functional behaviors, 29-30
functional classes of behavior, 91-92
functional contextualism, 7-8
functional knowledge, 145-149
functional relationships, 91
functionalism, 2
functionally equivalent behaviors, 91

G

generalization: operant conditioning and,
    102-103; psychotherapy and, 185-186, 198;
    respondent conditioning and, 70-71
generalized reinforcers, 86
geriatric patients, 53-54
goals: behavioral contract, 182; therapeutic,
    161-162

H

help to self-help, 152
holistic perspective, 147
hypothetical constructs, 29

I

imitative behavior, 87, 104-105
information processing, 2
infrequent behaviors, 39
insight, 59
internal stimuli, 68